P9-AOU-470

UNIVERSITY OF WINNIPEG
LIBRARY
515 PORTAGE AVENUE
WINNIPEG, MAN.   R3B 2E9
DISCARDED

CHRIST AND SATAN
A CRITICAL EDITION

PR
1630
.C6
1977

CHRIST AND SATAN

A Critical Edition

Robert Emmett Finnegan

Canadian Cataloguing in Publication Data

Christ and Satan.
 Christ and Satan

Text in Anglo-Saxon, introd. in English.
Bibliography: p.
ISBN 0-88920-041-6 bd. ISBN 0-88920-040-8 pa.

I. Finnegan, Robert Emmett, 1941-

PR1630.F55   829'.1   C77-001234-5

Copyright © 1977

Wilfrid Laurier University Press
Waterloo, Ontario, Canada
N2L 3C5

No part of this book may be translated or reproduced in any form, by print, photoprint, microfilm, microfiche, or any other means, without written permission from the publisher.

Cover design by Helen Lange

PREFACE

Christ and Satan was edited separately some fifty years ago by Merrel D. Clubb. Since 1925 it has appeared in Volume I of *The Anglo-Saxon Poetic Records: The Junius Manuscript,* 1931, edited by George Philip Krapp. Until recently the poem has not received overly much critical attention.

This edition is based upon a careful examination of the manuscript, and I have tried to present a text as close to Junius XI as possible. But such are the difficulties of dealing with *Christ and Satan* that an editor, even of a basically conservative bent, must, if he wishes to offer anything more than a transcription, become involved in weighing emendations: there is little purpose in perpetuating scribal lapses, or in hallowing unintelligibility. Whenever I have judged an emendation necessary, the original reading is given in the *Textual Notes* and the foundation of the emendation argued in the *Explanatory Notes.*

I have intentionally pared these notes close on matters of philology. Many discussions of forms and possible or probable variants are the dead leaves of Anglo-Saxon scholarship, and they ought to be allowed to rest. On occasion, to show the almost universal appeal of an emendation over a form in the manuscript, I have reference to Junius, Thorpe, Bouterwek, Dietrich, Cosijn et al. More rarely do I note in detail the attempt of older scholars to supply those lines they feel were dropped from the poem in one or other transcription: with an emendation we at least work from a known form, but to supply what the manuscript does not possess in any way is to work too much by the spirit.

I should here record my thanks to the Canada Council for a grant which allowed me to study the manuscript at Oxford, and to the Master and scholars of Campion Hall who made my visit most pleasant. The editors of *The Explicator, Modern Philology, Classica et Mediaevalia* and *Philological Quarterly* have kindly given me permission to use previously published material in this book.

The book has been published with the help of a grant from the Humanities Research Council of Canada, using funds provided by the Canada Council.

TABLE OF CONTENTS

Introduction

The Text

ABBREVIATIONS
USED IN THE BOOK

ANF   A. Roberts and J. Donaldson, eds., *The Ante-Nicene Fathers: Translations of the Writings of the Fathers Down to A.D. 325*. American reprint of the Edinburgh edition, revised and arranged by A. Cleveland Coxe, 10 vols. New York, 1916-1925.

Archiv   *Archiv für das Studium der Neueren Sprachen und Literaturen.*

Barnouw   A. J. Barnouw, *Textkritische Untersuchungen nach dem Gebrauch des Bestimmten Artikels und des Schwachen Adjectivs in der Altenglischen Poesie.* Leiden, 1902.

BGDSL   *Beiträge zur Geschichte der Deutschen Sprache und Literatur.*

Bliss   A. J. Bliss, "Single Half-Lines in O. E. Poetry," *N&Q,* 216 (1971), 442-49.

Bouterwek   K. W. Bouterwek, *Cædmon's des Angelsachsen biblische Dichtungen,* Vol. 1. Gütersloh, 1852.

Bright   J. W. Bright, "Jottings on the Cædmonian *Christ and Satan,*" *Modern Language Notes,* 18 (1903), 128-31.

Campbell   A. J. Campbell, *Old English Grammar.* Oxford, 1959.

Chr   "Christ" of *The Exeter Book*

CL   *Comparative Literature*

Clubb   M. D. Clubb, *Christ and Satan, An Old English Poem.* New Haven, 1925.

Cosijn   P. J. Cosijn, "Anglosaxonica III," *BGDSL,* 21 (1896), 21-25.

Dan   "Daniel" of *The Junius XI*

Dietrich   F. Dietrich, "Zu Cädmon," *Zeitschrift für deutsches Alterthum,* 10 (1856), 310-67.

DTC   A. Vacant, E. Mangenot and E. Amann, eds., *Dictionnaire de Théologie Catholique.* 15 vols. Paris, 1930-1950.

ELN   *English Language Notes*

ES	*English Studies*
Ettmüller	L. Ettmüller, *Engla and Seaxna Scopas and Boceras*. Quedlinburg and Leipzig, 1850.
Exo	"Exodus" of *The Junius XI*
Gollancz	Sir Israel Gollancz, *The Cædmon Manuscript of Anglo-Saxon Biblical Poetry*. Oxford, 1927.
Grein	C. W. M. Grein, *Bibliothek der angelsächsischen Poesie*, Vol. 1. Göttingen, 1857.
Grein-Köhler	C. W. M. Grein and J. J. Köhler, *Sprachschatz der Angelsächsischen Dichter*. Heidelburg, 1912.
Graz	F. Graz, "Beiträge zur Textkritik der sogenannten Cædmon'schen Dichtungen," *Englische Studien*, 21 (1895), 1-27.
Gu	"Guthlac" of *The Exeter Book*
Holthausen	F. Holthausen, Review of Grein-Wülker, 2, Part 2, *Anglia Beiblatt*, 5 (1895), 227-33.
Jul	"Juliana" of *The Exeter Book*
Junius	F. Junius, *Caedmonis Monachi Paraphrasis Poetica Genesios* .... Amsterdam, 1655.
JEGP	*Journal of English and Germanic Philology*
JTS	*Journal of Theological Studies*
Kock	E. A. Kock, *Jubilee Jaunts and Jottings: 250 Contributions to the Interpretation and Prosody of Old West Teutonic Alliterative Poetry*. Lund, 1918.
Krapp	G. P. Krapp, ed., *The Junius Manuscript*. New York, 1931.
MLN	*Modern Language Notes*
MP	*Modern Philology*
MLR	*Modern Language Review*
MS	*Mediaeval Studies*
Neophil	*Neophilologus*
NM	*Neuphilologische Mitteilungen*
NPNF	P. Schaff, ed., *The Nicene and Post Nicene Fathers*. First Series, 14 vols., Buffalo and New York, 1886-1890; Second Series, 14 vols., New York, 1890-1925 (edited by P. Schaff and H. Wace).
N&Q	*Notes & Queries*
Ogilvy	J. D. A. Ogilvy, *Books Known to the English, 597-1066*. Cambridge, Mass., 1967.

PMLA	*Publications of the Modern Language Association*
PG	J. P. Migne, ed., *Patrologiae graeca*. Paris, 1857-1866.
PL	J. P. Migne, ed., *Patrologiae latina*. Paris, 1844-1864.
PQ	*Philological Quarterly*
QJS	*The Quarterly Journal of Speech*
RES	*The Review of English Studies*
Rieger	M. Rieger, "Die Alt- und Angelsächsische Verskunst," *(Zacher's) Zeitschrift für Deutsche Philologie*, 7 (1876), 1-64.
RS	*Research Studies* (Washington State University)
RTAM	*Recherches de Théologie Ancienne et Médiévale*
Sievers-Cook	E. Sievers, *An Old English Grammar,* translated and edited by A. S. Cook. 3rd ed. London and New York, 1903.
Thorpe	B. Thorpe, *Cædmon's Metrical Paraphrase of Parts of the Holy Scriptures, in Anglo-Saxon*. London, 1832.
Wülker	R. P. Wülker, *Bibliothek der angelsächsischen Poesie,* Vol. 2. Leipzig, 1894.
XSt	"Christ and Satan" of *The Junius XI*

INTRODUCTION

I. THE MANUSCRIPT

Christ and Satan comprises the last seventeen pages of the late tenth to early eleventh century manuscript known as Junius XI, which contains as well the poems known as *Genesis, Exodus* and *Daniel*. Only *Genesis* bears a title, and that in a late hand. The manuscript is in the Bodleian Library, having been bequeathed that institution by Franciscus Junius, the Dutch philologist and antiquary. Junius received the manuscript from James Ussher, Bishop of Armagh and Primate of Ireland, probably in 1651, publishing an edition of the contents at Amsterdam in 1655. He believed the poems to be the work of Cædmon, as the title of the edition indicates.[1] Though modern criticism does not follow him in this, the first three poems[2] are quite close to Cædmon's practice as described by Bede.[3] It may be that the technique of vernacular biblical paraphrase associated with the name Cædmon established a poetic tradition in which *Genesis, Exodus* and *Daniel* may be placed.

The manuscript contains 116 parchment folios, numbered in a modern hand from 1-229; the first folio, which has a full-page illustration, is not included in the numbering. Each leaf is approximately 12″ x 7″ or 7-3/4″. The pages of the first three poems (*Genesis,* pp. 1-142, *Exodus,* pp. 143-71, *Daniel,* pp. 173-212) are ruled for twenty-six lines, *Christ and Satan,* pp. 213-24 and 226-28 for twenty-seven. Page 225 has a design on its lower half which obscures what rulings there may be, and the rulings on page 229, after the fourteenth and last line of text, cannot be determined because of the condition of the page.

Christ and Satan takes up almost all of the last gathering of the manuscript. Pp. 211-12, a blank page and the conclusion of *Daniel,* form one sheet with pp. 229-30. Pp. 213-14 are so connected with pp. 227-28,

---

[1] *Cædmonis Monachi Paraphrasis Poetica Genesios ac praecipuarum Sacrae paginae Historiarum, abhinc annos M. LXX....* The Junius XI is described in N. R. Ker's *Catalogue of MSS Containing Anglo-Saxon* (Oxford, 1957), pp. 406-08, under #334 (5123).

[2] I exclude, of course, *Genesis B,* ll. 235-851 of *Genesis* in Krapp's edition, which is an Anglo-Saxon translation of an Old Saxon original, the translation probably made by a continental Saxon. See M. Capek, "The Nationality of a Translator: Some Notes on the Syntax of *Genesis B,*" *Neophil,* 55 (1971), 89-96.

[3] Canebat autem de creatione mundi, et origine humani generis, et tota genesis historia, de egressu Israel ex Aegypto, et ingressu in terram repromissionis, de aliis plurimis sacrae scripturae historiis, de incarnatione dominica, passione, resurrectione, et ascensione in caelum, de Spiritus Sancti adventu, et apostolorum doctrina. Item de terrore futuri iudicii, et horrore poenae gehennalis, ac dulcedine regni caelestis multa carmina faciebat.... Venerabilis Baedae, *Historia Ecclesiastica Gentis Anglorum,* Liber IV, capitula 22, in C. Plummer, ed., *Baedae Opera Historica* (Oxford, 1969 reprint), pp. 260-61.

pp. 215-16 with pp. 225-26. There is a narrow strip between pp. 216-17 which is a projection of pp. 223-24, and a similar strip between pp. 222-23 which is a projection of pp. 217-18. These strips may indicate either that leaves of full folio sheets have been cut out, or that single leaves, half full folio sheets, have been bound in the gathering. There is no break in the text to suggest that any large section of the poem was lost through a hypothetical excision of the leaves. The gathering may be represented thus:

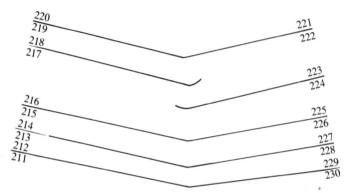

Since the poem ends on page 229, which is the right-hand half of the folio sheet containing on its left half pp. 211-12 (the conclusion of *Daniel*), the physical evidence indicates that the poem was intended as part of the manuscript, and was not bound in by chance. Pages 213-28 appear to have been folded in the middle from top to bottom. Gollancz believes that this occurred before the poem was copied, citing certain cramped lines on pp. 226, 227 and 228 to show that the scribe consciously avoided the ridge in his page.[4]

One scribe is responsible for the first three poems in the manuscript, while three hands are found in the text of the last: pp. 213-15 by one scribe, pp. 216-28 by another, page 229 by yet another. Though the styles of these scribes differ, they do not do so in any degree that would allow us to suppose that a significant interval separated their work. Clubb believes that Book I, the designation for *Genesis, Exodus* and *Daniel* extrapolated from the rubric *Finit Liber II* which concludes *Christ and Satan,* though copied earlier, is not separated by more than a generation from the copying of the last poem.[5]

The script is easy to read, though somewhat faded in parts. There is a large circular stain on page 224 which has run towards the bottom of the page. The design on the bottom of page 225 has run on to 224, further obscuring it. It appears that something was spilled on 224 (or that it was used as a coaster, for the stain looks like the base of a large tankard) and

---

[4] Gollancz, p. xcix.
[5] Clubb, p. xii.

the pages closed while wet. The script of pages 227, 228 and 229 is crabbed, and a bit more difficult to read than other pages of the poem. It seems that the scribes were hurrying to complete their task while attempting to conserve material, an idea supported by the large number of abbreviations these pages contain.

There are no illustrations as such in *Christ and Satan,* nor are there spaces for any. Gollancz assumes that the uncompleted design on page 225 was a trial drawing for the manuscript's cover, and so uses it in his collotype reproduction.[6] There is one zoomorphic capital on page 226, line 597a, *Hafað.* Other sections of the manuscript are richly illustrated with forty-nine drawings and a number of elegant capitals, though the spaces left for illustration by the scribe were not utilized after page 96. Three artists worked on the manuscript. The first ends his illustrations on page 68, but completes capitals on pp. 73 and 143; the second begins on page 73 and works through page 88; the third attempts drawings on pp. 31 and 96. The work of the first two artists is roughly contemporary with the manuscript—circa 1000-1025, while the third artist seems considerably later—circa 1150.[7]

There are numerous corrections, and some annotations and marginalia, in the manuscript, in hands other than those of the scribes responsible for the text. Someone, who has come to be identified as The Late West Saxon Corrector from a penchant for harmonizing particularly vowels to late West Saxon usage, has worked through *Christ and Satan* and *Genesis,* though his hand is much more active in the former than the latter, and in *Christ and Satan,* though the corrections continue to the poem's end, they are more frequent in the work of the first scribe. Another hand occasionally offers interlinear glosses and annotations, and this activity is ascribed to the Annotator. The only significant *marginalium* is found on page 219, where, to the right and approximately 1/2" above the first line of text, we have abbreviated: *omnis homo primum bonum.*

The most common form of punctuation in the manuscript is an acute accent, occasionally a double acute, over vowels and proper names. *Christ and Satan* has only the single acute in the form of a short slanting line. The first thousand lines of *Genesis* show this accent, as well as a longer slanting line which is continued through *Genesis, Exodus* and *Daniel,* but is not found in *Christ and Satan.* The accent is used initially with some consistency, only lines 8, 16, 23, 24 and 29 of our poem's first thirty lines being without at least one in the long line, while some lines have more than one: e.g., lines 22 and 26 have four, lines 11 and 25 have three. But there are significant groups of lines that have no

---

[6] Gollancz, p. xxxvi.

[7] F. Wormald, *English Drawings of the Tenth and Eleventh Centuries* (London, 1952), p. 76. But it may be that the third artist is of a different, though contemporary, school of illustration than the first two.

accent at all: e.g., lines 52-55, 67-70, 240-46, 250-53, 255-62, 542-66. Accents are far more frequent in the work of the first scribe than in that of the others.[8]

The *punctum* (.) or *punctus elevatus* (⁚), formed by conjoining the *punctum* with a *virgula*, is used with some regularity in most sections of the poem to indicate half-lines, with a preference for (⁚) to mark the caesura. Only rarely does the punctuator miss a line division, and then usually because the line is metrically exceptionable. Thus, although the failure to provide end punctuation for line 20 or note the caesura in line 66 contrasts unfavourably with his normal procedure, one cannot fault the punctuator too heavily, if at all, for incorrectly marking lines 89b, 624, or 638-39. Lines 279-305 form the only group without an attempt at consistent punctuation, there being but thirteen metrical indicators, all correctly used?

What appears to be a form of the *punctus versus* or semicolon (;) is the other significant punctuation in *Christ and Satan*. It is found in line 8b after *middangeard*, line 74b after *drugon*, where it marks the end of Section I of the poem, line 116b after *dyde*, line 118b after *sunu*, line 222b after *wuldorcyninge* where it marks the end of Section IV, line 278b after *dyde*, line 389b after *wæron*, line 450a after *wenan*, line 488b after *ðrowade*, line 492b after *gesette*, line 498b after *mihten*, line 641b after *sceoldon*.[10] The *punctus versus* is generally well used, even artistically so in lines 116b, 118b, 488b, 492b, and I have tried to take it into account in punctuating the text. Abbreviations in the poem are simple and familiar: 7 stands for *and/ond*, both prefix and conjunction; a letter or an ending left unwritten is indicated by a macron above the preceding letter; ꝥ is the normal abbreviation for *þæt*.

Only Sections II, III, V and VI are so marked in the manuscript; all these, including the first section, begin with large capitals. Section I ends with line 74b *drugon*, the first word of line 20, page 214. Approximately 2-1/4″ to the right we have .11.. Section II ends with line 124b *gelomp*, the second word of line 27, the last line on page 215. Approxi-

---

[8] George P. Krapp, in *The Vercelli Book: The Anglo Saxon Poetic Records* (New York, 1932), 2, gives the total number of accents in the Junius manuscript as "something over three thousand, or, in terms of percentage, .622 in proportion to the number of verse lines in the manuscript (p. lii)." For *Christ and Satan* he computes the percentage of accents in the work of the first scribe as 1.081, in the work of the second scribe as .301, in that of the third as .450.

[9] G. C. Thornley, "The Accents and Points of MS Junius XI," in *Transactions of the Philological Society* (1954), 178-205, argues convincingly that the punctuation in the manuscript is an early form of Gregorian recitative notation, an interesting idea, since it suggests that the poems were intoned or chanted. For a discussion of punctuation in early English manuscripts, see Peter Clemoes, *Liturgical Influence on Punctuation in Late O. E. and Early M. E. MSS* (Cambridge, 1952).

[10] Gollancz, p. xxiv, notes that a semicolon is misplaced in l. 91b after *gefærde*. The one in l. 450a seems dubious to me as well.

mately 2-1/2" to the right, we have 111 ·, the last two numerals very light. Section IV concludes with *wuldor cyninge,* line 222b, words seven and eight of line 10 on page 218. The line is full, *cyninge* being followed by a semicolon (;). Approximately 1" to the left of line 11, there is a *v* in very light ink. A faded capital begins the section. Section V ends with *hwile* of line 253b, the sixth word of line 4 of page 219. Approximately 1-1/2" to the right we have · VI ·.

Section IV, though not numbered, is clearly marked. Section III ends with *wide* of line 188b, the second word of line 13 on page 217. It is followed by two periods (. .) and the rest of the line is blank. Since the next line begins with a capital, sectional division IV is clear enough. Section VI concludes with *ende* of line 314b, line 14 of page 220. The word is exaggerated to take up a full inch of the line. It ends with a period and the remainder of the line is blank. Section VII is not provided with a capital, but the *e* for *Eala,* line 315a, is indicated by a small letter in the far left margin. Section VII ends with *mot* of line 364b, the third word of line 18 on page 221. It is immediately followed by a colon plus dash (:-); the rest of the line is blank. Section VIII begins with a capital and ends with *gesceafta,* line 440b, the tenth word of line 6 on page 223. There is no particular punctuation here, and the line is normally written, *gesceafta* being at the extreme right margin. Line 441a begins with a large capital, though, so a sectional division seems indicated. This Section IX concludes with *drihtne,* line 511a, the tenth word of line 18 on page 224. A period follows *drihtne,* and the remaining inch or so of the line is blank. The capital to begin Section X is not in the text, but room is left for it, lines 19 and 20 of page 224 being indented one space, and *s* of *Swa* indicated by a small letter in the left margin. This section concludes with þenceð, line 556b, the twelfth word of line 16 on page 225. This page, it will be recalled, has an incomplete design some 4-1/2" long and 5-1/4" wide running from line 16 to the bottom of the page. Lines 14-16 are crabbed, as if the scribe wanted to finish this section on the one page rather than to carry it on. This, of course, supposes that the design was on the page before the text was written, a practice at variance with the rest of the manuscript, where the text is in place and space is left for illustrations. Line 16 is full, þenceð being the last word in the extreme right margin. It is followed by a period and·a dash(.-). The capital for Section XI is not in the text, though room is left for it, lines 1 and 2 of page 226 being indented two spaces. I do not find the þ of þa indicated in the left margin. Section XI ends with *gestreonan,* line 596b, the third word of line 26 on page 227. It is followed by a period and a dash (.-), the remaining 3" of the line being blank. Section XII begins with the only zoomorphic capital in *Christ and Satan.* There is no indication in the text of a further division, and the poem ends with *teala,* line 729b, the third word of line 14 on page 229. It is followed by the rubric, in large letters: *Finit Liber .11. Amen.* With the possible exception of Section

VI, which comes in the middle of a speech by Satan, the divisions in the manuscript are structurally sound, marking major shifts in emphasis, point of view, or subject matter.

Small capitals are numerous:

13a Seolua	65a Swa	279a Swa	659a Swa
17b Hwa	84a þa	370a Satanus	705a Seoððan
20a Adam	100a Nagan	378b þa	712b Hwilum (?)
28a Saran	114a Ne	398a Hwearf	713b Hwilum
36b Hwær	163a Eala	408a Ic	714b Hwilum (?)
51a Ða	208a þonne	430a Aras	716a Ðonne
61a Atol	246b Ongan	450a Seoððan	727b Ongunnon
63a Segdest	248a Ic	585a Siteð	

Some, like *Seolua* of line 13a, *Hwa* of line 17b, *Saran* of line 28a, or the *Hwilums* of lines 712-714b, appear to be used for emphasis; others like line 65a *Swa,* line 163a *Eala,* line 208a þonne mark shifts of attitude, emotion or perspective within the larger structures of the sections. Only once does a small capital appear to be misplaced absolutely, line 450a, and this coincides with a peculiar use of the *punctus versus* (;) in punctuation. The scribe, I think, sought to read the lines *æfre moton/wenan; Seoððan ....* The sense of the lines requires a different structure. The only other instances in which one might quarrel with the small capitals are lines 716a and 727b, though they might be justified here by a desire to emphasize the actions of Satan and the devils on his ignominious return to hell after the temptation.

The scribes are responsible for the small capitals. The large capitals, of a homogeneous style but unlike the styles of those in Book I, were added to the text after it was copied, space being left for them and the letters to be copied indicated by a small letter in the left margin. These small letters, with the exception of Section XI where I can find no indication of þ, are visible where large capitals are absent, and I assume that they were either erased once the capitals were entered or that they were written over. The exception here is Section VI, where we have both small þ and capital Ð. The zoomorphic letter which begins Section XII is unlike any such in Book I. I conclude that two hands are responsible for the capitals of *Christ and Satan,* neither hand to be found in Book I. Why capitals were supplied for Sections I-VI and VIII-IX and not for Sections VII, X and XI, and why only Section XII should have a zoomorphic letter, are questions to which I have no answer.

We seem to be on firmer ground when we turn to discuss the person or persons responsible for the metrical markings, for there is a good deal of hard evidence in the manuscript. But, on the whole, it is quite complex and contradictory. There is, first of all, one large group of lines that has no metrical markings at all: lines 279-294, Section VI, line 20 of page 219 to line 1 of page 220. Two groups have the *punctum* but virtually no *virgula*: lines 1-50 of Section I, line 1 of page 213 to line 4 of page 214, shows *. only after line 30a *sceolun*, line 18 of page 213, and after line 49b *ham*, line 4 of page 214, although the *punctum* is regularly used; lines 223-257, all of Section V on pages 218-19 and the first three lines of Section VI, have no *virgula* at all, although again the *punctum* is used regularly. There are numerous indications on pages 227 and 228 that the markings, at least the *virgula*, have been added after the text was copied in its cramped script: the *virgula* is displaced markedly to the right or left of its *punctum* because of the initial letter of the following word, or the slash of the *virgula* cuts through the next letter. More, there are seven times in the last six lines of page 227 where both *punctum* and *virgula* are noticeably above the writing line, and three times when the *punctum* alone is so placed.

If we extrapolate from the evidence of pages 227 and 228 to the poem as a whole, we would be forced to conclude that the *virgula*, and quite likely the *punctum*, were added after the text was copied, but we would have no explanation for the section which has no punctuation at all, or the two that show the absence of the *virgula*. If we do not so extrapolate, and assume that the scribes were responsible for the metrical markings, we yet have those three sections to explain, and the evidence of pages 227-28 to conjure with as well. If we follow Gollancz and assume that the Corrector was responsible for the *punctum* and *virgula* when they occur together,[11] we fare no better. I have no resolutions for these difficulties, and am content perforce to note them.

There is a final problem to be discussed, quite as knotty in its way as the metrical markings: did the original plan of the Junius XI include *Christ and Satan*. The evidence of the manuscript as it now exists is not much help here, since all it can do is demonstrate that, *at the time it was copied*, the poem was intended to be an integral part of it. The condition of the poem's text, with pages having been folded and ruled for twenty-seven rather than twenty-six lines, with no large zoomorphic capitals or space for illustrations, and showing the hands of three scribes rather than one as in Book I, proves that it was not physically prepared for inclusion in the sumptuous Junius XI. But we ought recall here that the manuscript, even without Book II, is far from complete, and that the lack of such preparation for *Christ and Satan* may be explained in any number of ways that do not preclude an original plan that encompassed it: the scriptorium or the monastery which produced the manuscript might have fallen on hard times, or the patron for whom the volume was intended, or by whom it was commissioned, might have died or changed his mind. The physical evidence of the poem's folios is ambiguous, too, on closer analysis. The folded sheets and the incomplete design on page 225, both of which probably predate the copying of the text, need not

---

[11] Ibid., p. xxiii.

suggest that inferior materials were used for *Christ and Satan,* and that therefore neither the poem nor its inclusion in the manuscript were viewed by the makers of the book as important. We might just as well argue that the folios had been intended for some other work, a quarto volume perhaps, and were diverted for the use of *Christ and Satan,* being ruled for twenty-seven lines to save space and ensure that the complete poem would fit the resources at hand. The activity of three scribes, rather than one, may suggest not carelessness, but a task carried on under difficult conditions and with trying interruptions, a task that perforce took three hands to complete, and was, therefore, of some consequence. Internal evidence, then, can offer little direction to the discussion and, briefly, we must turn to a different line of argument.

I am inclined to believe that *Christ and Satan* may indeed have been in the projected plan of the manuscript, and I offer the following observations, conjectures really, as support. Aelfric, in his *Treatise on the Old and New Testament,*[12] deals at some length with the six ages of man in relation to biblical time. The first age he defines as the time from the creation to the flood, the second from the flood to Abraham, the third from Abraham to David, the fourth from David to Daniel, the fifth from Daniel to Christ, at whose coming the sixth age is inaugurated. It may be nothing more than coincidence, the meshing of biblical poetry in chronological order with a temporal frame based upon that biblical chronology, but the first three poems of the Junius manuscript fit this schedule rather well. *Genesis* encompasses the action of the first two ages; *Exodus* deals with a significant action within the third age, the crossing of the Red Sea, and contains a reference back to *Genesis* in the allusion to Noah's Ark; *Daniel* deals with an activity which borders the fourth and fifth ages, and the poem's opening lines harmonize quite well with the ending of *Exodus,* while its first significant action, the miraculous salvation of the three children in the furnace, might be seen as looking forward to the harrowing of hell in *Christ and Satan.* It may be worth recollecting too that all the Old Testament saints whose actions figure largely in Book I would be understood by one familiar with typology and biblical exegesis as prefigurations, in one way or another, of Christ. And Christ is the subject of the last poem in the manuscript. This, of course, may be no more than to say that Old Testament saints, given a sufficiently wide interpretation, will catch a Christic significance. But let me speculate further.

Christ and Satan begins with a brief account of the creation and the fall of the angels, thus recapitulating, as Alvin Lee has recently remarked,[13] similar material in *Genesis.* But while *Genesis* and the two

---

[12] S. J. Crawford, ed., *The Old English Version of the Heptateuch: Aelfric's Treatise on the Old and New Testament and his Preface to Genesis* (London, 1922), EETS. OS #160, pp. 23-71.

[13] Alvin Lee, *The Guest-Hall of Eden* (New Haven and London, 1972), pp. 20-21.

other poems of Book I detail the working out of the *heilsgeschichte* on the human level, *Christ and Satan* follows Satan to hell. There the reader remains, at least with the narrative and dramatic sections of the verse, through all of Part I and the beginning of Part II. Time is of no account in this hell, as befits an eternal place and condition, but there are some vague suggestions of time's passage in allusions by Satan to his ability, or inability, to capture men's souls. Where we find human time, in terms of Aelfric's biblical chronology of salvation, divided into various and discrete ages, in the hell depicted in *Christ and Satan* there are only two significant events: the establishment of hell itself at the edge of time with the angelic fall, and the harrowing, a fixed and datable event for the poet and his audience, which breaks hell's power. Aelfric, in addition to the six ages noted above, remarks a seventh age contemporaneous with the other six, running from the death of righteous Adam to the world's end.[14] It is a place and a condition rather than an age as such, for here remain the dead saints who await the eternal joy of the eighth age after the resurrection. Without commenting on Aelfric's eschatological millenarianism, I suggest that the first part of *Christ and Satan* presents us with the *heilsgeschichte* viewed from hell, the infernal correlative of Aelfric's seventh age. At the harrowing, in the person and actions of Christ, human, hellish and heavenly time fuse for an instant, and the way to Aelfric's eighth age, closed since Adam's fall, is opened. Part II of *Christ and Satan* deals, among other things, with the establishment of the church, that society which on earth is a mystical embodiment of heaven itself. Part III affords a picture of Christ the God-Man as a prime exemplar: by imitating his defeat of temptation, man remains a member in good standing of the church, and a participant in its future promise.

My conjectures, then, are these: that the original plan of the Junius manuscript had, as its rubric, something like the "ages of man," and that poems, including *Christ and Satan,* were collected accordingly. Something happened, though, and the work was not completed. The manuscript of *Christ and Satan,* after having been laid aside, was copied on folios added to what had been the last gathering of *Daniel.* All this is speculation, of course, but I trust that it is not totally idle.

---

[14] Crawford, p. 70.

II.   THE PROBLEM OF UNITY*

Two problems command the attention of the critic of *Christ and Satan*:[1] the un-chronological movement of the poem, and the presence in the work of different kinds of poetry. The action begins with the fall of the angels (ll. 1-364), moves through the harrowing of hell, the ascension, the coming of the Holy Spirit, and the last judgment (ll. 365-662), and concludes with the temptation of Christ in the desert (ll. 663-729). In the first two parts—i.e., the fall of the angels and the harrowing of hell—sections of dramatic dialogue, narrative, and monologue are interspersed in an apparently purposeless fashion with sections of homiletic exhortation. Yet the final part, the temptation, has no such exhortation, being essentially narrative and dramatic. This un-chronological movement and the mixture of verse types present an immediate challenge to any hypothesis that would find the last 729 lines of Junius XI a consciously structured, unified work.

Many critics have argued that *Christ and Satan* is not a single work at all, but a series of fragments from different poems, each fragment more or less incomplete. J. J. Conybeare, for example, believed that Book II contained several fragments which introduced an independent poem on Christ's harrowing of hell,[2] while Benjamin Thorpe remarked that a considerable portion of the Book's surviving fragments dealt with the same theme.[3]

Where Conybeare and Thorpe found traces of one poem and other fragments, M. Rieger found two, Bernhard ten Brink three, separate poems. Rieger's first poem, which he calls "Satan," ends with line 364; the second, which he compared with Cynewulf's *Christ* in terms of content and treatment, comprises lines 365-729.[4] Ten Brink's first poem, lines 1-364, to which he gives the name "The Fallen Angels," is complete; the second and third poems, lines 365-662 and lines 663-729, are fragmentary, the former resembling Cynewulf's *Christ,* the latter either a fragmentary poetic homily on the temptation or a part of some unspecified greater whole.[5]

---

* Much of the material in this section appeared in a different form in *Classica et Mediaevalia,* 30 (1969).

[1] Christian W. M. Grein first gave this title to the poem in *Bibliothek der angelsächsischen Poesie.*

[2] John Josias Conybeare, *Illustrations of Anglo-Saxon Poetry,* ed. W. D. Conybeare (London, 1826; rpt. New York: Haskell House, 1964), p. 189.

[3] Benjamin Thorpe, *Cædmon's Metrical Paraphrase of Parts of Holy Scripture* (London, 1832), p. xiv.

[4] M. Rieger, "Die Alt- und Angelsächsische Verskunst," *(Zacher's) Zeitschrift für deutsche Philologie,* 7 (1876), 6.

[5] Bernhard ten Brink, *History of English Literature,* vol. 1, trans. Horace M. Ken-

Friedrich Groschopp faults both Rieger and ten Brink for failing to offer cogent evidence for their respective positions, and for accepting in an uncritical spirit and without sufficient attention to detail the received text. He finds some virtue in ten Brink's division, in so far as it does away with the glaring anachronism of Rieger's analysis that would place the temptation after the ascension, but he finds ten Brink's argument unconvincing because it neglects to account for what are obvious and real links of thought and feeling connecting the three parts.[6]

Groschopp assumes that the text as it stands in the manuscript is faulty. He explains the difficulties of this faulty text—the peculiar structure, the somewhat mutilated condition of the manuscript, the seemingly random mixture of narrative-dramatic and hortatory-homiletic elements—by positing the existence of an Old English poem that dealt with the life of Christ in a manner similar to the Old Saxon *Heliand*. This poem, already in a fragmentary state in Anglo-Saxon times, was reworked by a pious though inartistic scribe who attempted to knit the fragments together.[7]

Groschopp excises those elements for which the restorer is responsible, primarily the hortatory-homiletic sections of Parts I and II, and, having thus arrived at the original fragments of his *Heliand,* arranges them in a coherent, that is, chronological, order. What remains of Part I is integrated with the harrowing material of Part II, while the temptation, Part III, is placed before. This temptation scene, and lines 573b-578, which, because Groschopp believed them to refer to the suicide of Judas before the crucifixion, are misplaced in the text as they stand, provide a foundation for Christ's ante-mortem activities. With the mention of the creation in lines 1-18, Groschopp discovers the fragments of an original poem that touched upon the Old Testament, but was principally concerned with narrating Christ's life and his activities after death.[8]

---

nedy (New York, 1883), pp. 86-88. Ten Brink's analysis of the poem was most influential; Albin Kühn, *Über die angelsächsischen Gedichte von Christ und Satan* (Halle, 1883); Eduard Sievers, "Zur Rhythmic des germanischen Alliterationsverses," *Beiträge zur Geschichte der deutschen Sprache und Literatur,* 10 (1885), 499; Betinck Smith, *Cambridge History of English Literature,* vol. 1 (London and New York, 1907), pp. 53-54, all accept his statements. Only Kühn adds anything of interest on this head in the form of lists counting how many times in each section certain key terms—e.g., for God, man, hell, salvation, etc.—are used. In such a way he hoped to buttress the tripartite division of the poem. Clubb, p. xliv, dismisses these lists as practically worthless as evidence, because Kühn failed to take into account the obvious differences in subject matter and length of the three sections.

    [6] Friedrich Groschopp, "Das angelsächsische Gedicht Christ und Satan," *Anglia,* 6 (1883), 251-52.

    [7] Ibid., pp. 251-52, 256.

    [8] Ibid., pp. 251-65. Richard L. Greene, "A Re-Arrangement of *Christ and Satan,*" *MLN,* 53 (1928), 108-10, argues for what is in effect Groschopp's position when he suggests that the structure of *XSt* could be improved by transposing the temptation between the laments of the devils and the harrowing of hell.

While C. Abbetmeyer agrees with Groschopp that the work—he calls it the "Satan poems"—is a compilation of previously existing material, he finds his predecessor's procedure "too arbitrary and most of his conclusions untenable."[9] Abbetmeyer contends that lines 1-364 of *Christ and Satan* are composed of "plaints of Satan," independent poems in a cycle which deals with the sufferings of the devil. This cycle seems to take its origin from the Latin works of Aldhelm, *De Lucifero* and *De Laudibus Virginum*: in the former Satan is seen "lamenting" his past glories and present pains; the latter rehearses the fall of the angels.[10]

Abbetmeyer's procedure is not unlike Groschopp's: both proceed by a series of cuts, the one to discover the original poem at the foundation of the present text, the other to separate the work into its independent parts. Abbetmeyer divides the first part into three sections, on the basis that each ends with an exhortation: lines 1-222, 223-314, 315-364. From lines 1-222 Abbetmeyer detaches lines 75-188, which he breaks into three monologues, each spoken "by the same fire-breathing demon": lines 75-124, 125-158, 159-188.[11]

The second part of the poem belongs to a different cycle of plaints than does Part I; it might originally have dealt with Christ's "exaltation" or have been a brief treatment of the second article of the creed, or "even the whole creed."[12] In the course of time the two cycles were amalgamated, the second having been influenced by the first, and by *Genesis A* as well. The final section of the poem, lines 663-729, is actually a "homily" on the temptation included because it yet again demonstrates a suffering of Satan. The last line of this section, line 729, is the beginning of another plaint.[13] In short, Abbetmeyer finds all of eight independent poems in the Second Book of the Junius manuscript: (1) 1-33, 189-192, 34-74, 193-222; (2) 223-314; (3) 315-364; (4) 75-124; (5) 125-158; (6) 159-188; (7) 365-662; (8) 663-729. These sections seem placed in genetic order, the first having in some way given rise to the others, the initial impetus of the set deriving from Aldhelm's Latin works.

While the suggestion that *Christ and Satan* is a series of more or less independent and incomplete fragments received support through the nineteenth, and, with Abbetmeyer, in the early years of the twentieth, century, that opinion has gradually given way before various attempts to discover in the lines a principle of unity. One of the earliest such attempts was that of Alois Brandl, who argued that the lines

---

[9] C. Abbetmeyer, *Old English Poetical Motives Derived from the Doctrine of Sin* (Minneapolis and New York, 1903), p. 10.

[10] Ibid., p. 17.

[11] Ibid., p. 11. Abbetmeyer appears to be using the Grein text as edited by Wülker. I have changed the line numberings to harmonize with my text.

[12] Ibid., p. 12.

[13] Ibid.

composed one poem that attempted to describe the redemption of man. The first section, the "laments of the fallen angels," contrasts with the second, the "harrowing of hell," the former detailing the punishments of those who oppose God, the latter the rewards of those loyal to him. Brandl believed that the concluding section, the "temptation," was included in the work because it presents the only direct contact between Christ and Satan depicted in the New Testament.[14]

M. D. Clubb is cautious in his remarks about the poem's unity. He writes, for example, that in view of "discrepant opinions" it would be "rash" to give a categorical answer to the question "is *Christ and Satan* a single unified poem,"[15] and he mentions in passing that lines 20-193 "seem most certain to have been taken more or less directly from another poem,"[16] a statement that hardly points towards a unified work. Finally he concludes that, since "Old English poets have never been commended especially for their constructive ability . . . the lack of articulation and centralization so evident in *Christ and Satan* need not prejudice us against the conclusion that the poem is the product of a single molding spirit."[17]

Clubb believes that the poet initially intended a short narrative on the activity of Christ after his crucifixion, Part II of the present text. He was struck, however, by the dramatic and poetic potential of the traditional material surrounding this activity, particularly that centred about the harrowing of hell. The terror of the devils at the coming of Christ to liberate the souls of the just held captive in hell suggested the possibility of constructing some lines on the original fall of the angels, which might be used as an introduction to the central material of the poem. But not only did the poet fail to integrate this introduction with the harrowing; he was so taken by it that he kept adding laments, descriptions, exhortations and hortatory passages until Part I became "almost an independent poem." The appeal of the characters he had created was such that the poet could not bear to tear himself from them, but decided to picture the "two great adversaries" in conflict yet again. So Part III was created, a gross anachronism since it is placed after the harrowing.[18]

Gollancz, in the introduction to his collotype reproduction of the Junius XI, follows Clubb, affirming that he can detect "the same type of mind at work in the various sections forming Book II," and concluding that these sections form a unity. This unity has two divisions, the lament of the fallen angels and the harrowing, to which has been added, "as an afterthought," the temptation. The manuscript used for the transcript of the poem that survives in the Junius was imperfect "in many respects":

---

[14] Alois Brandl, *Geschichte der Altenglischen Literatur* (Strassburg, 1908), p. 1046.
[15] Clubb, p. xlviii.
[16] Ibid., p. liv., fn. 80.
[17] Ibid., p. lvi.
[18] Ibid., p. lv.

the original manuscript had not been "reduced from its older Anglian forms," and was probably responsible for what Gollancz determines are "obvious omissions in the text." The ending of the manuscript from which *Christ and Satan* was copied was either imperfect or illegible, since "the poet did not end his poem with an abrupt recrimination of Satan by the fiends consisting of a speech of one line, and it seems odd that the third scribe's task should have been limited to 13-1/2 lines."[19]

George Philip Krapp, in his short introduction to the poem prepared for volume 1 of *The Anglo-Saxon Poetic Records,* states that *Christ and Satan* is a "set of lyric and dramatic amplifications" on common Christian themes.[20] Accepting Clubb's idea concerning the genesis of the work, he believes that the poet began composing with no set plan in mind, and as a result the poem grew in a totally random manner. Krapp incidentally laments the literary judgment of a scribe who would include a work of such inferior quality as *Christ and Satan* in a manuscript with *Genesis, Exodus,* and *Daniel.*

Recently there have been suggestions that the poem possesses an intelligible and purposeful structure that is supported by a definite thematic movement. So in the final chapter, "Conjectures," of his book *Doctrine and Poetry,* Bernard Huppé remarks that the peculiar chronology of *Christ and Satan* has caused some critics to doubt its unity, but that this doubt is caused by a failure to recognize the theme of the work, which he states as "the incommensurate might of God." He notes that the hortatory-homiletic sections of *Christ and Satan* contain "moral" applications of thematic material related in the narrative-dramatic lines. The third part of the poem, the temptation, is correctly placed, since it is the culmination of the moral teaching in the poem and pertains most particularly to man's relationship to the powers of evil, "how man, though burdened with the flesh, should imitate God."[21]

Neil D. Issacs sees the work unified by the "dramatic (and extra-chronological) arrangement of the material" which culminates in the temptation scene, and by the poet's "principle technique—the quoting of speeches." The structural principle of the poem is that "of using as many distinct voices as possible." Issacs suggests that, though the poem shows "substantial artistic endeavor," it has often been viewed as a "loose collection of biblical episode and moral application" because the poet was too enamoured of his technique, his "ventriloquism," to subdue it to the purpose of creating an artistic unity: "he [the poet] is using his material to sustain his art."[22]

---

[19] Gollancz, p. cv.

[20] Krapp, pp. xxxiv-xxxvi.

[21] Bernard Huppé, *Doctrine and Poetry: Augustine's Influence on Old English Poetry* (New York, 1959), pp. 227-31.

[22] Neil D. Issacs, *Structural Principles in Old English Poetry* (Knoxville, Tennessee, 1968), pp. 127-44.

This brief history of scholarship concerning *Christ and Satan* has discovered two attitudes toward the work: a critic, seizing upon the peculiar verse mixture and apparently confused chronology of the piece, either denies its unity, like Groschopp and Abbetmeyer, or affirms a unity other than organic, e.g., Clubb's statement that this work is the product of a "single molding spirit." With the exception of the five pages devoted to *Christ and Satan* by Huppé, and the chapter by Issacs, the critics who, like Brandl, opt for unity either fail to deal adequately with the structural problems raised by Groschopp and Abbetmeyer, or take, like Clubb, what is in fact an extreme genetic view of the poem, explaining its faulty structure by positing an incompetent artist.

While Huppé's remarks break new ground and are basically correct, they are, as they were intended to be, "conjectures," and leave much unanswered. For example: what is the relationship between the narrative-dramatic and homiletic-hortatory sections of the verse, how is this relationship manipulated, and why is it that Part III, the temptation, has no exhortation? Might Part III, then, be incomplete? Further, if *Christ and Satan* is one poem rather than a series of fragments, it should be possible to demonstrate a thematic progression that leads inevitably and necessarily from the first section, through the second, and is concluded in the third; one should be able to find the principle(s) of organic unity in just those places where Issacs denied them to be: in the arrangement of episodes in the narrative, in the formal system of contrasts between the title figures, in the dramatic progression of the thematic material. And, I would add, in the relation of the dramatic verse to the hortatory.

If we investigate the Latin and vernacular homilists with whom our poet may have been familiar, tracing in their devotional prose the use of the exemplum[23] as a pedagogical device, then the mixture of verse kinds in *Christ and Satan* is seen to be a problem more apparent than real. For in these works we find a collocation of the dramatic with the hortatory that is purposeful, and it is from such a collocation in the prose homilies that our poet, I think, took his inspiration for the verse mixture in *Christ and Satan,* a poem quite as devotional and as pedagogically oriented as many a homily.

Limitations of space require that an analysis of exempla in the work of the Latin homilists concentrate upon the writings of that most important figure for Anglo-Saxon Christianity, Pope Gregory the Great. But

---

[23] A handy definition of *exemplum,* should one be necessary, is offered by J-Th. Welter, *L'Exemplum dans la Littérature Religieuse et Didactique de Moyen Age* (Paris and Toulouse, 1927), p. 1: "Par le mot exemplum, on entendait, au sens large du terme, un récit ou une historiette, une fable ou une parabole, une moralité ou une description pouvant servir de preuve à l'appui d'une exposé doctrinal, religieux ou moral." See also J. A. Mosher, *The Exemplum in the Early Religious and Didactic Literature of England* (New York, 1911).

what is discovered in Gregory's work can also be found in the homiletic and polemical prose of Ambrose, Jerome, Augustine, Leo the Great, John Cassian, Isidore of Seville, and Boethius, to name the more important figures.[24]

While the Anglo-Saxon vernacular homilists took material from both Gregory's *XL Homiliarum in Evangelia* and *Dialogorum Libri IV, de Vita et Miraculis Patrum Italicorum,* the latter a storehouse of exempla, it was the former which provided them with the technical exemplar according to which they constructed many of their homilies.[25] While Gregory relies to a great extent on the technique of verse by verse explication of scripture, it appears that some part of his audience had to be exhorted to lead a Christian life by being given a concrete illustration of goodness and justice worthy of emulation. Such were the functions of exempla: they brought home the practical significance of explicated scripture passages. So in homily #3, which deals with the necessity of perseverance in the face of adversity, Gregory gives the story of the heroic Felicity; in homily #23, which emphasizes the necessity of Christian charity and hospitality, he tells the story of the man who received Christ himself, disguised as a beggar, into his home; homily #34 demonstrates the mercy and compassion of Christ's forgiveness of sins, and relates the tale of the sinner who joined Gregory's own monastery of Saint Andrew and became a saint.

Gregory places most of his exempla immediately before the homily's closing exhortation. The structure of these exhortations is interesting, since, by a repetition of certain forms and moods of the verb, they take on something of a formulaic aspect. Two examples will suffice to make the point. The closing charge of homily #3 reads:

> Consideremus, fratres, hanc feminam, consideremus nos, qui membris corporis viri sumus, in ejus comparatione quid existimabimur.... Sequamur ergo, fratres charissimi, districtam et asperam Redemptoris viam.... Despiciamus cuncta praesentia, nulla sunt etenim quae transire possunt. Turpe sit diligere quod constat citius perire.... Amore nostri, fratres charissimi, Redemptor noster occubuit, et nos amore ejus discamus vincere nosmetipsos.[26]

The prevailing mood of the verbs is hortatory subjunctive, quite as we might expect. The ending to homily #23 has much the same thrust, though here the significant verbs are in the imperative mood:

> Ecce Dominus non est cognitus dum loqueretur, et dignatus est cognosci dum pascitur. Hospitalitatem ergo, fratres charissimi, diligite, charitatis opera amate.... Ecce in judicium veniens, dicet: *Quod uni*

---

[24] Welter, pp. 12-27.

[25] For Gregory's influence on the formal aspects of Anglo-Saxon homiletics, see John Sala, *Preaching in the Anglo-Saxon Church* (Chicago, 1934).

[26] *PL* 76, cols. 1088-89.

ex minimis meis fecistis, mihi fecistis (Matth. xxv, 40). Ecce ante judicium cum per membra sua suscipitur, susceptores suos etiam per semetipsum requirit; et tamen nos ad hospitalitatis gratiam pigri sumus. Pensate, fratres, quanta hospitalitatis virtus sit. . . . Praebete modo peregrino Christo hospitium, ut vos in judicio non quasi peregrinos nesciat, sed ut proprios recipiat ad regnum, ipso adjuvante qui vivit et regnat Deus in saecula saeculorum. Amen.[27]

Gregory juxtaposed exempla with formulaic exhortation on the sixteen occasions he used them in *XL Homiliarum.* Formulaic closing exhortations may be found in Gregory without exempla; exempla cannot be found without closing formulaic exhortations.

When we look to the *Blickling* and *Vercelli Homilies,* and the *Catholic Homilies* of Aelfric,[28] we find exempla linked with closing exhortations in a manner similar to Gregory's. The vernacular exhortation takes the form most often of subjunctive and imperative verb forms, and a command infinitive construction with *wutan* or some other verb of obligation, e.g., *sculan,* plus an infinitive.

So, for example, in *Blickling Homily* #10, which contains the exemplum of the dead man's bones that warn his kinsman of approaching death, we find:

Magon we þonne, men þa leofestan, us þis *to gemyndum habban,* & þas bysene on urum heortum staþelian, þæt we ne *sceolan lufian* worlde glengas to swiþe ne þysne middangeard. . . . *Uton* we þonne geornlice *geþencean* & *oncnawan* be þyses middangeardes fruman. . . . *Uton* we þonne þæs *geþencean,* þa hwile þe we magon moton, þæt we us georne to gode þydon. *Uton* urum Drihtne *hyran* georne, & him þancas secggan ealra his geofena. . . .[29]

As with the Latin of Gregory the Great, the hortatory tone of this passage is a function of the verb constructions. The "magon we" + "to gemyndum habban" begins the exhortations which are carried by the "sceolan" + infinitive and the repeated "uton" + infinitive constructions to indicate necessity or obligation. In the eighth homily, which describes the death of a rich man with the attendant loss of properties and false friends, we have:"*Forðon,* men ða leofestan, *don we* soþe hreowe & bote ure synna, þa hwile þe we on þyssum life syn; *alesan we* ure saule þa hwile þe we þæt lif & þæt weorþ on urum gewealde habban."[30] Here the subjunctive mood of the verbs sets the tone. The

---

[27] Ibid., col. 1183.

[28] Even though a number of the homilies in the collections, especially those of Aelfric, were written later than *Christ and Satan,* all were composed within a well-established tradition. It is the tradition, rather than any individual work(s), that casts light on the technique of the *Christ and Satan* poet.

[29] R. Morris, ed., *The Blickling Homilies* (London, 1967), pp. 113-15.

[30] Ibid., p. 101. Morris glosses *don* and *alesan* as imperatives.

"Forðon" has a syllogistic function, drawing the moral as a conclusion from the material previously handled.

Much the same thing may be found in the *Vercelli Homilies,* and one example ought suffice. The sixth homily recounts the miracles which took place immediately preceding, and immediately following, the birth of Christ. The homilist considers that the miracles which provide his readers with evidence of the power and mercy of God are, in effect, exempla: "*Utan we* nu eorne *tilian,* þæt we þe selran syn, þonne we þylleca *bysena* usses Dryhtnes beforan us reccan 7 rædan ge gehyrað. *Utan we healdan* sybbe 7 lufan be-twiohs us: þonne gyldeð us God ece mede æt ussum ende."[31] The "utan" + infinitive formation is a pattern familiar from the *Blickling Homilies,* and it has a similar function here.

Aelfric's *Catholic Homilies* has a wealth of material: there are some forty occurrences of exempla, of which twenty-eight are fully developed narrative and dramatic pieces taking up between three-quarters of a page and two pages of text in the Thorpe edition. On occasion, though less frequently than in the *Blickling Homilies,* the exempla are followed by hortatory passages formulaic in structure. So in homily #28, vol. 1, "Dominica XI. Post Pentecosten," after recounting the story of the Velerian nobleman Chrysaurius who, at death, was carried off by devils, Aelfric concludes with the moral: "Ac *uton we beon carfulle,* þæt ure tima mid ydelnysse us ne losige, and we ðonne to weldædum gecyrran willan, ðonne us se deað to forðsiðe geðreatað."[32] The form "uton" + infinitive is familiar from the analysis of the other homily collections. Another illustration of the same technique, drawn from vol. 2, homily #3, "Sermo in Aepiphania Domini," occurs after the exemplum of the woman who prayed Christ to heal her sick daughter. Aelfric compares the function of the mother in the homily to the godparents of the Christian child at baptism, and exhorts the child upon becoming adult to learn how to guard his Christianity. He concludes: "*Uton don* forði swa swa se ylca apostol tæhte, 'Genealæcað to Gode, and God genealæhð to eow.' And se sealm-scop us mynegað eft, ðus cweðende, 'Eadig bið se wer seðe hine ondræt God, and awent his willan to his bebodum.'"[33]

But for the most part, Aelfric is more expansive in drawing his moral or doctrinal point than are the authors of the *Blickling* and *Vercelli* collections. Absent from many homilies that contain exempla is the succinct formulaic exhortation addressed to the people; Aelfric's is a more relaxed, free and literary treatment of illustrations. Following the exemplum there is often an explanation of it. The tone is always moral,

---

[31] Max Förster, ed., *Die Vercelli-Homilien* (Darmstadt, 1964), p. 137.

[32] Benjamin Thorpe, ed., *The Homilies of the Anglo-Saxon Church: The First Part Containing the Sermones Catholici, or Homilies of Aelfric,* 2 vols. (London, 1844-46), vol. 1, p. 414.

[33] Ibid., vol. 2, p. 52.

but formulaic phrases are usually wanting. For example, homily #23, vol. 1, "Dominica Secunda post Pentecosten," contains the exemplum of the monk who, while on a journey, carried on his back Christ disguised as a leper; the conclusion of the homily has no exhortation:

> Hwæt is on menniscum gecynde swa mærlic swa Cristes menniscnys? and hwæt is atelicor geðuht on menniscum gecynde þonne is ðæs hreoflian lic, mid toðundennesse, and springum, and reocendum stence? Ac se ðe is arwurðful ofer ealle gesceafta, he gemedemode hine sylfne þæt he wære gesewen on ðam atelican hiwe, to ði þæt we sceolon besargian menniscra manna yrmðe, and be ure mihte gefrefrian, for lufe ðæs mildheortan and ðæs eadmodan Hælendes; þæt he us getiðige wununge on his rice to ecum life, seðe us ahredde fram deofles hæftnydum....[34]

Another illustration of this technique can be found in the closing section of homily #6, vol. 2, "Dominica in Sexagesima," which recounts the story of Servelus and the paralytic who, by his constant prayer and holy activities in reading the scriptures, manifested the virtue of patience. The homily concludes:

> Mine gebroðra, understandað be ðisum hwilce beladunge hæbbe we æt Godes dome, gif we asleaciað from godum weorcum, we ðe habbað ure hæle and æhta, nu þes lama wædla buton handcræfte Godes beboda gefylde. Ic bidde eow, gebroðra, tihtað eower mod to gecnyrdnysse godra weorca, þæt ge mid geðylde godne wæstm to Godes handa gebringon, þæt ge mid him and his halgum þæt ece lif habban moton on ealra worulda woruld. Amen.[35]

The reason for the absence of hortatory elements is clear. Homily #23 concerns itself with a verse-by-verse explication of the parable of Dives and Lazarus, the burden of which is that Christians should beware of riches and have charity toward the poor. In his thorough fashion Aelfric goes over the moral implications of the parable repeatedly, demonstrating how much easier it is for the poor to enter heaven than the rich. The exemplum, in its setting, is the keystone of the sermon, since it shows that the risen Christ did not disdain to appear in the form of a leper, surely one of the poorest of the poor. The illustration is thus self-explanatory in context. Again, homily #6, vol. 2, is another verse-by-verse exegesis of Luke 8:4-15, the parable of the Sower, which emphasizes the necessity for the Christian to live free from sin and to perform good works in his station in life. This is treated so exhaustively that the culminating exemplum is self-explanatory. Most of the exempla in Aelfric's homilies are treated in similar fashion: they follow a thorough analysis of the gospel text, and they are chosen to illustrate the

---

[34] Ibid., vol. 1, pp. 336-38.
[35] Ibid., vol. 2, p. 98.

points under discussion with such care that no final exhortation is needed.

With Aelfric, then, we discover essentially the same elements, though approached in a more literary and scholarly fashion, that we found in the *Vercelli* and the *Blickling Homilies*: the use of exempla to point a moral or doctrinal argument, and occasional formulaic exhortation based on the exempla. With particular reference to Aelfric's usage, we have a more discursive approach to the manipulation of exempla, conditioned by the fact that, in context, certain illustrations are self-explanatory.

When we come to *Christ and Satan* with the analysis of the prose homilies in mind, the relationship between the narrative-dramatic and homiletic-hortatory verse becomes clear. The initial narrative-dramatic section, begun at line 34 and continued through line 188, describes Satan's and the fallen angels' reaction to the hell in which they find themselves, and rehearses the reason for their fall. The ensuing homiletic passage reads:

	Forþan sceal gehycgan	hæleða æghwylc
	þæt hē ne ābælige	bearn waldendes.
195	*Lǣte him tō bysne*	hū þā blācan fēond
	for oferhygdum	ealle forwurdon.
	Neoman ūs tō wynne	weoroda drihten,
	uppe ēcne gefēan,	engla waldend.
	Hē þæt gecȳdde	þæt hē mægencræft hæfde,
200	mihta miccle,	þā hē þā mænego ādrāf,
	hæftas of ðǣm hēan selde.	*Gemunan wē* þone hālgan drihten,
	ēcne alra gescefta;	*cēosan ūs* eard in wuldre
	mid ealra cyninga cyninge,	sē is Crīst genemned.
	Beoran on brēostum	blīðe geþōhtas,
205	sibbe and snytero;	*gemunan sōð and riht*
	þonne wē tō hēhselde	hnīgan þencað,
	and þone anwaldan	āra biddan.
	Ƿonne behōfað	sē ðe hēr wunað
	weorulde wynnum	þæt him wlite scīne
210	þonne hē ōþer līf	eft gesēceð,
	fǣgere land	þonne þēos folde sēo;
	is þǣr wlitig and wynsum,	wæstmas scīnað,
	beorhte ofer burgum;	þǣr is brāde lond,
	hyhtlicra hām	in heofonrīce,
215	Crīste gecwēmra.	*Uta cerran þider*
	þǣr hē sylfa sit,	sigora waldend,
	drihten hǣlend,	in ðǣm dēoran hām;
	and ymb þæt hēhsetl	hwīte standað
	engla fēðan	and ēadigre;
220	hālige heofenþrēatas	herigað drihten
	wordum and weorcum.	Heora wlite scīneð
	geond ealra worulda woruld	mid wuldorcyninge.

That which has been denied to the fallen angels because of their rebellion is offered to man, provided that he maintain a certain mode of life and level of conduct that will not anger the Son of God; the would-be citizen of the heavenly city must bear in his breast blessed thoughts, be mindful of truth and righteousness, have beauty (*wlite*) shining within. The pedagogical thrust of this passage is as clear as is the fact that it draws its power to convince from the description of the fallen angels presented in preceding lines. There are instructive formal similarities between this section of *Christ and Satan* and the exhortations discovered in the analysis of the Anglo-Saxon homilies. The "forþan" in line 193 has the same syllogistic function as the "forþons" in the *Blickling Homilies,* and the form "uta" + infinitive, line 215, is also familiar. The italicized verbs are in the subjunctive mood, a hortatory technique employed by both Anglo-Saxon and Latin writers.

The poem returns to narrative-dramatic verse after line 222, further developing in some fifty lines a picture of the pains of hell and the essential helplessness of its inhabitants. The second hortatory section in Part I, introduced by "forþon" + "mæg" + infinitive, contains a description of heaven as well as moral injunctions:

	Forþon mæg gehycgan,	sē ðe his heorte dēah,
	þæt hē him āfirre	frēcne geþohtas,
	lāðe leahtras,	lifigendra gehwylc.
285	*Gemunan symle on mōde*	meotodes strengðo;
	gearwian ūs tōgēnes	grēne strǣte
	ūp tō englum,	þǣr is se ælmihtiga god,
	and ūs befæðman wile	frēobearn godes
	gif wē þæt on eorðan	ǣr geþencað,
290	and ūs tō þām hālgan	helpe gelēfað.
	Þonne hē ūs nō forlǣteð,	ah līf syleð
	uppe mid englum,	ēadigne drēam.
	Tǣceð ūs se torhta	trumlicne hām,
	beorhte burhweallas.	Beorhte scīnað
295	gesǣlige sāwle	sorgum bedǣlde,
	þǣr hēo ǣfre forð	wunian mōten
	cestre and cynestōl.	*Uton cȳþan þæt!*
	Dēman wē on eorðan,	ǣrror lifigend,
	onlūcan mid listum	locen waldendes,
300	*ongeotan gāstlice!*	Ūs ongēan cumað
	þūsend engla,	gif þider mōton,
	and þæt on eorðan	ǣr gewyrcað.
	Forþon sē bið ēadig	sē ðe ǣfre wile
	mān oferhycgen,	meotode cwēman,
305	*synne ādwǣscan.*	Swā hē sylfa cwæð:
	"Sōðfæste men,	sunnan gelīce,
	fægre gefrætewod	in heora fæder rīce
	scīnað in sceldbyrig."	Þǣr sceppend seolf
	hēo befæðmeð,	fæder mancynnes,

310   āhefeð holdlice   in heofones lēoht,
           þær hēo mid wuldorcyninge   wunian mōton
           āwa tō aldre,
           āgan drēama drēam   mid drihtne gode,
           ā tō worulde   ā būtan ende.

Again the didactic intent of the passage is clear: negatively, the Christian must avoid evil thoughts and loathsome sins; positively, he must understand with the spirit, praise and demonstrate the hidden secrets of God while he is yet on earth. The general exhortations of the first homiletic section are the more specific here because the dramatic section to which this exhortation is attached and from which it draws its power contains details not only of the suffering of the hellish host, but also suggests the penetration of hell's evil into the land of men: since the devils are able to grapple the enemies of God to the bottom of the abyss (ll. 267-271), man must be ever the more wary. But having quenched sin, renounced evil, and, in general, pleased the Lord, he will receive the proper greeting in the heavenly city and thereafter shine, gloriously adorned, like the sun. We have here the essential elements of the hortatory structure already discovered in lines 193-222: verbs in the subjunctive mood, "forþon" and "uton" + the infinitive. The last line of the quotation, 314, resembles the closing formula used in many vernacular homilies.

     Lines 315-364 comprise a summation of all the material, both narrative and homiletic, presented in preceding verses. It contains another description of the pains and sufferings of the devils in hell and contrasts this with an affecting picture of the sublime joy of the heavenly host. Emphasis is placed on man's ability to gain heaven if he obeys the Saviour: "Blǣd bið ǣghwǣm / þǣm ðe hǣlende hēran þenceð, / and wel is þām ðe þæt wyrcan mōt" (ll. 362b-364).

     Part II begins with a brief recapitulation, lines 365-378a, of the fall of the angels and Lucifer's punishment in hell. The poet seizes upon the idea of suffering to provide the transition to the harrowing, at which time the pains of the devils increased. Christ appears in hell to bind the devils and release the souls of the just; Eve, upon successfully pleading with the Saviour, is included in the number of those who journey to the "mǣran byrig." To emphasize the fact of the true resurrection, the poet stresses Christ's appearance to Peter and Thomas, and it is only after this that a homiletic passage appears:

545   Fǣger wæs þæt ongin   þæt frēodrihten
              geþrōwode,   þēoden ūre.
              Hē on bēame āstāh   and his blōd āgēat,
              god on galgan,   þurh his gāstes mǣgen.
              Forþon men sceolon   mǣla gehwylce
550   *secgan* drihtne þanc   dǣdum and weorcum,
              þæs ðe hē ūs of hæftum   hām gelǣdde
              ūp tō ēðle,   þǣr wē āgan sceolon

drihtnes dōmas,
and wē in wynnum   wunian mōton.
555   Ūs is wuldres lēoht,
torht ontȳned,   þām ðe teala þenceð.

The "ongin" mentioned in line 545 encompasses the whole of the previously recounted action of Part II: i.e., the harrowing, true resurrection, appearance to the apostles, for which salvific events man ought offer thanks. The hortatory pattern is "forþon" + "sceolon" + "secgan." There are no subjunctives, and the section is relatively short.

Two further exhortations occur in Part II, each having the structure "uton" plus infinitive, the second having a hortatory subjunctive as well, each emphasizing the necessity to obey Christ:

                                Uton teala hycgan
þæt wē hælende   hēran georne,
Crīste cwēman.   Þǣr is cūðre līf
þonne wē on eorðan mægen æfre gestrēonan. (ll. 593-596)

Uton, lā, geþencan   geond þās worulde,
þæt wē hælende   hēran onginnen!
Georne þurh godes gife   *gemunan gāstes blēd.* . . . (ll. 642-644)

The direction of the argument on the difficulties presented by the mixture of verse kinds in *Christ and Satan* should be clear. The poet has so structured the narrative-dramatic verses of his work that they serve as exempla to which he attaches and from which he draws his exhortations in the homiletic-hortatory sections. The structure of these hortatory lines closely parallels the pattern of homiletic exhortation which accompanies the use of exempla in the prose homilies. The quantitative disparity between the number of lines devoted to such material in Parts I and II seems conditioned by the fact that the scenes described and the dialogue dramatized in the second part have a relatively clear moral burden: the implications of these scenes for the conduct of man's life are apparent. The events in Part I, or at least the manner in which the poet wished his audience to approach them, are not so readily comprehended.

Part III presents a seemingly insoluble problem for the thesis that verse mixture in *Christ and Satan* is consciously structured, since it contains no homiletic-hortatory elements, but is consistently narrative-dramatic. To deal with this last part it is necessary to demonstrate that, in context, it is self-explanatory, and thus a closing homiletic charge would be superfluous. This requires an analysis of the thematic movement of the poem to clarify the tentative argument for unity developed so far. Such an investigation shows that the poem in all its parts supports the dual theme of the development and revelation of the character of Christ, and the implications of this revelation for man's moral life.

Bernard Huppé believes that *Christ and Satan* exemplifies the Trinitarian nature of the Deity.[36] The theme of the poem, then, to follow the argument of his book, might be amended to something like "The Might of the Triune God." Huppé's translation of the poem's initial eighteen lines supports his analysis of the theme:

> It was manifest to mankind
> that the Master had might and strength
> when He fashioned the fields of earth.
> Selfsame He set the sun and the moon,
> 5   the stars and the earth, the stream in the sea,
> the water and the sky, through His wondrous might.
> The deep expanse entirely encompasses He,
> the Master in His might, and all the middle-earth;
> He Godself may gaze through the sea,
> 10   the deeps in heaven, the dear Son of God,
> and reckon He can the rain showers,
> singly each drop: the sum of all days
> Selfsame He set through His soothfast might.
> So the Creator through the Holy Spirit
> 15   planned and set in six days
> the earthly regions, up in heaven,
> and the deep waters. Who is it that knows
> the skill entirely except Eternal God?[37]

The word Huppé renders as "Master," line 2, is, in the Anglo-Saxon, "meotod," and Huppé probably intends this for the Father. Completing the Trinity we have the Son, line 10, and the Holy Spirit, line 14. But in neither Bosworth-Toller nor Grein-Köhler is such a translation of "meotod" given as a possible choice; rather the term is more often to be translated as "creator," with specific identification to be gained from context. The mention of the Holy Spirit, line 14, appears a mistranslation. The Anglo-Saxon reads þurh his wuldres gāst, but Huppé renders "his" as "the." There is no confusion in the manuscript about the "his," and in fact þurh his wuldres gāst of line 14 is a structural parallel to þurh his sōðan miht in line 13, which in turn takes its force ultimately from godes āgen bearn of line 10b, as do the somewhat unspecified subjects of the first nine lines—e.g., "meotod" and "Seolfa he." Though one may quarrel with the artistic technique of the poet which keeps the adequate specification of the subject until line 10, it can hardly be argued that he intended anything other than the second person of the Trinity as the creative agent.

A superficial reading of *Christ and Satan,* though, offers an immediate difficulty to the thematic movement the opening lines suggest. It is a natural assumption that since Christ is introduced as the creative

---

[36] Huppé, p. 228.
[37] Ibid., p. 228.

agent in the initial lines, his character, activities and history would provide the sustaining interest. Such does not seem to be the case. Part I, for example, concerns itself with the laments of the devil(s), detailing the horrors of hell in contrast to the lost joys of heaven, and exhorting readers or listeners to "do good and avoid evil." As an active character, as a centre of interest, Christ does not appear.

But though he is not an active character, his presence is felt and his omnipotence is emphasized in the total defeat of the devils. There is no question that anyone other than Christ expelled the angels from heaven, a fact stressed by repetition throughout Part I, by the poet-narrator, the devil, and his subordinates. The first specific reference is contained in a narrative section, lines 67b-68a: "Crīst hēo āfirde drēamum bedēlde." In the initial altercation between the Devil and his followers, there is a somewhat enigmatic statement in which they indicate the nature of their chief's offense: "Segdest ūs tō sōðe þæt ðīn sunu wære/meotod moncynnes. Hafustū nū māre sūsel!" (ll. 63-64). Clubb interprets "ðīn sunu" as a reference to the Antichrist, a figure believed by some early commentators to be the son of Satan,[38] while Gollancz cites in explanation a section from the Gospel of Saint Bartholomew in which Satan "takes counsel with his son Salpsan."[39] But these putative allusions lead nowhere: neither the Antichrist nor Salpsan is again alluded to in the more than 700 lines of the work. But if we understand the "meotod mancynnes" as a reference to Christ, then the passage would be intelligible within the structure of the poem and Satan's sin would be an attempt to subordinate the Son to himself by usurping the position of the Father.[40]

That the sin of Satan was in some manner or other directed against Christ is affirmed in succeeding statements. Lines 85-87 mention his desire to overthrow the "wuldres leoman, bearn haelendes";

> þæt ic wolde tōwerpan   wuldres lēoman,
> bearn hēlendes,   āgan mē burga gewald
> eall tō æhte,   and ðēos earme hēap....

This enormity is further specified by mention of a desire to wrest control of heaven from Christ. There is conscious irony here in the yoking of such a bold attempt with the qualification of those angels in league with Satan as "ðēos earme hēap." There follows, in lines 89-124, a detailed description of the pains of hell and the frustrations of the devils, similar in essentials, though not particulars, to that in lines 36b-64. The pain is clearly imposed by Christ. Again, in lines 172-173, Satan affirms the reasons for his fall: "ðæs ic wolde of selde sunu meotodes,/drihten

---

[38] Clubb, p. 62.

[39] Gollancz, p. civ.

[40] See notes to these lines, and my brief "*Christ and Satan*, 63-64," *The Explicator*, 31, No. 2 (1972), article 10.

ādrīfan, and āgan mē þæs drēames gewald." Lines 180b-183 express the same idea, but add an affirmation of the awesome power of Christ:

	Wāt ic nū þā
þæt bið alles lēas	ēcan drēamas
sē ðe heofencyninge	hēran ne þenceð,
meotode cwēman.	

There is a wide application to Satan's remarks. "Anyone" who refuses to honour and obey the king of heaven is without eternal joy, not only those devils who have refused, but others, angelic or human, who might refuse. This more general statement, and the fiercely lyrical nature of the laments in lines 163-188, with the contrast between the pains of hell and the joys of heaven they contain, appears to be a consciously structured introduction to the first lengthy homiletic section, lines 193-222. The formulaic nature of these verses and their connection with the techniques of the prose homilies has been dealt with above. It is sufficient to point out here that they continue the theme of the power of Christ adumbrated in the narrative and dramatic sections, but direct it to the condition of man by drawing out the implications of such power for the moral life of the reader or audience. In this segment there are three references to Christ, line 194b "bearn waldendes," line 203b "sē is Crīst genemned," and lines 213b-215a: "þær is brāde lond,/hyhtlicra hām in heofonrīce/Crīste gecwēmra." These allusions inform other somewhat less specific substantives in the section. The didactic purpose is to remind man to bear in his breast "blīðe geþōhtas, sibbe and snytero . . . sōð and riht" (ll. 204b-205) when he seeks the "ōðer līf" (l. 210a), the life denied Satan because of his sin but made available to man, conditioned always on his conduct. Such moral implications have meaning and become intelligible only in terms of the activity of Christ in the utter defeat of Satan described in the narrative-dramatic sections. Lest man take too lightly the homiletic exhortations to the good life, he has before him the pains of hell and the total frustration of the devils as a reminder of the fate of those who fail to obey the Son.

With the intention of further emphasizing his moral, the poet returns to the description of the pains of Satan. In a somewhat confused section that seems at once a recollection and a prevision, lines 228-244, Satan admits his sin and, again detailing the loss of heavenly joys, remarks that the glories once given him and his are now available to man. Though the syntax is cloudy, the intention of the poet is clear: a concrete example of the defeat of those who fail to obey the law of Christ, and the possibility of heavenly bliss for those who do. The succeeding lines, 245-278, have the same general thrust, but without the textual difficulties. Satan again indicates the nature of his sin, and the immediate and devastating response it elicited:

| Ðā gewearð ūsic | þæt wē woldon swā |
| drihten ādrīfan | of þām dēoran hām, |

cyning of cestre.   Cūð is wīde
þæt wreclāstas   wunian mōton
grimme grundas. (ll. 254-258a)

The stark juxtaposition of the attempted coup with the immediate and
unqualified defeat of the devils suggested in "Cuð is wīde . . . grimme
grundas" indicates the omnipotence of the One they chose to disobey.
Lines 282-314 comprise the second homiletic section which emphasizes
that the reader should remember "meotodes strengðo." This is an
effective adjuration, since illustrations of such strength are given
throughout Part I. As before, the moral exhortations are conditioned by
the actions described in the dramatic verses; both sections body forth
the power of Christ and develop his character in relation to Satan and to
man. The substantives in these lines are not as clearly directed to the
Son as in the first homiletic section, and in isolation such terms as
"drihten" line 255a, "cyning" line 256a, "God seolfa" line 258b,
"hælend God" line 280b could refer to the Father or to the Trinity.
These terms, however, are not in isolation, but in a context that has
established for some 200 lines that Christ is their exact referent.

Following the second homiletic division, the poet recounts in narrative form what had been presented previously in dramatic verse in the
body of Part I: the sufferings of Satan in the pains of hell and lost joys of
heaven, and the availability of these joys for man if he will follow certain
general moral precepts. Here again there is adequate reference to the
fact that Satan's sin was a revolt against Christ, and that Christ remained
in control of the heavenly kingdom:

                                         Hēofon dēop gehygd,
þā hēo on heofonum   hām staðelodon,
þæt hīe woldon benǣman   nergendne Crīst
rodera rīces,   ah hē on riht gehēold
hīred heofona   and þæt hālige seld.
                                         (ll. 343b-347)

Part I closes with a description of the heavenly joys available to man.

There may be much to criticize in the technique of the poet in Part I.
His most obvious peculiarity is repetition: he states and restates the
background of the fall and its consequences; he draws the explicit moral
implications of such events not once, but twice; he concludes Part I with
a section combining both themes. Such repetition may be an artistic
flaw. But if I am correct in assuming that *Christ and Satan* is primarily a
didactic work, the *raison d'être* of such repetition should be apparent,
since Gregory and Aelfric, for example, within a single homily emphasized repeatedly the moral implications of their doctrines. Here the
poet does essentially the same thing. The repetitions, both narrative-
dramatic and homiletic-hortatory, are just that: none of them deviates
from the theme established in their respective first sections, no new
doctrine is adumbrated, no new characters introduced. The poem pro-

ceeds in terms of these repetitions by increments of meaning, each repetition based upon the previous one, not superseding it, but adding something to it. Finally a fully articulated picture is formed of the sufferings of the devil(s), the sin which caused this suffering, the character of Christ in so far as he reacts against the fiends in the heavenly rebellion, and the obligation of man to lead a moral life in terms of the rewards and punishments of the next, with the vivid scenes of hell providing him at least a negative motivation.

It is in terms of this negative motivation that we may see an aesthetic and psychological justification for the verse mixture of the poem, Part I particularly, to complement the pedagogical explanation offered so far. In *Christ and Satan* we have a shifting perspective, a dual point of view, the elements of which are found in the narrative-dramatic and homiletic-hortatory verse. In Part I, hell is described with highly detailed visual and auditory images, primarily by and through Satan's monologues. The reader is brought within the scope of the action, into hell itself, and becomes identified artistically with Satan, seeing and feeling things as he does. In the homiletic-hortatory sections a totally different point of view is established. These verses initiate a retrogressive movement which brings the audience back from hell and the company of Satan, while maintaining both as objects of contemplation. The aesthetic distance thus achieved allows an objective perspective in which to extrapolate from the experience of Satan and the felt description of hell general moral precepts for the conduct of a Christian life. Part II has fewer homiletic passages than Part I, but then the material dealt with in the narrative-dramatic verses of the second part has a more immediately apparent implication for man's moral life. Still, the relationship between the kinds of verse in Part II is essentially the same as in Part I, the homiletic-hortatory sections finding a similar pedagogical, aesthetic, and psychological justification.

Though he is prominent as the conqueror of Satan, Christ never actually appears as a character, never personally intervenes in the action "onstage" in Part I; but as the laments of Satan and his troop suggest, he is most energetic and active "offstage." Christ's character here is defined almost exclusively in terms of power, his omnipotence demonstrated in the immediate and absolute defeat of the devils.

The situation in Part II is quite different: Christ is an actual participant in the action, takes physical part in the harrowing of hell, releases the souls of the just, binds more securely the devils. In this section the poet strives to give Christ attributes over and above the single omnipotence described in Part I. That he is still omnipotent is demonstrated by the fact that the devils fear him, and with good reason: his advent in hell is the prelude to their destruction. But the poet seems absorbed with something other than a glorification of the power of Christ. The details surrounding the conflict in hell are given in some twenty lines, 378-397, and the actual binding of the devils is narratively described in lines 442-454. Such subjects present perfect opportunities for amplification, and, as Part I has indicated, the poet is capable of embroidering. That he did not do so when the opportunity presented itself argues that he was concerned with something else.

In fact the most affecting scenes of the harrowing are devoted not to a glorification of Christ's power, but to a manifestation of his charity and love. Such appears to be the poet's intention in Eve's long speech in which she recounts the circumstances of her and Adam's fall, indicates her contrition, and pleads for release from hell. Her final appeal is one of generative relationship with Christ through Mary who is her daughter. This technique is not unlike that used to define the character of Christ in Part I, where he is revealed through the eyes of others and measured in his activities toward them. Eve's speech strikes a responsive chord in Christ: just as Satan's suffering indicates his omnipotence, his response to Eve manifests his charity, mercy, and forgiveness. There is even a "stage direction" in the speech, a slight thing, but indicative of the mood the poet was attempting to create: "Ræhte þā mid handum tō heofencyninge,/bæd meotod miltse þurh Marian hād..." (ll. 435-436). Something emotionally affecting is caught here: Eve stretches her hand towards Christ just before voicing her final and successful plea for mercy, a plea which inextricably involves her with the person of the Saviour.

Christ's compassion is illustrated in the long section, lines 469b-511a, where he explains to the holy souls that his incarnation, passion, and death was the condition of their salvation. Rehearsing the fall of man from the divinity's point of view as a complement to Eve's narration of it, he has only sorrow for man's plight: "þā mē gehrēaw þæt mīn handgeweorc/þæs carcernes clom ōrōwade" (ll. 487-488). Primary responsibility for the fall is placed on the Tempter, "se balewa," "handþegen helle," "se atola": man is more sinned against than sinning.

The poet mentions certain activities of Christ after the harrowing, all of which point to the reality and truth of the resurrection, as an earnest, I think, of the Christian's final reward. Such is the intention of Peter's statement, lines 535-538a:

> "Eart þū þis, drihten, dōme gewurðad?
> Wē ðē gesāwon æt sumum cyrre;
> þec gelegdon on lāðne bend
> hǣþene mid hondum...."

and the doubt of Thomas as well, in lines 540-543:

> Sume hit ne mihton mōde oncnāwan:
> þæt wæs se dēora Didimus wæs hāten
> ǣr hē mid hondum hǣlend genōm
> sylfne be sīdan þǣr hē his swāt forlēt.

The following homiletic section, lines 545-556, refers to the preceding activities and emphasizes the cost at which man was liberated from hell. It stresses man's duty to Christ in relation to the price paid for salvation.

Part II continues with a brief mention of the ascension and the descent of the Holy Spirit. It is interesting to note that this latter is considered from an exclusively Christocentric perspective:

þā gȳt nergende Crīst
ymb tēne niht
mid his gāstes gife,

Þā hit þus gelomp,
gecwæð þæt hē þæs
twelf apostolas
gingran geswīðde.
(ll. 568b-571)

That which descends upon the apostles is not a separate person of the Trinity, but the spirit of Christ. This descent of the spirit, since it is traditionally understood to be the formal founding of the church, that mystical body of Christ membership in which ensures man of salvation, may be seen as yet another example of Christ's concern for men. Those possessing such membership need fear nothing at the time of the final judgment, to which cataclysm the poet turns to conclude Part II.

Here again one might question the poet's architectonics, since, as in Part I after the second homiletic section, a case could be made for ending this part before the description of the judgment. But if the primarily didactic thrust of the poem be remembered, then its inclusion can be justified on pedagogical grounds. The poet has presented in Part II a picture of Christ which stresses the human virtues of charity, compassion, and mercy. As a corrective, perhaps, to a possibly over-sanguine view of Christ, he includes the last judgment and his final justice.

Thus far analysis has included Parts I and II, and has demonstrated that the narrative-dramatic sections emphasize the development and revelation of Christ's character, while the homiletic-hortatory sections stress the implications of this revelation for the conduct, in broad terms, of man's life. We have seen an initial emphasis on Christ's omnipotence, a subsequent revelation of his charity, compassion, and mercy. Paralleling and supporting this revelation of Christ's character is the chronological movement of the poem, the progression of the time sequence. The action of Part I takes place in hell, the eternal aspect of the scene putting the action, as it were, "out of time." In this part, Christ does not actually appear, but is revealed through the awesome effects of his power. The initial scene of Part II, the harrowing, again is situated in hell, though it is conditioned by an actual historical event, the crucifixion, alluded to by both Christ and the poet-narrator, though not described as such. Here Christ is physically present, his ability to harrow hell attesting to his divine power, the circumstances surrounding the crucifixion, as well as Eve's speech and his own explanation of the incarnation, passion and death, attesting to his mercy and charity. There is a movement in Part II from eternity to time in the appearances to Peter and Didymus. One might also say that the ascension is itself an historically dated event.[41] By the end of Part II, then, the poem has moved from the eternal to the temporal, from a conception of Christ as exclusively divine omnipotence to one which, while recognizing his power, emphasizes certain charitable characteristics. Part III provides at once the poem's final temporal movement, concludes the revelation of the character of Christ, and gives a concrete exemplum of how man should implement his duty to God when confronted by temptation.

Part III deals with the temporal event of Christ's temptation in the desert by Satan, thus bringing the chronological progression of the work from the eternity of Part I well into the realm of historical time. The fact that Christ is tempted at all is sufficient manifestation of his humanity, the fact that he is able so easily to crush the Devil after the third temptation indicates his divinity. This is the final development of the character of Christ: he is the God-Man. There is no further need to emphasize in the poem Christ's human nature, since the audience already would be familiar with the doctrine of Christ's two natures. There is need, though, to anchor the somewhat broad moral generalizations contained in the hortatory-homiletic sections of Part I and II to concrete action. This is the final function of Part III: man should act, when tempted, in a manner mirroring Christ's reaction to the Devil in the desert. Part III, unlike the preceding parts, has no hortatory-homiletic lines, no exhortations, because there need be none; like certain exempla in the homilies of Aelfric, this exemplum in context is self-explanatory.

This movement of the poem follows *Matthew* 4:1-11, though with significant modifications. In his handling of this scene, the poet appears to have assumed that his audience would be familiar not only with the gospel passage itself, but also recognize its particular exemplary character. This assumption was probably well founded, since a tradition of such handling can be traced to Jerome and Augustine, and followed through the *Blickling Homilies* and the *Catholic Homilies* of Aelfric.[42] In all instances, *Matthew* 4:1-11 is used to demonstrate how man should react to temptation: if he follows Christ's example, he will be saved.

The poet avails himself of the irony inherent in a situation where his audience knows more than one of his literary characters: from their

---

[41] The last judgment, since its appearance is primarily pedagogically conditioned, does some violence to this scheme. Even so, the broad outlines of the temporal movement are not obscured.

[42] See, for example, Jerome, *Letters, NPNF,* Second Series 6, letter 38, p. 48, letter 130, p. 266; Augustine, *City of God,* Book 9, chap. 21, *NPNF,* First Series 2, p. 177; *The Trinity, NPNF,* First Series 3, p. 78; sermon 73, *NPNF,* First Series 6, p. 473; *On the Gospel of John, NPNF,* First Series 7, p. 288; Gregory the Great, *XL Homiliarum in Evangelia,* #16, *PL* 76, cols. 1134-38; *Aelfric's Catholic Homilies,* vol. 1, "Homily for the First Sunday in Lent," pp. 174, 176-78; *The Blickling Homilies,* "Homily for the First Sunday in Lent," p. 31.

general biblical knowledge, reinforced by the material presented in
Christ and Satan so far, the audience recognizes that Satan is doomed.
And the poet handles the irony well. The first temptation falls within the
bounds of the *Matthew* tradition:

>   Brōhte him tō bearme   brāde stānas,
>   bæd him for hungre   hlāfas wyrcan—
>   "gif þū swā micle   mihte hæbbe." (ll. 670-672)

The last line is particularly effective, since the previous 600 lines have
adequately disclosed the power of Christ. Most of Christ's response is
lost, as is the material of the second temptation, probably owing to a
copying oversight or a scribal lapse of some sort which is further responsible for three misplaced lines: 676-678. Enough of the second rejoinder
to Satan survives, however, to indicate that it too was in keeping with
the *Matthew* tradition:

>   Þā him andswarode   ēce drihten:
>   "Wēndest þū, āwyrgda,   þæt āwriten nǣre,
>   nymþe mē ænne.... (ll. 673-675a)

The third temptation follows the *Matthew* account in essence, but
makes significant expansions:

>   Þā hē mid hondum genōm
>   atol þurh edwīt,   and on esle āhōf,
>   herm bealowes gāst,   and on beorh āstāh,
>   āsette on dūne   drihten hǣlend:
>   "Lōca nū ful wīde   ofer londbēwende.
>   Ic þē geselle   on þīnes seolfes dōm
>   folc and foldan.   Fōh hider tō mē
>   burh and breotone   bold tō gewealde,
>   rodora rīces,   gif þū sēo riht cyning
>   engla and monna,   swā ðū ǣr myntest."
>   (ll. 679b-688)

There is nothing in the gospel of the Devil putting hands on Christ or
heaving him onto his shoulder. The expansion magnifies Satan's offense. The temptation speech itself is subtly changed. *Matthew* 4:9
reads: "And he said to him, 'All these things will I give thee, if thou wilt
fall down and worship me.'" The poet's expansions describe the Devil
attributing mean ambition to Christ, and make his lordship a function of
þegnscip to Satan. Clubb's remark on lines 683-688, that Satan is
attempting to articulate what he believes to be in the mind of Christ, is
well taken.[43] What Clubb does not explain is why these expansions take
place.

The expansions allowed the poet to integrate Part III into the
economy of the work by yet another, more striking, modification of

---

[43] Clubb, p. 132.

tradition. The temptation scene was traditionally treated as an exemplum of how man should react to personal temptations of the Devil: specifically, he should manifest heroic patience. But the poem has stressed the all-encompassing power of Christ, his function of creator, expeller of Satan, saviour of mankind. The temptation thus becomes a monstrous hybris. With the expansions of the third temptation, the emphasis on the physical action of the Devil's grappling Christ, and his ascription of mean ambition to him, the violent response of Christ, itself to be found in no source, becomes perfectly intelligible, perhaps even psychologically and aesthetically necessary.

Since there is nothing like this response in any of the sermons, homilies or commentaries readily available to the poet, it may well be his own artistic creation. And it is most effective. For the hybris of the temptation, the Devil is condemned to measure, to fully experience (*āmetan*), the vastness of the sufferings of hell. The strength of Christ's spurning of Satan is a function of the imperatives in which he speaks:

"Gewīt þū, āwyrgda,   in þæt wītescræf (l. 690)
                                        Cer ðē on bæcling! (l. 697b)
Wite þū ēac, āwyrgda,   hū wīd and sīd
helheoðo drēorig,   and mid hondum āmet.
Grīp wið þæs grundes;   gang þonne swā
oððæt þū þone ymbhwyrft   alne cunne.... (ll. 698-701)
                                        Gong ricene tō.... (l. 707b)

This is powerfully done.

There follows a narrative description of Satan fulfilling Christ's command. The rhetoric here is as effective as the imperatives detailed above:

                                        Hwīlum mid folmum mæt
wēan and wītu;   hwīlum se wonna læg
læhte wið þes lāþan;   hwīlum hē licgan geseah
hæftas in hylle;   hwīlum hrēam āstāg,
ðonne hē on þone atolan   ēagum gesāwun. (ll. 712b-716)

Finally, in keeping with the command of Christ, lines 694-695, that he not bring a message of hope to the hell-dwellers, Satan returns to his "werigan gastas." They greet him with a curse: "'Lā, þus bēo nū on yfele!/Noldæs ær teala!'" (l. 729a-b). The poem concludes with the rubric "Finit Liber II. Amen."

The final section of the poem completes the revelation of Christ. As the commentators remark, the temptation expresses his dual nature: he is the God-Man. It completes the chronological movement of the poem, bringing the action into the realm of real time. It provides a striking example, a concrete illustration, of how man is to react to the devil, thus informing the general moral exhortations in Parts I and II. The culminating position of the temptation, and the probability that its exemp-

lum nature was recognized by the audience, precludes the necessity for
homiletic exhortation. That the conduct illustrated by the poet is somewhat different from that usually understood by commentators on
Matthew 4:1-11 is at once a measure of the poet's independence in
relation to sources, a guide to his sense of aesthetics, and, perhaps, an
indication of his personal theological beliefs as to how man should
confront temptation.

It can be fairly said that the poet of *Christ and Satan* is an innovator
of some note. His innovations are two: he adapts the technique of the
exemplum as a teaching device from the works of the Latin and vernacular homilists and makes it the structural principle of his poem; he
manipulates the received linear chronology of Christianity to demonstrate what for want of a better term may be called moral chronology.
The two innovations are mutually supporting: the structure bodies forth
the dual theme of the revelation of Christ to man, and man's moral
obligation with respect thereto; the theme's dual implication supports
the poem's structure: theme, chronology, and verse alternation find
their point of fusion in the culminating movement of the work, the
temmptation. Rather than a series of greater or lesser poetic fragments,
then, I suggest that we have in *Christ and Satan* a bold, and a largely
successful, pedagogical poem.

III. SOURCES

Christ and Satan draws its inspiration from many things: the Latin and vernacular homiletic tradition; the canonical Gospels generally, but particularly Matthew; apocryphal works like *Nicodemus,* probably the *Vision of Paul,* perhaps the visions of Drihthelm and Furseus; the commentaries of various churchmen, particularly, I think, Gregory the Great, perhaps Bede. Unlike some Old English poems—for example, the *Metres of Boethius, Christ II, Elene, The Phoenix*—we can find no single work, Latin or vernacular, that provides the intellectual underpinning of the poem, nor can we be sure that the poet came into contact with his ultimate sources immediately. Therefore, the most that can be attempted in a source study of *Christ and Satan* is the reconstruction of the ideational atmosphere within which the poet composed, with the intention of discovering what materials were available, what ideas current, on given topics. By analyzing the poem in relation to this atmosphere, it should be possible to follow the choices of traditions, attitudes and ideas the poet probably made. The analysis is divided into two parts, following the natural sense division of the poem. For an analysis of Part III, lines 663-729, see above, section II, pp. 33-36.

PART I, LINES 1-364

THE ANGELIC FALL

During the first three Christian centuries, ideas concerning the reason for the angelic fall were influenced by the Jewish Apocrypha, especially the *Book of Jubilees,* the *Book of Enoch (1 Enoch),* and the *Book of the Secrets of Enoch (2 Enoch).* These works viewed the fall in terms of *Genesis* 6:1-4,[1] and interpreted the "sons of God" who lusted after the "daughters of men" as angels, thus making the fall a function of lust. So in *1 Enoch* 6:1-8, a book that was accepted as canonical until the fourth century, Semjaza, the leader of the fallen angels, descends to Mount Hermon with two hundred of his followers to

---

[1] When men began to multiply on the earth, and had daughters born to them, the sons of God saw that the daughters of men were fair, and they took wives for themselves, as many as they wished. Then the Lord said, "My spirit shall not remain in man forever, since he is flesh. His lifetime shall be one hundred and twenty years."

There were giants on the earth in those days, and also afterward, when the sons of God had relations with the daughters of men, who bore children to them. These were the mighty men who were of old, the men of renown.

choose wives from the daughters of men.[2] The *Book of Jubilees* 5:1-2[3] and *2 Enoch A* 18:3-6[4] follow this tradition, but *2 Enoch A* 29:4-5 maintains that the sin of Satanil, the leader of the fallen host, was an attempt to be like God.[5]

The explanation of the angelic fall as a function of lust is found in early Christian documents: the *Apology* of Justin Martyr,[6] the *Plea for Christians* of Athenagoras,[7] the *Pedagogus* of Clement of Alexandria,[8] and the *Recognitions of Clement*.[9] But early on we discover dissatisfaction with the crassness of the idea. Athenagoras, for example, distinguishes the fall of Satan from that of the other devils: the former was placed in charge of physical creation by God, proved neglectful, and fell in some unspecified manner; the latter lusted after the daughters of men. Tertullian concedes that the devils fell through lust,[10] but is unsure of the reason for Satan's fall. He theorizes that Satan was created good by God, and fell by an exercise of his free will. Satan's fault appears to be contemporaneous with his temptation of man, a temptation founded on impatience, jealousy and envy because God had created man in his divine image and subjected all creation to him.[11]

Theologians subsequently moved towards an explanation of the angelic fall based on the intellectual sin of pride. The Enoch tradition, though, was still strong enough in the late fourth century to have Ambrose accept essentially the same syncretistic position as Athenagoras and Tertullian,[12] and to have Augustine offer a serious rejoinder to it.[13] With the writings of Gregory the Great, however, pride became established as the reason for the fall of both angels and men.[14]

The poet of *Christ and Satan* follows a Gregorian interpretation of the angelic fall. There is no indication that he knew the Enoch tradition,

---

[2] R. H. Charles, ed., *The Apocrypha and Pseudepigrapha of the Old Testament in English* (Oxford, 1913), 2, p. 191.

[3] Ibid., p. 20.

[4] Ibid., pp. 439-40.

[5] Ibid., p. 447. The tradition viewing lust as the cause of the fall necessitates a chronology which places it after the creation of man.

[6] Justin Martyr, *Apologies*, 2, trans. Thomas B. Falls (New York, 1948), p. 124.

[7] *ANF* 2, chapter 24, p. 142.

[8] Clement of Alexandria, *Christ the Educator*, Book III, c. 2, trans. Simon Wood (New York, 1954), p. 211.

[9] Book IV, chapter 26, *ANF* 8, p. 140.

[10] *De Cultu Feminarum*, Liber I, caput 2, *PL* 1, cols. 1419-20.

[11] *Adversus Marcion*, Liber II, caput 10, *PL* 2, cols. 322-24; *De Patientia*, caput 5, *PL* 1, cols. 1367-70.

[12] *Exposition in Psalmum CXVIII*, sermo 7, 8, *PL* 15, cols. 1350-51, 1388-89.

[13] *De Genesi ad Litteram*, Liber XI, caput 14-17, 23, *PL* 34, cols. 436-38, 441-42; *De Sancta Virginitate*, Liber I, caput 31, *PL* 40, col. 413; *De Civitate Dei*, Liber III, caput 5, *PL* 41, cols. 81-82; ibid., Liber XV, caput 22, 23, cols. 467-70.

[14] *In Primum Regum Expositiones*, Liber III, caput 5, *PL* 79, cols. 205-06; ibid., Liber IV, caput 1, cols. 222-23; *Moralium*, Liber XXVIII, caput 2, *PL* 76, col. 452; ibid., Liber XXXIV, caput 23, col. 744; ibid., Liber XXIX, caput 8, col. 487.

UNIVERSITY OF WINNIPEG
LIBRARY
515 PORTAGE AVENUE
WINNIPEG, MAN.   R3B 2E9

nor is there an attempt to separate the fall of Satan from that of his angels. Lines 22-24a state that the angels fell because they aspired to heights above their nature; in lines 53-64 the fallen angels testify that Satan suborned them with lies, initially maintaining that they should not obey the Saviour, subsequently stating that he himself was the creator, finally assuming the fathership of the lord and creator of mankind. Pride as the cause of the fall is mentioned prominently in lines 50, 69, 196, 226. In the brief recapitulation of circumstances surrounding the angelic fall which serves as the preface to Part II, lines 365-372a, it is pride that changes the angel of light into the demon of darkness.

The angelic rebellion is directed against Christ, and takes the specific form of an attempt to drive him from his throne (ll. 172-173) and wrest from him control of the heavenly kingdom (ll. 85-87, 254-256). This theme, which provides the underpinning for the first part of the work and furnishes the foundation upon which the other sections are reared, can be found in three other Old English poems,[15] but the citations are quite brief, and afford little support for an assertion that the idea was common in Anglo-Saxon England.

The search for Patristic sources for such a handling of the heavenly rebellion discovers surprisingly negative results. There is almost unanimous agreement among the commentators that the rebellion was directed against God and that it was suppressed by him. It might have had a number of purposes: to drive God from his throne, to become like or independent of God, to set up a rival throne in the north of heaven.[16]

Some support for the modification of tradition in *Christ and Satan*[17] may be found in the *Epistle of Jude* 6:

> And the angels also who did not preserve their original state, but forsook their abode, he [Jesus] has kept in everlasting chains under darkness for the judgment of the great day.

Bede, the only significant commentator[18] on this Jude verse who would

---

[15] C. Abbetmeyer, p. 14, initially noted these occurrences: *Juliana*, ll. 420-424; *Guthlac A*, ll. 596-598; *Prayer IV*, ll. 54ff.

[16] Almost all of these points can be discovered in the *Genesis* poems of the Junius manuscript. In *Genesis A* and *B*, lines 22 and 262ff., pride is remarked as the cause of the fall of the angels. *Genesis A*, line 32, mentions that Satan intended to build a throne in "norðdæle," while *Genesis B* locates the throne "west and norð," line 275. Neither work specifies that the rebellion was directed against Christ, or that he had a significant role in its suppression. *Genesis A*, line 34, and *Genesis B*, line 270, state only that "god" was offended by the activity of Satan and moved to crush him.

[17] Clubb, p. 64, mentions the study by Stephanie von Gajšek, *Cædmon und Milton*, where it is suggested that the heavenly rebellion in both *Christ and Satan* and Milton's *Paradise Lost* is derived from the Apocalypse, having been transposed from the end to the beginning of time by the poets.

[18] After the citation of Bede, the next significant comments I can find by Latin writers concerning Christ's activity in the heavenly rebellion are contained in the twelfth-century works of Bernard of Clairvaux and Rupert of Deutz, particularly *Sermones de Tempore*,

have been readily available to the poet, writes:

> ... Jesus Dominus noster praevaricatores angelos punivit. Qui enim homo in fine saeculorum de Virgine natus, Jesu nomen angelo dictante, accepit, ipse ante omnia saecula natus ex Patre Deus, omnem creaturam cum Patre, ut voluit, disposuit, et a principio superbientes angelos ita sub caligine aeris hujus damnavit, ut eosdem in die judicii graviores reservaret ad poenas.[19]

Here we find essential elements for part of the heavenly rebellion depicted in *Christ and Satan*. The Jude verse contains the germ of the idea that the angels opposed Christ by not maintaining their original state; Bede supplies the detail that the proud apostate angels were defeated by Christ the Son.[20]

In Adventu Domini sermo 1, *PL* 183, col. 36, and *De Victoria Verbi, PL* 169, cols. 1221-40 respectively. Rupert avers that Satan rebelled against the Word, was condemned by him, defeated by the loyal angels, and thrown from heaven. Bernard remarks that God hurled Satan from heaven because he, Satan, wished to be equal to the Father in dignity and exaltation, an equality proper only to the Son. Much later, the Spanish philosopher-theologian Francisco Suarez (1548-1617) explains that Satan rebelled because he was angry that the Word would be united to man at the Incarnation, Satan believing himself the more worthy recipient of such a divine union. Among Satan's many other original sins, Suarez lists hatred and envy of Christ and men. (For the ideas of Suarez on this head, see E. Mangenot, "Démon d'après les scolastiques et les théologiens poetérieurs," *DTC* 4, pt. 1, 398-400.) Geoffrey Shepherd, "Scriptural Poetry," in *Continuations and Beginnings,* ed. E. G. Stanley (London and Edinburgh, 1966), p. 26, notes, with reference to the treatment of the fall in *Genesis A,* the possibility of a formative influence from Eastern Christian literature, specifically the homilies of Epiphanius of Salamis, a late fourth-century writer. Shepherd suggests that *Genesis* shows a syncretistic elaboration of the fall tradition similar in technique to the Ascension Day homily of Epiphanius. The section Shepherd quotes from the homily bears some similarity to *Christ and Satan*: "What shall I do, unhappy that I am? All those I had bound down forever, in a flash have been snatched from me. He holds me back to earth, stripped of flight and abandoned. The Son of Mary has deceived me.... While I ponder, I see him in all glory and majesty rise up to the heavens, whence I with great disgrace and dishonour have been cast out. I seek to catch him, and see, as with a lead weight I am dragged down. I seek to seize him and by a strange force I am held back. What in my misery can I do? He has driven me out from every place. *From the heavens he threw me down to earth* [italics mine] like a little whirling stone" (*PG* 43, cols. 481-84). Such an influence as Shepherd suggests for *Genesis A* is not at all impossible, either for it or *Christ and Satan*; Theodore of Tarsus and Abbot Hadrian were well acquainted with Eastern Christian writings, and it can be assumed that they brought knowledge of them to England. Further, C. J. Godfrey, in *The Church in Anglo-Saxon England* (Cambridge, 1962), pp. 174-78, notes the presence of marked Eastern influence in the art and architecture of pre-Danish England, particularly with respect to the erection of standing crosses, and the Syrian and Byzantine technique of a centrally planned church, e.g., St. Mary's at Hexam built by Wilfrid.

[19] *In Epistolam Judae, PL* 93, col. 125.

[20] There is a possibility that the Christocentricity of the poem is a reaction to the Adoptionist heresy of the late eighth century. This controversy may have provided the ambience in which the poet composed, but it did not, so far as I can tell, provide any sources as such. See below, "Language and Date," section IV, pp. 60-63.

Complementing Jude and Bede, there is a statement suggesting Christ's defeat of the angelic rebellion in *Felix's Life of Saint Guthlac*: the devils who have been tormenting the saint are ordered by him to cease "in the name of Jesus Christ who banished you from heaven...."[21] We also have an exorcism attributed to St. Ambrose from a Vatican manuscript of the late sixth or early seventh century, which reads, in part:

> Omnipotens Domine, Verbum Dei Patris, Christe Jesu, Deus et Dominus universae creaturae, qui sanctis apostolis tuis potestatem dedisti calcandi supra serpentes et scorpiones: qui inter caetra mirabilium tuorum praecepta dignatus es dicere: "Daemones effugate" (Matt. x, 8); *cujus virtute victus tanquam fulgar de caelo Satanus cecidit....*[22] [Italics mine.]

Again, in *Exameron Anglice,* or *The Old English Hexameron,* written by Aelfric, we discover the normal interpretation of the creation, with God deemed the creator of the world, who brings all things into being through the agency of his Son. Aelfric says that the angelic fall, which occurred simultaneously with the creation of man, took place because Satan refused to honour his creator.[23] May we see here, and in other treatises on the creation which posit either God the creator working through the Son as creative agent, or stress the role of the Son in the creation so as to make that event his very attribute, a rich ambiguity that allows a poet to emphasize the Son-Jesus Christ-Creator synthesis, thus making the failure of Satan to honour his creator a personal encounter between Christ and Satan? In any event, the commanding position given Christ in the angelic rebellion by our poet is scarcely a doctrinal impropriety, though we can hardly affirm, on the basis of the evidence I have been able to collect, that it was the normal and accepted view of the affair circa 790-830. Perhaps the poet, directly or indirectly, was aware of the sources I cite; perhaps the interpretation he offers in the poem, which was to become in later years more or less an orthodox position, was just "in the air" at the time of composition. But it is just as likely

---

[21] *Vita Sanctii Guthlac Auctore Felice,* ed. and trans. Bertram Colgrave (Cambridge, 1956), p. 117. The Latin reads: "idcirco imperio tibi in nomine Iesu Christi, qui te de caelo damnavit...."

[22] *PL* 17, cols. 1109-10.

[23] S. J. Crawford, ed., Aelfric's *Exameron Anglice or The Old English Hexameron* (Darmstadt, 1968), ll. 47-48, 297-308. In the treatise *On the Old and New Testament* (ed. Crawford in *The Heptateuch,* p. 19), Aelfric seems to suggest some sort of direct engagement of the Son in the angelic fall when he remarks that Lucifer would neither acknowledge his creator as his Lord, "nor continue in the truth of the true Son of God who made him so fair..." [ne he nolde þurhwunian on ðære soþfæstnisse ðæs soðfæstan Godes sunu, þe hine gesceop fægerne...], from MS Laud Misc. 509(L). Here the Son appears to be responsible both for the creation of the angels and their maintenance in grace. It must be admitted, though, that in most contexts Aelfric is a firm articulator of the involvement of the Trinity in creation.

that, wishing to structure a work that would reveal adequately the character of Christ as he understood it to his audience or readers, the poet took the licence of his craft in moulding materials to fit his need.

THE LOCATION AND DESCRIPTION OF HELL

The Jewish Apocrypha contain traditions concerning the location and description of hell that remain viable well through the time of Bede. *2 Enoch,* for example, mentions that the fallen angels are bound and suffering in the third heaven, while their chief is chained in the fifth. This placing of the heavenly rebels in some aerial confinement with the pains of hell, though prepared, reserved until after the last judgment had a significant influence on early writers: variations of the idea may be found in *2 Peter, Jude,* Paul's *Epistle to the Ephesians,* and the writings of Justin Martyr, Tertullian, Irenaeus, and Hippolytus of Rome, to mention the more important.[24]

Of Latin writers who were more familiar to the Anglo-Saxons, Ambrose believes that the fallen angels inhabit the space between the air and the earth, and that eternal fire is reserved for them.[25] Augustine is cautious about apodictic statements on the nature and location of hell, and the remarks he makes are somewhat confusing and contradictory. In a commentary on Psalm 86, for example, he distinguishes a heaven above the earth, which is the abode of the blessed, from two levels of hell, one which corresponds to the surface of the earth, the other subterranean. This subterranean hell encompasses two levels, one of which contained the just souls who awaited release at Christ's harrowing.[26] In other works Augustine seems to accept the tradition of the angels imprisoned in the air:

> Propterea ad ista caliginosa, id est ad hunc aerem, tanquam ad car-cerem, damnatus est diabolus, de apparatu superiorum Angelorum lapsus cum angelis suis: nam Apostolus hoc de illo dicit: "*Secundum principem potestatis aeris hujus, qui nunc operatur in filiis diffidentiae* (Ephes. II, 2)". Et alius apostolus dicit: "*Si enim Deus angelis peccan-tibus non pepercit, sed carceribus caliginis inferni retrudens, tradidit in judicio puniendos servari* (2 Petr. II, 4)": infernum hoc appellans, quod inferior pars mundi sit.[27]

---

[24] For a handy digest of ideas on the location of hell, see M. Richard, "Enfer," *DTC* 5, pt. 1, 28-120. This early tradition gave rise to the idea that it was necessary to delay at least the full punishment of the damned, if not the joys of some of the blessed (martyrs, for example, were thought to be accepted into heaven immediately upon their death), until after the judgment. This heresy, known as the *Delatio Inferni,* was formally condemned only at the Council of Florence, 1439.

[25] *Expositio in Psalmum cxviii,* sermon 8 and 20, *PL* 15, cols. 1388-89, 1567-68.

[26] *On the Psalms, NPNF,* First Series 8, Psalm 86, p. 416.

[27] *Ennaratio in Psalmum cxlviii, PL* 37, col. 1943.

and again:

> Although they [the fallen angels] have already penally received this hell, that is, an inferior smoky air as a prison, which nevertheless since it is also called heaven, is not that heaven in which there are stars, but this lower heaven by the smoke of which the clouds are conglobulated, and where the birds fly....[28]

Gregory the Great, particularly in the *Dialogorum,* writes of a subterranean hell already inhabited by devils, and notes that the souls of the damned go there immediately after death, as the souls of the blessed ascend to heaven.[29] However, at least once in the *Moralium* he suggests that Satan and his angels fell, not into a subterranean hell, but into an aerial prison: "Et scimus quod immundi spiritus, qui e caelo aethereo lapsi sunt, in hoc caeli terraeque medio vagantur."[30] Bede, too, is familiar with the tradition which places the devils in an aerial prison. To the commentary on the sixth verse of the *Epistle of Jude,* already cited, can be added a section from the commentary on the *Second Epistle of Peter*:

> Ostendit ergo adhuc angelis apostatis ultimi judicii poenam debri, de qua Dominus dicit: "*Ite in ignem aeternum qui paratus est diabolo et angelis ejus* (Matt. xxv)," quamvis jam poenaliter hunc infernum, hoc est inferiorum caliginosum aerem, tanquam carcerem acceperint.[31]

However, in a comment on the *Catholic Epistle of James,* Bede places some of the fallen angels in the air, some on the earth, some under the earth in what appears to be a subterranean hell:

> A gehenna dicit a diabolo et angelis ejus, propter quos gehenna facta est, et qui ubicunque vel in aere volitant, vel in terris aut sub terris vagantur, sive detinentur, suarum secum ferunt semper tormenta flammarum, instar febricitantis, qui et si in lectis eburneis, et si in locis ponatur apricis, *fervorem* tamen vel *frigus* insiti sibi languoris evitare non potest.[32]

The poet of *Christ and Satan* has chosen to place the devils immediately in a subterranean hell. There is no suggestion that any delay ensued from the time of the offense in heaven until the punishment in hell. The hell to which the devils are consigned is an underground cavern, "niðær under nessas in ðone neowlan grund (l. 31)," a description that is repeated more or less exactly in lines 90 and 134. In lines

---

[28] *Nature of the Good, Against the Manichaeans,* chapter 33, *NPNF,* First Series 4, p. 358.

[29] *Dialogorum,* Liber IV, caput 25, 28, 29, 42-45, *PL* 77, cols. 356-57, 365, 400-05.

[30] *Moralium in Job,* Liber II, caput 47, *PL* 75, col. 590. See also Liber VIII, caput 23, *PL* 75, col. 824.

[31] *PL* 93, col. 75.

[32] *PL* 93, col. 27. The detail that makes even those devils flying in the air bearers of their own hell finds a point of contact in *Christ and Satan,* ll. 261-264.

130a, 135b and 331b hell is referred to as a hall, "sele." There are indications that some of the devils are to remain in hell, while others, perhaps Satan himself, are available to tempt man: lines 111-112, 261-263, 269-271.

The physical pains in hell are the traditional ones associated with the subterranean location: fire, ice, snakes and darkness. But the poet has described psychological sufferings as well. Time and again Satan laments the loss of his glory, the very memory of which is made more lacerating because of his present surroundings. He goes so far as to state that he is worse for ever having known heavenly bliss (ll. 140-142a). A novel addition to the psychological torments of hell is the eternally vacillating hope of Satan that he will somehow secure release:

Ic hēr geþolian sceal   þinga æghwylces,
bitres nīðæs   beala gnornian,
sīc and sorhful,   þæs ic seolfa wēold,
þonne ic on heofonum   hām staðelode,
hwæðer ūs se ēca   æfre wille
on heofona rīce   hām ālēfan,
ēðel tō æhte,   swā hē ær dyde. (ll. 272-278)

Groschopp believed that this passage was indicative of the confusion permeating the whole poem, since, in terms of other passages which demonstrate Satan's knowledge of the enormity of his offense and the eternal nature of its punishment, for example, lines 97, 114-116, 137-139, it appears a gross inconsistency.[33] But the poet has structured particularly psychological torments for Satan in other sections of Part I: in lines 129-130, Satan laments that he cannot hide in hell, in lines 144b-146, 267-268 he acknowledges that he can bring to hell only the heathen, those whom God will not have. In the context of torments such as these, lines 272-278 are intelligible, and describe yet another subtle pain of hell.

For the mixture of fire and ice, the extremes of heat and cold, as a punishment of hell in the Christian tradition,[34] one need look only to the citation of Bede, noted above, where hell's pains are remarked to be "fervorem vel tamen frigus." Of the visions contained in Bede's *History,* the Vision of Drihthelm mentions extremes of temperature as an element in the suffering of those in the neighbourhood of hell. Though this suffering is essentially purgatorial rather than eternal, that distinction might not have occurred to an Anglo-Saxon reader or listener. The separation of hell and purgatory in the Vision is purely linear: Drihthelm, having seen the souls punished by the extremes of fire and ice in a deep abyss, moves some little further on, and there sees hell proper

---

[33] Groschopp, 252.

[34] See *Genesis A,* l. 43; *Genesis B,* 315-317; *Christ III,* ll. 1627b-1629a; *Judgment Day II,* l. 192. The prose citations include *Blickling Homily* #5, "Dominica V. in Quadragesima," p. 61 (Morris), *Vercelli Homilies* #4, pp. 74-75, and #8, p. 157 (Förster), Aelfric's "Dominica III Post Epiphania," 1, p. 132 (Thorpe).

where Satan is chained. The punishment of purgatory, and it is not so called in the text, is in the same general location as that of hell, in its very vestibule. A poet struck by the effectiveness of the image might well have passed over such a distinction.

Another possible source for many of the details found in the poem's description of hell, one which might even have influenced the Vision of Drihthelm, is the *Apocryphal Vision of Paul,* a third-century Greek composition, which, in a Latin translation, had a "tremendous vogue in the West."[35] The earliest full Latin version of the *Vision* was copied in France in the eighth century; the material contained in the manuscript has been ascribed on philological grounds to the fifth or sixth centuries.[36] Of the forty-seven surviving manuscripts of shortened redactions of the *Vision,* twenty-one are of English provenance, and date between the ninth and twelfth centuries.[37]

The *Vision* was known in England in the seventh century, as the following quotation from Aldhelm's *De Laudibus Virginitatis* indicates:

> ... nonne ob purae integritatis praerogativam, tertium polum peragrans, supernorum civium arcana castis obtutibus contemplatur, et coelestis militiae abstrusa ineffabili rerum relatu rimatur, licet Revelatio, quam dicunt Pauli, in nave aurea florentis paradisi delicias eumdem adisse garriat. Sed fas divinum vetat catholicae fidei sequipedas plus quidpiam quam canonicae veritatis censura promulgat credere, et caetera apocryphorum deliramenta velut horrisona verborum tonitrua penitus abdicare et procul eliminare, orthodoxorum Patrum scita scriptis decretalibus sanxerunt.[38]

The Blickling Homilies draw two exempla from the *Vision*[39] and the fourth homily of the collection, *Dominica Tertia in Quadragesima,* contains a statement based upon the long Latin version.[40] Aelfric in the Preface to his homily "In Letania Majore, Feria Tertia," inveighs against those who persist in reading it: "humeta rædað sume men ða leasan gesetnysse, ðe hi hatað Paulus gesihðe, nu he sylfe sæde þæt he ða digelan word gehyrde, þe nan eorðlic mann sprecan ne mot."[41] A

---

[35] Montague Rhodes James, trans., *The Apocryphal New Testament* (Oxford, 1924), p. 525. See also R. P. Casey, "The Apocalypse of Paul," *JTS,* 34 (1933), 1. For a complete analysis of the *Vision*'s influence on Mediaeval Western literature, see Theodore Silverstein, *Visio Sancti Pauli* (London, 1935), especially chapter 1. See also T. D. Hill's "Satan's Fiery Speech: 'Christ and Satan' 78-79," *N&Q,* 217 (1972), 2-4, and my "Three Notes on the Junius XI *Christ and Satan,*" *MP,* 72 (1974), 175-81.

[36] Casey, 2.

[37] Silverstein, pp. 9-12.

[38] *PL* 89, col. 121-22. Quoted in Silverstein, p. 6.

[39] Max Förster, "A New Version of the Apocalypse of Thomas in Old English," *Anglia,* 73 (1955), 7, mentions *Visio Pauli* as the source for exempla in *Blickling Homilies* 4 and 13.

[40] Silverstein, p. 7.

[41] Thorpe, 2, p. 332.

short version of the *Visio* is erroneously attributed to Bede by Migne, and marked homily one hundred, *PL* 94, col. 501-502.[42] Yet another short version, this one Anglo-Saxon, is contained in a collection of homilies edited by R. Morris from a twelfth-century manuscript.[43] Rudolph Willard notes the existence of a fragmentary Anglo-Saxon translation of the long Latin text in a manuscript of the eleventh century, Junius 85, 3r-11v.[44]

Both versions, full and abbreviated, contain descriptions of hell and its torments which include serpents, worms and the extremes of heat and cold, contain, in a word, many of the elements found in the description of hell in *Christ and Satan*. The following quotations are taken from M. R. James's translation of the eighth-century long Latin version in *The Apocryphal New Testament* (Oxford, 1924):

> And I saw another man in the river of fire sunk up to his knees: and his hands were stretched out and bloody, and worms issued out of his mouth and nostrils. (p. 543)

> And I saw a multitude of pits in the same place, and in the midst thereof a river filled with a multitude of men and women, and worms devoured them. (p. 544)

> And again I beheld there men and women with their hands and feet cut off and naked, in a place of ice and snow, and worms devoured them. (p. 544)

> And thereafter I saw men and women clad in rags full of pitch and brimstone of fire, and there were dragons twined about their necks and shoulders and feet. (p. 546)

> And I looked from the north unto the west and saw there the worm that sleepeth not, and in that place was gnashing of teeth. And the worms were of the measure of one cubit, and on them were two heads, and I saw there men and women in cold and gnashing of teeth. . . . And I inquired and said: Lord is there no fire nor heat in this place? And he said unto me: In this place is nothing else but cold and snow. . . . Even if the sun rose upon them, they would not be warmed because of the excessive cold of this place and the snow. (p. 547)

The short Latin version ascribed to Bede compresses the exquisitely detailed torments of the full version, but still retains its essentials:

> Et iterum vidit fornacem ignis ardentem septem flammis, et multi puniebantur in ea, et septem plagae erant in circuitu fornacis. Prima nix, secunda glacies ... quinta serpentes.... Et vidit alium locum in quo erant puellae nigrae, habentes vestimenta nigra ... et dracone, et serpentes, et viperas circa colla habebant.[45]

---

[42] P. Meyer, "La Descent de Saint Paul en Enfer," *Romania*, 24 (1895), 359.

[43] R. Morris, *Old English Homilies* (London, 1868), p. 43.

[44] Rudolph Willard, "The Address of the Soul to the Body," *PMLA*, 50 (1935), 957-58.

[45] *PL* 94, col. 501-02.

The Anglo-Saxon version contained in Morris' collection of homilies compresses the torments even further: "Efter þon he him sceawede þe sea of helle and innan þan sea weren. vii. bittre uþe. þe forme wes swnan (scribal error for *snaw*) þat oðer is, þet þriddle fur. þet feorðe blod. þe fifte neddren."[46]

There is one detail in the Paris manuscript of the *Visio* which may inform a striking section of the poem. Line 78 of *Christ and Satan* contains the detail that Satan emitted sparks when he spoke: "Hē spearcade, ðonne hē spreocan ongan/fȳre and ātre." The long Latin version of the *Visio* contains a section which describes the angels appointed to torment sinners: "et de capillis capitis eorum scintille ignis exiebant, sive de ore eorum."[47] Grein-Köhler *Sprachschatz*, p. 625, gives *scintillas ejicere* as the Latin equivalent of *spearcian*. The only other use of the term in the Anglo-Saxon corpus occurs in the gloss to Aldhelm's *De Virginitate*, where the form *sparcendum* translates *scintillante*.[48] The possible sources and analogues from Christian writings that Clubb gives for line 78, *Jer.* 5:14; *Ecclus.* 48:1; *4 Esdras* 13:10; *Rev.* 11:5,[49] are essentially unsatisfactory: the *Jeremias* citation refers to that prophet's mission to the Israelites; the *Ecclesiasticus* citation refers to the prophet Elias; the *Revelation* citation refers to the two olive trees that stand before the Lord of the earth, which, if anyone offer to harm them, emit sparks from their mouths; the *Esdras* relates the activity of the Messiah in defeating the hosts which rise against him. None of the references has any connection with hell or Satan. While the *Visio* citation does not specify the devil himself, it does refer to the angels who, in hell, torment the evil souls.

Recently Hugh Keenan has suggested that the source of Satan's sparking is to be found in Evagrius' Latin translation of the *Vita Beati Antonii*,[50] specifically a section from chapter 16:

> Crebro denique Antonius talem a se visum diabolum asserebat, qualem et beatus Job, Domino revelante, cognoverat (*Job* XLI). Oculi ejus ac si species Luciferi, ex ore ejus procedunt lampades incensae. Crines quoque incediis sparguntur, et ex naribus ejus fumus egreditur, quasi fornacis aestuantis ardore carbonum. Anima ejus ut pruna, flamma vero ex ore ejus glomeratur....[51]

The *Vita* was known in Anglo-Saxon England, as was the *Visio*. It may be that both works contributed to the picture of Satan we have in the poem.

---

[46] Morris, p. 43.

[47] Montague Rhodes James, "Visio Pauli, Chapter 11," *Apocrypha Anecdota, Texts and Studies*, 2, No. 3 (Cambridge, 1893), 15.

[48] Bosworth and Toller, p. 899.

[49] Clubb, p. 65.

[50] Hugh Keenan, "Satan Speaks in Sparks: 'Christ and Satan' 78-79a, 161b-162b, and the 'Life of St. Antony,'" *N&Q*, 219 (1974), 283-84.

[51] *Vitae Patrum*, Liber I, *Vita Beati Antonii Abbatis*, c. 16, *PL* 73, col. 138.

THE CHARACTER OF SATAN

The artistic antipodes of the representation of the character of Satan in Old English poetry are established by *Genesis B* and *Christ and Satan.* In the former, to quote an early critic, we see "... the wild Northern freedom! It is a great earl speaking, whose pride in personal beauty, whose insolence of individuality, has sent him into haughty anger against his lord.... This is pure heathen, and the comfort of vengeance was never better put";[52] in the latter, to quote another early critic, we have a Satan who "falls quite out of character and speaks like a weak repentant sinner, at times even like a preacher."[53] These polarities are inherent in the works, and are still with us. But the process of critical evaluation has been modified in time, and, though one may yet be impressed by the defiance of Satan in *Genesis B,* and even hypothesize that it exhibits the *zeitgeist* of the Teutons, one no longer affirms necessarily that the Satan of *Christ and Satan* is an inferior artistic creation by comparison.

Stanley B. Greenfield recognizes many of the qualities of both poems apprehended by earlier critics, noting that in *Genesis B* Satan "is the same proud rebellious tyrant-hero as he is in *Paradise Lost....* Even in defeat he is the undaunted Germanic warrior... bound in iron bands... he yet hurls defiance at the almighty," remarking that the Satan of *Christ and Satan* is a "wretched figure."[54] But Greenfield correctly sees this wretchedness as a "negative capability [which provides a] fitting beginning for the great theme of the poem, the 'incommensurate might of God.'"[55] Indeed, anything but such wretchedness would have ill-suited the theme, which I define as the revelation of the character of Christ and man's moral obligation in relation to this revelation. Had the Satan of *Christ and Satan* been a character in the epic mould, spiritually akin to the Satan of *Genesis B,* he might have shifted the audience's interest away from the omnipotence of the Son to the dangers of the heavenly battle, and, perhaps, to the putative moral victory of a devil who, though defeated, refuses to submit. It is at least possible that the audience for whom the poem was intended would have been taken with an epic Satan in much the same way as were the early critics, or the uninitiated modern reader of *Paradise Lost.* Thus the purpose of the poem would have been thwarted.

I have found no sources properly so-called for the Satan of *Christ and Satan.* The seven lines from Aldhelm's *De Virginitate* and the three lines from his *De Lucifero* that Clubb, following Abbetmeyer, suggests as a possible source lack sufficient weight to explain the development of

---

[52] Stopford Brooke, *The History of Early English Literature* (London, 1892), p. 328.
[53] Ten Brink, p. 328A.
[54] Stanley B. Greenfield, *A Critical History of Old English Literature* (New York, 1965), pp. 151, 143.
[55] Ibid., p. 143.

the character in the poem, and reference to Avitus of Vienne's *De Originali Peccato* is, as Clubb states, to a speech that is in the definant manner of the Satan of *Genesis B*.[56] Patristic commentators are not much help here, since they generally believed Satan to be the unregenerate foe of God and man, not unlike the essential Satan we see in *Genesis B*, though lacking all grandeur.

It may be that Clubb is correct in suggesting that the poet took his inspiration from works dealing with the harrowing of hell:[57] in *Nicodemus* we at least have a fearful devil. If so, the poet ought to be credited with the artistic wisdom of having transposed this Satan to the border area between eternity and time wherein the angelic rebellion took place, and having expanded the character greatly. Such a transposition and expansion, viewed in the light of what the poet probably tried to accomplish with his poem, is by no means a minor achievement.

PART II, LINES 365-622

The source of the initial ninety lines of Part II is *The Descent into Hell*, the second section of the *Gospel of Nicodemus*, sometimes termed the *Acts of Pilate*, an apocryphal composition originally written in Greek, probably before the fifth century, and subsequently done into Latin.[58] Translations from the Latin into Old English survive in three late manuscripts: Cambridge University Library Ii. II. 11; Cotton Vitelius A XV; Cotton Vespasian D XIV.[59]

Critical opinion has been divided over whether the poet was immediately familiar with a Latin or vernacular text of *Nicodemus*, or

---

[56] Clubb, p. xxv; Abbetmeyer, p. 18. Clubb (pp. xxvii-xxix) believes that Part I of *XSt* has a close though indeterminable connection with *Guthlac A*, and argues that lines 22-192 of the former, specifically lines 22-31, show some similarity in thought, tone and diction to lines 548-643 of the latter. But in the absence of a significant number of formulaic expressions common to both sections of the poems, and taking into account the fact that most of the citations from *XSt* are drawn from a compact section of the work, while the citations from *Guthlac A* are scattered through almost one hundred lines, I do not see the necessity to follow Clubb and conclude either that the poet of *Guthlac A* borrowed from the poet of *XSt* or that both poets were indebted to a common source. Given what we have learned during the continuing debate on the hypothesis of the oral-formulaic character of Old English poetry, particularly about the traditional and formulaic character of verse composed by a poet in a written as well as oral ambience (see particularly Larry D. Benson, "The Literary Character of Anglo-Saxon Formulaic Poetry," *PMLA*, 81 [1966], 334-41), the most, and the least, that we can say is that in certain instances both poets seem to have been drawing upon a similar fund of ideas, themes, and, occasionally, phrases.

[57] Clubb, pp. liv-lv.

[58] James, p. 96.

[59] W. H. Hulme, "The Old English Version of the Gospel of Nicodemus," *PMLA*, OS 13 (1898), 464. In "The Old English Gospel of Nicodemus," *MP*, 1 (1903-04), 589, Hulme notes the existence of a homily dealing with the harrowing written in the margins of MS CCCC 41.

came into contact with the harrowing tradition through the mediation of homilies. Groschopp believed that the poet had neither the Bible nor the *Nicodemus* before him, but composed the whole work from his inferior memory,[60] while Kühn maintained that both Gospel and *Nicodemus* were immediate sources for Part II.[61] B. ten Brink suggested that the poet had treated "the weightier points of the Creed," and had used as an immediate source an Easter homily like *Blickling #7.*[62] Abbetmeyer found Part II an exposition of "the second article, or even the whole Creed."[63] Max Förster believed that the 160th Pseudo-Augustinian sermon and the *descensus* tradition as preserved in the *Book of Cerne* were the sources of the harrowing material in *Christ and Satan* and the foundation of the *Exeter Book's* "Descent into Hell."[64] Clubb rather warily accepted the possibility of a homiletic source for Part II, but maintained that it must have been remarkably different from any yet proposed. His final statement on the source of Part II is that the poet, though demonstrating a fair general acquaintance with the Bible and other religious literature, was probably composing from memory.[65]

If the poet was immediately familiar with the *Gospel of Nicodemus,* he edited and compressed it freely before using it in his poem. There is, for example, nothing of the apparatus by which the gospel comes to be written, nor anything of the many remarks by Old Testament prophets and personages in hell, for example, Adam, Seth, David, Isaias, concerning their foreshadowing of the harrowing. There is no mention of Seth's journey to the gates of Paradise to find the oil of mercy for Father Adam and the prophecy of the Redeemer he received from the angel guardian in its stead. There is no indication of a personification of hell, and no dialogue between it and Satan over the advisability of accepting Christ within hell's walls. The command of Christ that the gates of hell be opened that the King of Glory might come in, and the subsequent questions of the devils concerning the identity of the King, elements given a most prominent place in the *Gospel,* are absent from the poem.[66]

The *Gospel* account of the actual spoiling of hell includes the breaking of the gates of brass and iron, Christ's remanding Satan to the keeping of Hell, the loosing of the prisoners, an address by Christ to Adam who, in company with the saints, hymns the praises of the lord. The final action before the ascension of the host is the establishment of the cross, the sign of victory, in hell, with appropriate remarks by Old Testament prophets. This is detailed by the Greek and Latin A text in

---

[60] Groschopp, p. 262.

[61] Kühn, pp. 11-15.

[62] Ten Brink, p. 87.

[63] Abbetmeyer, p. 12.

[64] Max Förster, "Altenglische Predigtquellen I.i. Pseudo-Augustin und die 7. Blickling Homily," *Archiv,* 116 (1906), 301-07.

[65] Clubb, pp. xxxvi-xxxvii.

[66] All references are to James.

three, the Latin B text in four, chapters. Similar material in the poem is compressed into lines 378b-440.

In common with the *Gospel* we have an emphasis on noise, "dyne for deman," and on the brightness brought by Christ's arrival. Both *Gospel* and poem depict him as coming at the head of an army. In place of the extended exclamations of the Old Testament worthies, the joy of the inhabitants of hell is indicated in a line and a half, 380b-381. The dialogue between Hell and Satan is replaced by a general lament of all the devils which serves to qualify the harrower and emphasize the results of the harrowing. The function of this precision is to focus attention exclusively on the significant action of Christ: the many circumstances surrounding the harrowing in the *Gospel* are not without interest, but they serve more to generate expectation and suspense than to clarify and reveal his character. It can be said with some justice that he shares the stage with Satan, Hell, and the Old Testament worthies, since each, at one time or another, becomes the centre of dramatic attention. By placing the description of Christ's coming in the mouths of a rabble of undifferentiated devils, the poet is able to gain a sense of drama, since their exact words are reported, and still maintain focus exclusively on Christ, because no single character is present to draw attention from him. The actual strife in hell receives two lines, 401b-403a, and its result is given in one and a half, 405-406a. There is no mention of the barring of hell-gate, or the address of Adam and the saints to Christ. Instead, there is the long speech by Eve.

Of singular interest is the poet's substitution of Judas Iscariot for John the Baptist as the precursor who announces Christ's imminent arrival in hell. Traditional commentaries, as well as the *Gospel of Nicodemus* itself, provide the Baptist with essentially the same mission in hell as he had on earth—to prepare the way for the coming of Christ.[67] I have found no source for this substitution, and it just may be the poet's original invention. It is a happy stroke of economy since, without the apparatus of the Baptist which takes up almost all of chapter 2 of the second part of the *Nicodemus,* the poet is able to describe the joyful expectation of the souls in hell and provide an ironic occasion to demonstrate the encompassing power of Christ, whose betrayer becomes, in effect, his messenger.

The binding of the devil receives full treatment by the poet, though it is handled narratively, without the direct address Christ gives to Hell in the *Gospel*. This fullness is conditioned by the emphatic position Satan holds in Part I of the work; thematically considered, the elabora-

---

[67] John Arnott MacCulloch, *The Harrowing of Hell* (Edinburgh, 1930), p. 244. Gregory the Great, in the sixth homily of the collection *XL Homiliarum in Evangelia, PL* 76, cols. 1095-96, maintains that just as John went before Christ on earth, so he would go before him into hell. Cf. *The Gospel of Nicodemus*: Latin A II(XVIII), 3; Latin B V(XXI), 2; Greek II(XVIII), 3. *The Descent into Hell* of *The Exeter Book* follows this tradition.

tion of the binding allows the poet to demonstrate Christ's absolute power over his adversary. Here the power that was implicit in Part I is made explicit: lines 441-454.

The *Gospel of Nicodemus* follows the spoliation of hell with the establishment of the victory sign of the cross within its confines and the ascension of Adam and the souls, with appropriate comments by the Old Testament prophets. Christ delivers them to the care of Michael, who brings the host to Paradise where they encounter Enoch, Elias and the Good Thief. *Christ and Satan* focuses exclusively on the ascension,[68] lines 455-467, with passing mention of prophets in lines 458-459, 461b-462.

The speech of Christ to the saints, lines 469b-511, is not in the *Nicodemus.* It appears conditioned by the same artistic consideration which caused the poet to centre attention on Eve, an interest in delineating character. This relatively long speech stresses Christ's beneficent role in creation and salvation.[69]

There are certain correspondences between Part II and the seventh *Blickling Homily* which are not to be found in a comparison of the poem with the *Gospel of Nicodemus.* The homily describes the just souls in hell as suffering torments, a point of some debate among the commentators. Such a detail is absent from the *Gospel,* but suggested by lines 416b-419 and 430-434 of the poem. The homily depicts the saints, Adam and Eve, making separate pleas for release to Christ. Eve's prayer takes essentially the same form as in the poem: a maternal connection with Mary as her daughter, and, through her, with Christ. Yet a further parallel is the appearance of the risen Christ to his apostles. Though mentioned briefly in the homily, it serves the same function as in the poem, i.e., to demonstrate the true resurrection and thus further clarify the character of Christ.[70] The poet describes two separate appearances, one to Peter, the other to Thomas (ll. 534-544); the *Nicodemus* has nothing like it.

Perhaps the most striking similarity between poem and homily is, as might be expected, with respect to tone and structure. The homilist approaches his narrative and dramatic material in much the same manner as does the poet, both writers using it as the foundation for exhortations. The homilist maintains that the deeds he recounts, the Lord's resurrection, harrowing, etc., were performed "for our example":"forþon þe Drihten of deaþe aras mancynne to bysene"

---

[68] It would appear that this ascension is not to heaven proper, but to an intermediate place of repose. See note to line 401a.

[69] See above, section II, p. 31.

[70] *Blickling Homily* #7, pp. 89-91. "... he hine his gingrum æteowde, forþon þe he wolde ælcne tweon of heora heortum adon. & he eac æteowde þa wunda & þara nægla dolh þæm ungeleaffullum mannum, forþon þe he nolde þæt ænig ortrywnes wære emb his æriste...."

(p. 83). Hortatory statements, quite like those discussed in section II, are found immediately after a brief statement covering the ascension. The burden of these is that man should be mindful of the debt he owes Christ for salvation.[71] With the mention of the "last days" and the arrival of Christ to collect the debts owed him by man, the homily moves naturally into an extended analysis of the signs before doomsday, and the fate of those who are then unrepentant.

Immediately after a description of Christ's encounter with Thomas, we move into the first homiletic section of Part II (ll. 545-556) which emphasizes man's duty to repay Christ for the sacrifice he made. This is re-enforced by the mention of the cross, a scene not narratively treated, merely alluded to, in the dramatic section of the poem. Following a description of the ascension and the descent of the Holy Spirit, we find the second homiletic section, which stresses man's duty to Christ for the sacrifice which opened heaven (ll. 593b-595a).

The poem concludes Part II with a description of the last judgment; the homily closes with a similar scene. The latter deals at length with the traditional signs associated with that event, while the former centres attention on the confrontation between Christ and the souls. This economy is similar to that found in an analysis of the harrowing material: the apparatus may in itself be significant, but in the poem it is subordinated to a delineation of the character of Christ. Both poem and homily terminate the last judgment with an exhortation emphasizing man's obligation to gain merit with Christ:

homily

> Uton nu, men þa leofestan, þas þing geþencean swiþe snotorlice & wislice, þæt we þurh soþfæste dæda & þurh mildheortnesse weorc urne Deman mildne gemeton. . . . (p. 97)

poem

> Uton, lā, geþencan   geond þās worulde,
> þæt wē hǽlende   hēran onginnen!
> Georne þurh godes gife   gemunan gāstes blēd. . . .
>   (ll. 642-644)

Max Förster believed that the Pseudo-Augustine Sermon 160 was the ultimate source of *Blickling Homily* #7, the March 26 entry of the *Mercian Martyrology,* the apocryphal harrowing of hell with which the *Book of Cerne* ends, and *Christ and Satan,* lines 435ff.[72] But

---

[71] Ibid., p. 91. "Uton we ealle wynsumian on Drihten we þe his æriste mærsiaþ. . . . Uton we forþon geþencean hwylc handlean we him forþ to berenne habban, þonne he eal þis recþ & sægþ æt þisse ilcan tide, þonne he gesiteþ on his dom setle. . . . Uton nu geþencean hu mycel egsa gelimpeþ eallum gesceaftum on þas ondweardan tid . . . ."

[72] Max Förster, "Altenglische Predigtquellen: I. i. Pseudo-Augustin und die 7. Blickling Homily," *Archiv,* 116 (1906), 301-07. Förster includes *The Descent into Hell* of *The Exeter Book* among those things influenced by Sermon 160, but the points of contact between it and *XSt* are too slight to warrant extended comment here.

Sermon 160 as we have it[73] lacks anything that might have served our poet as a source for Eve's appeal to Christ: there is no distinction among appellants in the sermon, the supplications to Christ at the harrowing being the corporate efforts of the undifferentiated just. In the *Mercian Martyrology*, though Adam is mentioned by name and there is a brief collective appeal to Christ by all the just, Eve's is the final, and hence the most dramatic, appeal in the series, the longest, and the only one to be personally identified.[74] *Blickling* #7 has collective supplication, and separate appeals by Adam and Eve.[75]

The similarities among these appeals by Eve are interesting:

XSt, lines 435-440

Ræhte þā mid handum	tō heofencyninge,
bæd meotod miltse	þurh Marian hād:
"Hwæt, þū fram mīnre dohtor,	drihten, onwōce
in middangeard	mannum tō helpe.
Nū is gesēne	þæt ðū eart sylfa god,
ēce ordfruma	ealra gesceafta."

Martyrology, p. 50

... Eua hine halsode for sancta Marian mægsibbe þæt he hire miltsade. Heo cwæð to him: 'gemyne, min drihten, þæt seo wæs ban of minum banum ond flæsc of minnum flæsce; help min forðon.'

Blickling Homily #7, p. 89

Ic þe halsige nu, Drihten, for þinre þeowene, Sancta Marian, þa þu mid heofonlicum wuldre geweorþodest . . . þu wast þæt þu of minre dehter, drihten, onwoce; & þæt hire flæsc is of minum flæsce, & hire ban of minum banum. Ara me nu . . . ara me . . . & min Scyppend miltsa me, & genere me of þysses deaþes bendum.

There is no verbal similarity between *Martyrology* and the poem, though both support the same idea: a maternal appeal to Christ through Mary. But *Blickling* #7 has both ideational and verbal elements in common with *Christ and Satan* and *Martyrology*.

The harrowing of hell material in *Cerne* is so close to the like scene in the *Blickling* #7 as to be the parent, or derived from the parent, of which the Old English is a veritable translation. Although, then, the ending of *Cerne* is missing a quire or more, we may follow Förster in assuming that part of the lost material dealt with essentially the same matter as the Blickling homily. But though Förster convincingly demonstrates the similarity between parts of *Blickling* #7 and Sermon 160, and parts of *Cerne* and *Blickling* #7, it is a shaky deduction that those elements—to wit, the specific appeals of Adam and Eve at the harrowing—found in *Cerne* and *Blickling* #7 ought to be accepted as

---

[73] *PL* 39, cols. 2059-61.

[74] G. Herzfeld, ed., *An Old English Martyrology* (London, 1900), p. 48.

[75] *The Blickling Homilies,* pp. 87-89.

having been derived from an ancestor of the Latin homily we now possess, which ancestor was the source of the harrowing material in a good number of things.

David Dumville, dealing with the same problem as Förster, posits "x," a Latin homily based on Sermon 160 but including additional matter relating to the role of Adam and Eve in the harrowing.[76] This "x," Dumville argues, was the source of *Blickling #7*, the harrowing section in the original *Cerne,* of which the *Book of Cerne* is a poor copy, and possibly the entry in the *Mercian Martyrology.*

If we assume that the poet of *Christ and Satan* was familiar with either Dumville's "x," or Förster's ancestor of Sermon 160, or with a Latin or vernacular homily based thereupon, we find a likely source for Eve's appeal to Christ in lines 435ff. That the poet may have approached this possible source creatively is in keeping with his attitude extrapolated so far toward putative sources. The change in tradition which centres attention exclusively on Mother Eve to the exclusion of Father Adam and other Old Testament worthies demonstrates artistic economy, is emotionally affective, and, in a typological sense, serves to bind together the action of Part II of the poem.[77]

---

[76] David Dumville, "Liturgical Drama and Panegyric Responsory from the Eighth Century? A Re-examination of the Origin and Contents of the Ninth Century Section of the Book of Cerne," *JTS,* 23 (1972), 386-87.

[77] See my article in *MP,* 72 (1974).

IV. LANGUAGE AND DATE

Kenneth Sisam answers a resounding "no" to the question "Do linguistic tests now available enable us to determine the dialect in which any longer piece of Old English poetry was composed."[1] He suggests that, rather than using the normal spoken or written dialect of any given area, poets had recourse "to a general Old English poetic dialect, artificial, archaic, and perhaps mixed in vocabulary, conservative in inflections that affect the verse structure, and indifferent to non-structural irregularities...."[2] Sisam arrives at this hypothesis by arguing that for the earlier poetry, i.e., for works composed in the seventh, eighth and early ninth centuries, there is insufficient evidence of what various dialects were like to make comparisons meaningful; that there is the possibility, even the likelihood, that a poem composed in one dialect would, in the course of time, find its way to another dialect area, and, through oral transmission or recopying by a scribe whose dialect was different from that of the original composer, lose something of its original linguistic characteristics; that the tests of vocabulary and phonology usually employed to determine the original dialect can only be inconclusive. This seminal hypothesis has not been challenged effectively, and in fact provides the assumption upon which some editors of Old English poems make an analysis of the language of their texts.[3] In the light of Sisam's argument, it would be of dubious utility to attempt to discover by linguistic analysis the original dialect of *Christ and Satan,* or to locate geographically its point of origin.[4] It seems more fruitful to analyze objectively the language of the poem as it stands in the manuscript, taking account of the activity of the Annotator, and particularly the Corrector, as such activity supports or modifies Sisam's hypothesis.

A. VOWELS IN STRESSED SYLLABLES

1. We see a confusion between *æ* and *e* from West Germanic *a* in closed syllables when the vowel is not influenced by other sounds: e.g.,

---

[1] Kenneth Sisam, *Studies in the History of Old English Literature* (Oxford, 1953), pp. 119-39, particularly 119.

[2] Ibid., p. 138.

[3] See, for example, Rosemary Woolf, ed., *Juliana* (London, 1955), p. 4; N. F. Blake, ed., *The Phoenix* (Manchester, 1964), pp. 3-4.

[4] The most exhaustive and still useful of the earlier investigations of the language of *Christ and Satan* is that by Theodor Frings, "*Christ und Satan,*" *Zeitschrift für deutsche Philologie,* 45 (1913), 216-36. Clubb, pp. xvii-xxiv, bases his analysis on Frings's. I lean on the researches of both. Frings and Clubb conclude that *Christ and Satan* was originally composed in a Mercian-Northumbrian border dialect.

scref lines 26, 73; *scræf* lines 128, 417, 724; *wītescræf* line 690; *gefestnade* line 3; *gefæstnod* line 515. Unaffected *e* in a closed syllable gives *e* or *æ*: e.g., *swegles* line 23, *swægles* line 123; *selde* line 661; *rægnas* line 11. Unaffected *ā* gives *æ* or *ē*: *blǣd* line 412, *blēd* lines 592, 644; *nǣddran* lines 336, 410, *nēdran* line 101; *wǣron* variously, but *wēron* line 23. Unaffected *i* is usually retained, but we find *y* in *hym* line 70, *syndon* line 149, *synd* line 357, *fyrndagum* line 461. *Self* is spelled variously with *e*, *y*, and *eo*.

2. *a* before nasals is variously *o* or *a*: *land* line 211, *lond* line 213; *mancynnes* line 666, *moncynnes* line 64; *handum* line 705, *hondum* line 538; *gelamp* lines 24, 174, 476, *gelomp* lines 124, 532, 568.

3. *a* before *l* or *r* + a consonant, or *h*, is either *ea* or *a*, with one case of *e* as the redaction of *a* + *h*: e.g., *waldend* line 216, *wealdendes* line 576; *swearte* line 370, *swarte* line 638; *leahtrum* line 262; *esle*, emended to *ehsle* by the Corrector, line 680. *e* before *r* + consonant is either *eo* or *e*: e.g., *eorðan* line 16, *eorlas* line 476; *tōwerpan* line 85, *tōweorpan* line 391; *weorcum* line 221, *wercum* line 48. *e* before *h* + consonant is *i*: e.g., *six* line 15; *riht* lines 205, 687. *i* before *r* + consonant is *eo*: e.g., *beornende* line 157.

4. The *i* umlaut of *a* before *l* or *r* + consonant is, variously, *æ*, *e* or *y*: e.g., *wælm* line 30, *welme* line 39, *hylle* line 431, *helle* line 70; *wærgðu* line 89, *āwyrgda* line 315; *cyrre* line 536, *cer* line 697. The *i* umlaut of *i* before *r* + consonant is *y* or *i*: e.g., *wirse* line 24, *wyrse*, lines 124, 174; *āfirde* line 67, *āfyrde* line 477. The *i* umlaut of *u* is *y* or *i*: e.g., *drihten* line 47, *dryhtene* line 44; *hyhte* line 70, *hihte* line 175. The *i* umlaut of *ai* is either *ǣ* or *ē*: e.g., *ǣhte* line 87, *lǣhte* line 714, *mǣndon* line 384; *clēne* lines 7, 18, *gedēlde* line 19, *hēlende* line 54, *hǣlend* line 217. The *i* umlaut of *au* is either *ī*, *ȳ*, *ǣ* or *ē*: e.g., *līge* line 324, *lǣg*, changed by erasure to *lēg*, line 713; *gelȳfdon* line 414, *gelēfde* line 244; *hēran* line 54, *bēgde* line 380. The *i* umlaut of *iu* is either *ȳ*, *ī*, or *ēo*: e.g., *lȳhteð* line 104, *gelīhtan* line 429; *ðēostræ* line 38, *dēore* line 82.

5. The *u* umlaut of *a* is *ea*: e.g., *eaples* line 409. The *u* umlaut of *e* is usually *eo*: e.g., *meotod* lines 2, 8, 64, *metod* line 666; *heolstres* line 100, *geseotu* line 601; between *w* and *r* we have *eo*, *o* or *e*: e.g., *weoroda* lines 187, 197, *werud* line 33, *weroda* line 251; *worulde* line 93, *weorulde* line 209. The *u* and *o/a* umlaut of *i* is *eo*: e.g., *cleopað* line 615, *leomu* line 154, *neoman* line 197 (glossed to *niman* by the Annotator), *weotod* line 691. The *u* and *o/a* umlaut of *e*, when it occurs, is *eo* or *ea*: e.g., *fela* lines 400, 495, *feolo/a* lines 419, 475; *teala* lines 556, 593; *spreocan* line 78; *ongeotan* line 300.

6. *au* before *c*, *g* or *h* becomes *ēa*, *ē* or *ǣ*: e.g., *hēahgetimbrad* line 29, *hēhenglas* line 600, *hēhfæder* line 654; *ēagum* lines 139, 169, *ēgum* line 725; *þēah* lines 431, 516, *þǣh* line 264. Old English *ēo* before a palatal or velar fricative gives *ēo* or *ī*: e.g., *lēoht* lines 28, 366; *līht* lines 68, 360, 677. *a* after palatals is, variously, *ea*, *æ*, *e*, but usually *y* when

affected by *i* umlaut: e.g., *gesceafta* line 440, *gescæft* line 138, *gesceft* line 662, *scyppend* line 242, *scypend* line 57, *sceppendes* line 105. *e* after palatals is *i, y* or *e*: e.g., *gife*, line 571, *gylp* line 252, *bescyrede* line 342, *sceldbyrig* line 308.

B.   INFLECTIONS

1. We find *æ* for *e* in *niðær* line 31, *ðeostræ* line 38, *gelærdæst* line 53, *wyrsæ* line 140, *drēamæs* line 181, *lǣdæð* line 360 (in these last three cases the *æ* is the result of the Corrector's emendation of *e*), *noldæs* line 729.
2. *un* instead of *an/on* as the pret. ind. plural ending is found in *sceolun* lines 30, 41, *gesāwun* line 716.
3. The tense stem *-ed-* for the second weak conjunction instead of *-ad-* or *-od-* is seen in *staðeledon* line 25, *gnornedon* line 279, *cwānedon* line 319, *þanceden* line 532, *firnedon* line 619.

C.   CONSONANTS

1. We see an intrusive *h* in *hrefnan* line 498, while initial *h* is dropped in *reðre* line 98, *nīgan* line 206, *insiðgryre* line 454, *gerēaw* line 487, *rēam* line 715.
1.A. *u* is used for *f* in *seolua* in lines 13, 711. *d* replaces *ð* in *sidas* line 188 and *gecȳdde* line 199. *sidas* is in all probability a scribal error; *gecȳdde* is an acceptable grammatical form. *h* is used more often than *c* in *ac*, while *h* appears instead of final *g* in *āstāh* lines 547, 562 (but see *āstāg* lines 715, 726). *g* becomes *i* in *eisegan* line 36, and is omitted in *menio* line 474 (but see all other instances where *g* is retained, e.g., lines 83, 110, 261, etc.), and *middaneard* lines 164, 271 (but see, e.g., *middangeard* lines 8, 438, etc.). Finally the doubling of consonants has not taken place in *ātre* line 79, *nēdran* line 101, *tūdor* line 657 (but see *āttre* lines 40, 128, 162, etc., *næddran* lines 336, 410, *hlūddre* line 600, *ærror* lines 150, 298. Other forms requiring specific mention are remarked in the "Explanatory Notes."

The Annotator makes few changes in the text, his activity being confined to the first five pages, of which page 213 has one annotation, page 216 one, page 217 three, page 218 three. His additions seem to be attempts to clarify the poem's sense: e.g., *þær* line 212, *mycele* line 211, *some* line 190. But with the possible exception of *þær* in line 212, such additions are unnecessary, the poem being intelligible at these points. Of his other corrections, line 227 offers the dative plural *oðrum wordum* for the text's *oðre worde. cwidum* of line 159 for MS *cwide*, which I emend to *cwīðde*, seems based upon a misreading of what is admittedly a difficult text at this point; the gloss *buton* for MS *nymðe* line 18 and the change of MS *neoman* to *nīman* line 197 may be attempts to harmonize these elements of the poem to Late West Saxon norms. The change of *anwaldan* line 207 to *ealwaldan* appears both substantive and dialectical.

The Annotator's eight emendations provide a slim foundation for any but the most general remarks concerning his purpose in working with the poem. Such, happily, is not the case with the other revising hand to be found in the text, that of the Late West Saxon Corrector. Though the quantity of his activity tends to fall off in the middle of the text, pages 216-20,[5] there is not one page that contains less than three corrections by him, and most contain many more. The quality of his activity is consistent, though the quantity changes: there is a conscious attempt to bring the language of *Christ and Satan* into conformity with the Late West Saxon dialect.

The Corrector is particularly interested in the West Saxon result of breaking: hence his emendations in lines 21, 34, 52, 71, 86, 92, 117 (thrice), etc. He changes MS *ē* to *ǣ* as the normal West Saxon form of the *i* umlaut of West Germanic *ai*: lines 19, 32, 54, 86, etc. He emends *līht* to *lēoht* in line 68 and *sīc* to *sēoc* in line 274, changes *wēron* to *wǣron* in line 23, and *seolfe* and *selfe* to *sylfe* in lines 23 and 646. But his activity is uneven. There are other examples in the poem of, e.g., *waldend, līht* and *seolf* that are not changed. Again, though he modifies *clēne* to *clǣne* in line 18, he allows the *clēne* in line 7 to remain, emends neither *meotod* nor *cester,* forms that are non-West Saxon (it may be that *meotod* had become a common form, but see *metod* line 666), is probably responsible for changing the *gelamp* of line 24 to *gelomp* and the *gelomp* of line 124 to *gelamp,* changes the *hworfon* of line 71 to *hweorfon,* but emends the *tōwerpan* and *wercum* of lines 85 and 48 to *tōwiorpan* and *wiorcum.* Still, the thrust of his purposeful activity is clearly to modify the dialect of the poem in the direction of West Saxon.

The Corrector's activity provides the stuff of a footnote to Sisam's hypothesis. Even if one grant the sometimes whimsical character of Old English scribal practice, it remains that the Corrector has a definite attitude toward the manuscript text, and that attitude is to change its dialect. Why? Is he a hack who does not recognize the poetic koine when he sees it? He may not have been a poet, but he was certainly literate and something of a linguist in the bargain, and he did exercise some care in

---

[5] Gollancz, pp. xxviii-xxix, believes this is due to the fact that the second scribe, who is responsible for pages 216-28, transcribed more successfully from one dialect to the other, presumably from Anglian to West Saxon, leaving the Corrector relatively less to do than in the sections transcribed by scribes one and three. A radical example of such transcription, perhaps, is *rægnas,* line 11b, and *dæles,* line 16a, forms that are quite Late West Saxon. If we accept a date for the poem any time before the early tenth century, these forms would not be normal. They may, of course, be scribal errors. See the notes to the lines.

working through a large collection of poetry. Was he preparing the manuscript for an exclusively West Saxon audience? But would they themselves not have recognized the poetic koine, and if so, why change it? Of course, the koine may have fallen into desuetude by circa A.D. 1000; or perhaps the Corrector was just satisfying his sense of propriety. In any event, we have in *Christ and Satan* a text in which non-West Saxon forms are intentionally modified to conform to the West Saxon dialect. This fact does not invalidate, or seriously question, Sisam's hypothesis, and in fact serves to support the assertion that it is all but impossible to determine the original language, be that language a poetic koine or a dialect properly so called, of an Old English poem. For it is clear that, had the poem been recopied with the Corrector's changes incorporated in the text, the character of the language would have been much more West Saxon than it is now, and we would have been at yet another remove from the language of original composition. I hesitate to speculate at how many removes from the original our text now stands.

An attempt to discover the date of original composition of an Old English poem is a task similar in difficulty to an attempt to locate geographically its point of origin or to discover the original dialect of composition: such tasks are all but impossible. With the exception of a few poems whose general date and circumstances of composition have been preserved—I think here, for example, of *Cædmon's Hymn* in Bede's *History, Brunanburh* in the *Chronicle,* the verse *Metres of Boethius,* and Alfred's verse epilogue to Gregory's *Pastoral Care*—there is little firm basis for an opinion, and we proceed, therefore, by guesswork more or less inspired.

Different inspiration has allowed different critics to place *Christ and Satan* within a time frame of A.D. 680-950. The methodology traditionally employed is an analysis of the poem's language; an analysis of the poem's artistry to locate it in relation to the "Cædmonian" poems, for example, *Genesis,* and the works of Cynewulf, or a combination of these two. Theoretically, of course, the *terminus ad quem* for *Christ and Satan* is the compilation and composition of the manuscript itself, approximately A.D. 1000, while the *terminus a quo* is the earliest recorded example of vernacular Christian poetry, approximately A.D. 680. Within this wide range, there is little or no external evidence for placing the poem. It would be presumptious to suggest that I have found that evidence which dates *Christ and Satan* exactly; I offer the following consideration as circumstantial evidence that tends to limit the *a quo,* and perhaps the *ad quem.*

Christ and Satan is one of the more Christocentric of Old English poems, distinct from other works such as the *Christ* poems of the *Exeter Book* by reason of its unique structure and theme. Should we find that this Christocentricity requires explanation, and should we turn to the theological history of Western Europe to discover a time when the ideational atmosphere might have been conducive to the composition of such a work, we are drawn to the controversy caused by the Adoptionist heresy at the close of the eighth, the beginning of the ninth, centuries.

Elipandus, bishop of Toledo, and Felix, bishop of Urgel, fomented this heresy, which was not unlike that of Nestorius. The Adoptionists believed that Christ as God was the true and natural son of the Father, but that Christ as Man was the adopted son, a son by grace, "filius adoptivus," "nuncupativus," "per metaphorem."[6] Since the territory in which this doctrine was initially popularized was contiguous to the domain of Charles the Great, and since the heresy seems to have spread through Gaul, Germany and Acquitaine, Charles became instrumental in its suppression. He called three, possibly four, councils to deal with it: Narbonne, A.D. 788; Ratisbon, A.D. 792; Frankfort, A.D. 794; Aix-la-Chapelle, A.D. 799.[7] Frankfort was a *synodus universalis,* convened with the apostolic authority of Pope Hadrian, who personally dealt with the heresy in letters to the Spanish bishops in A.D. 785, and to Charles in A.D. 794. The most famous Englishman involved in the dispute was Alcuin, who wrote numerous letters and treatises defending the orthodox position.[8] At least as important for our purposes is the fact that English ecclesiastics, unfortunately not identified, are mentioned by Charles in a letter to Elipandus as having attended the Council of Frankfort.[9] I think we can assume, then, that the English church was aware of the problems raised by the Adoptionists. I suggest that by causing a re-investigation of the relationship of the Son to the Father, and to man, the Adoptionist dispute might have provided the atmos-

---

[6] For an analysis of the doctrinal content of this heresy, and the history surrounding its suppression, see C. J. Hefele, *Histoire des Conciles* (Paris, 1910), 3, pt. 2, pp. 1001-60, trans. from the German by Dom L. Leclercq; H. Quillet, "Adoptianisme au viiie Siecle," *DTC,* 1, 403-13. Primary concilar documents may be found in J. D. Mansi, ed., *Sacrum Conciliorum,* 13 (rpt. Graz, Austria, 1960).

[7] Hefele, pp. 1024-27, argues persuasively that the acts of the Council of Narbonne were altered after the fact to include a condemnation of Felix and the Adoptionist heresy.

[8] For example: Libellus adversus Felicis Haeresim; Adversus Felicem Libri Septem; Contra Epistolam sibi ab Elipando Directam Libri Quatuor; Epistola Albini ad Laidradum et Nefridium episcopos et Benedictum abbatem; Epistola altera ad eosdem; Epistola Albini ad Elipandum; Epistola Alcuini ad filiam in Christo. All works listed may be found in *PL* 101.

[9] From "Caroli Magni Regis Epistola ad Elipandum et ceteros episcopos Hispaniae," in Arthur W. Haddan and William Stubbs, eds., *Councils and Ecclesiastical Documents Relating to Great Britain and Ireland,* vol. 3 (Oxford, 1871 [rpt. 1964]), p. 481, I quote the following selections relating to the attendance of English clergy at the Council of Frankfort: ". . . Nec non et de Britanniae partibus aliquos ecclesiasticae disciplinae viros convocavimus, ut ex moltorum diligenti consideratione veritas catholicae fidei investigaretur, et probatissimis sanctorum patrum hinc inde roborata testimoniis absque ulla dubitione teneatur. . . . Post haec tenet et tertius orthodoxam sanctorum patrum episcoporum et virorum venerabilium fidem, qui in Germaniae, Galliae, Aquitaniae et Britanniae partibus dignis Deo deserviunt officiis, vestrisque objectionibus sanctarum scriptuarum testimoniis roboratas obtinet responsiones."

phere in which such a Christocentric poem as *Christ and Satan* was written.

I do not mean, of course, that the poem is a doctrinal response to the heresy in any sense. Yet by mentioning the Sonship of Christ but depicting him as the active divine person, for example, as the creative agent, the object and the suppressor of the angelic rebellion, the harrower of hell, etc., the poet manages to support at once the orthodox conception of the filiation of the Son and the equality of the persons of the Trinity, at least of the first two, while centring attention on the divinely omnipotent and salvific actions of Christ. Indeed, such is the emphasis on his power and position that there is a danger of seeing him as *primus inter pares,* a natural reaction if one assumes that the poem was written in an atmosphere aware of a theological speculation that diminished the position of the Son. Further, the affecting scene in Part II in which Eve claims a maternal connection with Christ through Mary, lines 435-440, affirms at once the humanity and divinity, in a word the hypostatic union, of the harrower:

Ræhte þā mid handum	tō heofencyninge,
bæd meotod miltse	þurh Marian hād:
"Hwæt, þū fram mīnre dohtor,	drihten, onwōce
in middangeard	mannum tō helpe.
Nū is gesēne	þæt ðū eart sylfa god,
ēce ordfruma	ealra gesceafta."

In the event, we see that the character of Christ remains essentially the same throughout the three parts of the poem: different facets of that character are revealed in different circumstances, but Christ in all his divinity remains Christ, even when, through the mystery of the Incarnation, he is seen as man in Part III. It may be coincidence, or the natural result of the similarity of a formal expression of orthodox belief and the representation of that belief by an orthodox poet, that the culminating revelation of Christ's character as God-Man in Part III of the poem, and the statement of the Council of Frankfort with respect to the Incarnation, are alike: *Mansit vero persona Filii in Trinitate, cui personae humana accessit natura ut esset et una persona Deus et homo, non homo Deificus et humanatus Deus, sed Deus homo et homo Deus:....*[10]

The Adoptionist heresy did not long outlive its most famous supporters, and seems to have lost all force before the death of Felix in A.D. 818. Assuming that the character of the heresy was known in England at about A.D. 792, when Charles recalled Alcuin from York, and that it was a topic of discussion through the beginning of the ninth century, receiving added interest in about A.D. 818 when it was discovered that Felix, after an apparently sincere retraction of his heresy, retracted his retraction in a document written the very year of his death,

---

[10] *PL* 101, col. 1337.

then the time frame of *Christ and Satan,* based on the admittedly circumstantial argument I have put forth, would be somewhere between about A.D. 792-820. It is interesting to remark that M. D. Clubb, working from a completely different set of assumptions, dates the poem between A.D. 790-830.[11]

---

[11] Clubb, p. lx.

THE TEXT

The Text

Yogh and wynn have been replaced by *g* and *w*, *ę* by *æ*. Abbreviations for þæt (þ) and for *and* (7) are expanded without comment. Inflectional endings are abbreviated in the manuscript by a macron over the preceding letter: e.g., line 623a *englū* = *englum*. The majority of abbreviations are for *m*, though I note *wæt* for *wæter* in line 6a, *scās* for *sanctas* in line 238a, *æft* for *æfter* in line 628a. All such abbreviations are expanded without comment. Bold type in the text indicates either that the word(s) does not appear in the manuscript or that an emendation has been incorporated.

In presenting the text I have tried to take into account the manuscript's metrical markings and punctuation, particularly the *punctus versus* (;), where such indicators give a coherent reading. Only rarely has this been impossible. Ultimately, though, the text rests upon my understanding of the poem.

The Textual Notes

The letters C, S, or A in a bracket after an entry suggest that the Corrector, Scribe, or Annotator is responsible for the particular change. "Gollancz" refers to Sir Israel's facsimile reproduction, particularly pages cxv-cxix wherein he catalogues and assigns to various hands the modifications of the text. For the most part, my analysis of the manuscript agrees with his.

THE POEM

Þæt wearð underne
þæt meotod hæfde
ðā hē gefestnade
Seolfa hē gesette
5 stānas and eorðan,
wæter and wolcn,
Dēopne **ymblyt**
meotod on mihtum,
Hē selfa mæg
10 grundas in heofene,
and hē ārīman mæg
dropena gehwelcne;
seolua hē gesette
Swā se wyrhta
15 serede and sette
eorðan dæles
hēaum holme.
orðonc clēne
   Drēamas hē gedēlde
20 Ādām ǣrest,
engla ordfruman,
Ðūhte him on mōde
þæt hīe wēron seolfe
wuldres waldend.

eorðbūendum   [I]
miht and strengðo
foldan scēatas.
sunnan and mōnan,
strēam ūt on sǣ,
ðurh his wundra miht.
clēne ymbhaldeð
and alne middangeard.
sǣ geondwlitan,
godes āgen bearn,
rægnas scūran
daga enderīm
þurh his sōðan miht.
þurh his wuldres gāst
on six dagum
ūp on heofonum
Hwā is þæt ðe cunne
nymðe ēce god?
duguðe and **geoguðe**:
and þæt æðele cyn,
þæt þe eft forwarð.
þæt hit mihte swā,
swegles brytan,
Him ðǣr **wirse** gelamp,

---

1 **wearð** originally **wearþ**, with ð written over partially erased þ; MS reads **eorð buendum**, with an e erased between words, thus **eorðebuendum**. Above and to the right of the erased e is a faint **a**, visible under ultraviolet light.

2 **hī** = **him** superscript after **meotod** (probably C).

6 MS reads **wolcᵉ/n** (probably C).

7 MS reads **ybmlyt**, with a small mark after **t**, probably caesural.

9 **sǣ** from earlier **se** (Gollancz offers "S?").

10 **heofene** from earlier **heofeno**, with final **o** from earlier **e**, and **n** added above o/e (C).

17 **hēaum**: MS reads **henne** with **a** over first **e** (probably S).

18 **clēne**, with **e** altered to **æ**, thus **clǣne** (C); **nymðe** with ·**i**· **buton** superscript, where "i" = **id est** (A).

19 **gedēlde**, with **æ** above second **e** (C); **geoguðe**: MS reads **geþeode**.

21 **forwarð**, with **e** above **w** (C).

22 **him**, with **eo** above **i** (C).

23 **wēron**, with **e** altered to **æ**; **seolfe**, with **y** above first **e** (C).

24 **wirse**: MS reads **wise**, with **ors** above **ise** (probably C); **gelamp**, with **o** over **a** (Gollancz offers C or S).

25 ðā hēo in helle   hām staðeledon,
    ān æfter ōðrum   in þæt atole scref,
    þǣr hēo brynewelme   bīdan sceolden
    sāran sorge;   nales swegles lēoht
    habban in heofnum   hēahgetimbrad,
30 ac gedūfan sceolun   in ðone dēopan wælm,
    niðær under nessas,   in ðone neowlan grund,
    grēdige and gīfre.   God āna wāt
    hū hē þæt scyldige werud   forscrifen hefde.
        Cleopað ðonne se alda   ūt of helle,
35 wriceð wordcwedas   wēregan reorde,
    eisegan stefne: "Hwǣr cōm engla ðrym,
    þe wē on heofnum   habban sceoldan?
    Þis is ðēostræ hām   ðearle gebunden
    fæstum fȳrclommum;   flōr is on welme,
40 āttre onǣled.   Nis nū ende feor
    þæt wē sceolun ætsomne   sūsel þrōwian,
    wēan and **wērgu**,   nalles **wuldres** blǣd
    habban in heofnum,   hēhselda wyn.
    Hwæt, wē for dryhtene iū   drēamas **hefdon**,
45 song on swegle   sēlrum tīdum,
    þǣr nū ymb ðone ēcan   æðele stondað,
    heleð ymb hēhseld,   herigað drihten
    wordum and wercum.   And ic in wīte sceal
    bīdan in bendum,   and mē **bettran** hām

---

26 **þæt**: abbreviation ꝥ with a following e, visible under ultraviolet, erased.
27 **sceolden**: MS reads **sceoden**, with l above o, o above second e (probably C, though
    Gollancz attributes the l to the Scribe).
28 **swegles**, with o erased between e and g.
29 **habban**, with the second b superscript (S).
30 **dēopan wælm**: MS reads **deop anwælm**, with a line across the separation connecting
    the bottoms of p and a.
31 **under**, with a cedilla below the e, thus **undær** (C).
32 **grēdige**, with æ above first e (C).
33 **scyldige**, with ge superscript; **hefde**, with cedilla under first e, thus **hæfde** (C).
34 **Cleopað**: MS reads **cleopad**; **alda**, with superscript e before a (C).
35 **wordcwedas**, with **word** superscript over **cwedas** (S).
37 **þe**: MS reads ða þe.
38 **is ðēostræ** with þe erased between the words, and æ from a (S).
42 **wērgu**: MS reads **wergum**; **nalles**, with a above an e marked for cancellation (C or S);
    wuldres: MS reads **wulres**.
44 MS reads **hefdom**, with the 3rd stroke of the m clear enough under magnification,
    unmistakable under ultraviolet.
46 **ēcan**, with e from æ by erasure.
47 **heleð**, with first e changed to æ (C); **ymb**: MS reads **ym** with b added above m,
    probably by the Scribe, in what appears to be a lighter ink. The b is not, as Gollancz
    maintains, erased.
48 **wordum**: MS reads **wordun**; **wercum**, with io above er, the e marked for deletion (C).
49 **bettran**: MS reads **(b)ættran**, with the b erased and the æ marked with a dot to

50   for oferhygdum   ǣfre ne wēne."
         Đā him andsweradan   atole gāstas,
      swarte and synfulle,   sūsle begrorenne:
      "þū ūs gelǣrdæst   ðurh lyge ðīnne
      þæt wē hēlende   hēran ne scealdon.
55   Đūhte þē ānum   þæt ðū āhtest alles gewald
      heofnes and eorþan,   wǣre hālig god,
      scypend seolfa.   **Nū earttū sceaðana sum**
      in fȳrlocan   feste gebunden.
      Wēndes ðū ðurh wuldor   ðæt þū woruld āhtest,
60   alra onwald,   and wē englas mid ðec.
      Atol is þīn onsēon!   Habbað wē alle swā
      for ðīnum lēasungum   lȳðre gefēred.
      Segdest ūs tō sōðe   þæt ðīn sunu wǣre
      meotod moncynnes.   Hafustū nū māre sūsel!"
65   Swā firenfulle   fācnum wordum
      heora aldorðægn   **on reordadon,**
      on **cearium** cwidum.   Crīst hēo āfirde,
      drēamum bedēlde.   Hæfdan dryhtnes līht
      for oferhygdum   ufan forlēton;
70   hæfdon hym tō hyhte   helle flōras,
      beornende bealo.   Blāce hworfon
      scinnan forscepene;   sceaðan **hwearfedon**,
      earme ǣglēcan,   geond þæt atole scref,
      for ðām anmēdlan   þe hīe ǣr drugon.

75   Eft reordade   ōðre sīðe   II
      fēonda aldor.   Wæs þā **forht** agēn
      seoððan hē ðes wītes   worn gefēlde.
      Hē **spearcade**   ðonne hē spreocan ongan
      fȳre and ātre: ne bið swelc fǣger drēam

---

       indicate a mistake; **for** cancelled before **ham.**
52   **swarte**, with e above a (C).
54   **hēlende**, with æ above first e: **scealdon** with o above ea (C).
57   MS reads **nu eart tu earm sceaða**, with a following **na sum** erased.
63   **Segdest**, with first e altered to æ (C).
66   **on reordadon**: MS reads **unreaordadon.**
67   **cearium**: MS reads **cearum.**
68   **bedēlde**, with middle e erased and æ added above the erasure; **līht**, with eo above erased i (C).
69   **ufan**, with f over an erasure; **forlēton**: MS reads **forlæten** with æ from e, e from o (C).
71   **hworfon**, with e above and after w (C).
72   **hwearfedon**: MS reads **hwearfdon.**
74   **anmēdlan**, with **an** superscript before **m** (Gollancz offers "?C," but the hand seems to be the Scribe's).
76   MS reads **wæs þa for worht agen.**
77   **ðes**, with e erased and æ superscript (C).
78   MS reads **sweartade**, with **t** written over c (S).

80 ðonne hē in wītum
  "Ic wæs iū in heofnum
  dryhtene dēore;
  micelne for meotode,
  Þā ic in mōde
85 þæt ic wolde tōwerpan
  bearn hēlendes,
  eall tō æhte,
  þe ic hebbe tō helle
  Wēne þæt tācen sutol
90 niðer under nessas
  Nū ic ēow hebbe tō hæftum
  alle of earde.
  wloncra wīnsele,
  nē ængla ðrēat,
95 āgan mōten.
  fȳre onæled;
  Æce æt helle duru
  hāte on reðre;
  Is ðæs wālica hām
100 nāgan wē ðæs heolstres
  in ðissum neowlan genipe.
  wyrmas gewunade;

þā word indrāf:
hālig ængel
hefde mē drēam mid gode,
and ðēos menego swā some.
mīnum hogade
wuldres lēoman,
āgan mē burga gewald
and ðēos earme hēap
hām gelēdde.
þā ic āseald wes on wærgðu,
in ðone neowlan grund.
hām gefærde,
Nis hēr ēadiges tīr,
nē worulde drēam,
nē wē ūpheofon
Is ðes atola hām
ic eom fāh wið god.
dracan eardigað,
hēo ūs helpan ne magon.
wītes āfylled;
þæt wē ūs gehȳdan mægon
Hǣr is nēdran swǣg,
is ðis wītes clom

---

79 **ātre**, with additional **t** superscript after **a** (C); **ne**, with **n** from **h** by erasure.
80 **þā word**: **þā** not in MS.
82 **dryhtene**, with first **e** cancelled, second **e** added (C).
85 **ic wolde**, with an erasure between the words, probably **in**; **tōwerpan**, with **io** above **e** (C); **wuldres**: MS reads **wulres**.
86 **hēlendes**, with **æ** above first **e**; **gewald**, with **e** superscript before **a** (C).
87 **ðēos** from altered **ðes** (S).
88 **gelēdde**, with second **e** altered to **æ** (C).
89a **wēne**, with **ge** above **ne** (C).
89b MS reads **and wærgðu þa ic of aseald wes**.
90 **nessas**, with **e** cancelled by a dot and **æ** superscript (C); **ðone** is **ðonne** in the MS, with the first **n** erased.
91 **gefærde**, with original **æ** changed to second **e**, another **e** superscript after **r**, giving **geferede** (C).
92 **alle**, with superscript **e** before initial **a** (probably C).
93 **winsele**, with **y** above **i** and final **e** changed to **a** (C).
94a **ængla**, with the first half of **æ** erased to give initial **e**.
94b **we** superscript after **ne**, additional **p** superscript after **up** (C).
95 **āgan mōten**, with **ne** superscript between; **ðes**, with **os** erased and **s** written over (C).
96 **fȳre**, with final **e** added (probably C).
97 **Æce**, with **Æ** altered to **E** (C).
98 **hēo**, with **e** and **o** dotted for correction, **y** superscript above **e** (C).
99 **ðæs**: MS reads **ðes**, with **e** from altered **æ**.
100 **nāgan**: first **n** over some erased large letter; **mægon**, with second half of **æ** erased.
101 **Hǣr**, with the first half of **æ** erased; **swǣg**, with first half of **æ** erased.

feste gebunden; fēond seondon rēðe,
dimme and deorce, ne hēr dæg lȳhteð
105 for scedes scīman, sceppendes lēoht.
Nū āhte gewald ealles wuldres;
þær ic mōste in ðeossum atolan æðele gebīdan
hwæt mē drihten god dēman wille,
fāgum on flōra. Nū ic fēran cōm
110 dēofla menego tō ðissum dimman hām;
ac ic sceal on flyge and on flyhte ðrāgum
earda nēosan, and ēower mā
þe ðes oferhȳdes ord onstaldon.
Ne ðurfon wē ðes wēnan þæt ūs wuldorcyning
115 æfre wille eard ālēfan,
æðel tō æhte swā hē ær dyde.
Ēce onwald āh him alles gewald
wuldres and wīta, waldendes sunu!
Forðon ic sceal hēan and earm hweorfan ðȳ wīdor,
120 wadan wræclāstas, wuldre benēmed,
duguðum bedēled, nænigne drēam āgan
uppe mid ænglum, þes ðe ic ær gecwæð
þæt ic wære seolfa swægles brytta,
wihta wealdend.'' Ac hit him wyrse gelomp.

125   Swā se wērega gāst wordum sæde   III
his earfoðo ealle ætsomne,

---

103 feste, with a cedilla under first e, thus fæste (C).
104 and, an expansion of the scribal 7, which 7 is written over on erased; dæg, with final e erased; lȳhteð, with teð added above and to the right of lyh.
106 āhte gewald, with ic superscript between words (C).
107 æðele, with the first half of æ erased (Gollancz offers "?S").
108 wille, with dotted y above i (C).
111 ac, with c over erased h.
113 onstaldon, with a dotted for cancellation and e superscript (C).
114 MS reads Ne/ður-fon; ðes, with e marked with a cedilla, thus ðæs.
115 ālēfan, with y above e (C).
116 æðel, with first half of æ erased (Gollancz offers "?S").
117 Ēce, with n superscript between c and e; onwald, with e superscript between w and a; alles, with e superscript before a; gewald, with superscript e over a (C).
118 wuldres, with d superscript between l and r (S); waldendes, with superscript e between w and a (C).
119 ic hēan, with sceal superscript between words (C); earm, with m added after r, ma following underlined as error (Gollancz offers C or ?S); hweorfan, with eo dotted for cancellation and superscript y over o (C); wīdor, with additional d superscript over o (C).
122 ænglum, with first half of æ erased; þes: with the e marked with a cedilla, thus þæs.
123 swægles, with first half of æ erased.
124 wihta wealdend, with ihta wealdend in the hand of the second Scribe, over an erasure; Ac, with c altered from h; gelomp, with o dotted for cancellation and a superscript (C).

fāh in fyrnum.
geond þæt atole scræf
"Ic eom limwæstmum
130 on þyssum sīdan sele,
Hwæt! hēr hāt and ceald
hwīlum ic gehēre
gnornende cynn,
niðer under næssum;
135 winnað ymb wyrmas.
eall inneweard
Ne mōt ic hihtlicran
burga nē bolda,
ne mōt ic æfre mā
140 Is mē nū wyrsa
uppe mid englum
song on swegle,
habbað ēadigne bearn
seolfa mid sange.
145 ænigum sceððan
būtan þām ānum
þā ic mōt tō hæftum
bringan tō bolde
Ealle wē syndon
150 þonne þe wē iū in heofonum
wlite and weorðmynt.
brōhton tō bearme
þær wē ymb hine ūtan
leomu ymb lēofne,
155 drihtne sædon.
gewundod mid wommum;
beoran beornende
hāt on helle,
Þā gȳt feola cwīðde
160 atol æglæca,
wītum wērig;
āttre gelīcost,

Fȳrlēoma stōd
āttre geblonden.
þæt ic gelūtian ne mæg
synnum forwundod.
hwīlum mencgað;
hellescealcas,
grundas mænan
hwīlum nacode men
Is þes windiga sele
atole gefylled.
hāmes brūcan,
nē on þā beorhtan gescæft
ēagum starian.
þæt ic wuldres lēoht
æfre cūðe,
þær sunu meotodes
ealle ymbfangen
Nē ic þām sāwlum ne mōt

þe hē āgan nyle;
hām geferian,
in þone biteran grund.
ungelīce
hæfdon ærror,
Ful oft wuldres swēg
bearne hælendes,
ealle hōfan,
lofsonga word
Nū ic eom dǣdum fāh,
sceal nū þysne wītes clom
in bæce mīnum,
hyhtwillan lēas."
firna herde,
ūt of helle,
word spearcum flēah,
þonne hē ūt þorhdrāf:

---

133 **gnornende**, with superscript **i** between second **n** and **e** (C).
135 **ymb**, with superscript **e** after **b** (C).
140 **wyrsa**, with **a** altered to **æ** (C).
146 **hē āgan nyle**: MS reads **he to agan nyle**.
151 **swēg** not in MS.
152 **bearne**: MS reads **bearn**.
159 **cwīðde**: MS reads **cwide**, with abbreviation for **vel** (ł) and **dum** superscript over **e** (A); **herde**: MS reads **herede**, with a letter, "perhaps a" (Gollancz), above first **e**.
162 **þorhdrāf**, with **o** dotted for cancellation and **u** superscript above **o**; words separated (C).

"Ēalā drihtenes þrym!   Ēalā duguða helm!
Ēalā meotodes miht!   Ēalā middaneard!
165 Ēalā dæg lēohta!   Ēalā drēam godes!
Ēalā engla þrēat!   Ēalā ūpheofen!
Ēalā þæt ic eam ealles lēas   ēcan drēames,
þæt ic mid handum ne mæg   heofon gerǣcan,
nē mid ēagum ne mōt   ūp lōcian,
170 nē hūru mid ēarum ne sceal   æfre gehēran
þǣre byrhtestan   bēman stefne;
ðæs ic wolde of selde   sunu meotodes,
drihten ādrīfan,   and āgan mē þæs drēames
                               gewald,
wuldres and wynne.   Mē þǣr wyrse gelamp
175 þonne ic tō hihte   āgan mōste.
Nū ic eom āscēaden   fram þǣre scīran driht,
ālǣded fram lēohte   in þone lāðan hām.
Ne mæg ic þæt gehicgan   hū ic in ðǣm becwōm,
in þis neowle genip   **nīðsynnum** fāh,
180 āworpen of worulde.   Wāt **ic** nū þā
þæt bið alles lēas   ēcan drēamas
sē ðe heofencyninge   hēran ne þenceð,
meotode cwēman.   Ic **þæs morðres** sceal,
wēan and wītu   and wrace drēogan,
185 gōda bedǣled,   iūdǣdum fāh,
þæs ðe ic gebōhte ādrīfan   drihten of selde,
weoroda waldend;   sceal nū wreclāstas
settan sorhgcearig,   **sīðas** wīde."

Hwearf þā tō helle   þā hē gehēned wæs,   [IV]
190 godes andsaca;   dydon his gingran swā,
gīfre and grǣdige,   þā hīg god bedrāf
in þæt hāte hof   þām is hel nama.
Forþan sceal gehycgan   hæleða ǣghwylc

---

165 **lēohta**, with the o altered from **d**.
169 **ūp**, with **g** erased after **p**.
171 **bēman**, with y superscript above **e** (C).
178 **becwōm**, with two dots under the **w** (C or S).
179 **nīð**: MS reads **mid**.
180 abbreviation for **þæt** added after **ic**.
181 **ēcan**, with a cedilla under **e**, thus **æcan**; **drēamas**, with the second **a** changed to **æ** (Gollancz offers ?S and ?C respectively).
183 **þæs**: MS has the abbreviation for **þæt**; **morðres**: MS reads **morðre**.
188 **sīðas**, from MS **sidas**.
190 **swā** followed by abbreviation for **vel** (ɫ) and **some** superscript (A).
191 MS reads **he** with superscript **ig** over the **e** (C). Gollancz notes that the **e** is dotted for cancellation, but my examination of the manuscript did not confirm his remark.

þæt hē ne ābælige
195 Lǣte him tō bysne
for oferhygdum
Neoman ūs tō wynne
uppe ēcne gefēan,
Hē þæt gecȳdde
200 mihta miccle,
hæftas of ðǣm hēan selde.

ēcne alra gescefta;
mid ealra cyninga cyninge,
Beoran on brēostum
205 sibbe and snytero;
þonne wē tō hēhselde
and þone anwaldan
Þonne behōfað
weorulde wynnum
210 þonne hē ōðer līf
fǣgere land
is þǣr wlitig and wynsum,
beorhte ofer burgum;
hyhtlicra hām
215 Crīste gecwēmra.
þǣr hē sylfa sit,
drihten hǣlend,
and ymb þæt hēhsetl
engla fēðan
220 hālige heofenþrēatas
wordum and weorcum.
geond ealra worulda woruld

bearn waldendes.
hū þā blācan fēond
ealle forwurdon.
weoroda drihten,
engla waldend.
þæt hē mægencræft hæfde,
þā hē þā mænego ādrāf,
Gemunan wē þone hālgan drihten,
cēosan ūs eard in wuldre
sē is Crīst genemned.
blīðe geþōhtas,
gemunan sōð and riht
hnīgan þencað,
āra biddan.
sē ðe hēr wunað
þæt him wlite scīne
eft gesēceð,
þonne þēos folde sēo;
wæstmas scīnað
þǣr is brāde lond,
in heofonrīce
Uta cerran þider
sigora waldend,
in ðǣm dēoran hām;
hwīte standað
and ēadigre;
herigað drihten
Heora wlite scīneð
mid wuldorcyninge.

Ðā gēt ic furðor gefregen **fēondas** ondetan: V

---

194 **ābælige**, with the first half of **æ** erased (Gollancz offers ?C or S).
197 **neoman**, with abbreviation for vel (ꝉ) and **i** superscript over **eo** (A).
198 **uppe:** MS reads **upne**.
202 **ēcne . . .** , MS reads: **ecne in wuldre mid alra gescefta.**
206 **hnīgan**, with **h** added in the margin (probably C).
207 **þone:** MS reads **þonne**, with second **n** erased; **anwaldan**, with abbreviation for vel (ꝉ)
    and **eal** as a variant above **an** (A); **āra**, with second **a** changed to **æ** (probably S).
211 **fǣgere:** MS reads **fægre**, with ·s· (i.e., **scilicet**) **mycele** superscript (A).
212 MS reads: **is wlitig and wynsum**, with ·s· **þær** above **is** (A).
214 **hyhtlicra**, with a final **n** erased.
215 MS reads: **ut^on/a-cerran**, with the **on** in the hand of the Corrector.
218 **ymb**, with a final **e** added (C).
220 **hālige**, with an **r** erased between **g** and **e**.
222 **wuldorcyninge**, with final **e** added (probably C).
223 **fēondas:** MS reads **feonda.**

wæs him eall ful strang,
225 wom and wītu;   hæfdon wuldorcyning
for oferhigdum   ānforlǣten.
Cwǣdon eft hraðe   ōðre worde:
"Nū is gesēne   þæt wē syngodon
uppe on earde.   Sceolon nū ǣfre þæs
230 drēogan dōmlēase gewinn   drihtnes mihtum.
Hwæt, wē in wuldres wlite   wunian mōston
þǣr wē hālgan gode   hēran woldon,
and him sang ymb seld   secgan sceoldon
þūsendmǣlum.   Þā wē þǣr wǣron,
235 wunodon on wynnum,   gehērdon wuldres swēg
bēman stefne.   Byrhtword ārās,
engla ordfruma,   and tō þǣm æþelan
hnigan him sanctas;   sigetorht ārās
ēce drihten,   ofer ūs gestōd
240 and geblētsode   bilewitne hēap
dōgra gehwilcne: and þes se dēora sunu,
gāsta scyppend.   God seolfa wæs
eallum andfeng   þe ðǣr ūp becōm,
and hine on eorðan   ǣr gelēfde."
245 "Þā ðæs ofþūhte   þæt se þēoden wæs
strang and stīðmōd.   Ongan ic þā steppan forð,
āna wið englum,   and tō him eallum spræc:
'Ic can ēow lǣran   langsumne rǣd,
gif gē willað mīnre   mihte gelēfan.
250 Uta oferhycgan   helm þone micclan,
weroda waldend,   āgan ūs þis wuldres lēoht,
eall tō ǣhte.   Þis is īdel gylp
þæt wē ǣr drugon   ealle hwīle.'

Ðā gewearð ūsic   þæt wē woldon swā   VI
255 drihten ādrīfan   of þām dēoran hām,
cyning of cestre.   Cūð is wīde
þæt wreclāstas   wunian mōton
grimme grundas.   God seolfa him
rīce haldeð.   Hē is āna cyning,

---

227 ōðre worde, with Ꝉ (vel) um above the last two letters of each word (A).
228 syngodon, with ge above sy (C).
231 in added above and before wuldres (C).
234 wǣron added above and before wunodon (l. 235a) (C).
241 MS reads and his se deora sunu.
244 gelēfde, with y above second e (C).
249 w erased after gif; mīnre, with n superscript between i and r (S or C); mihte: MS reads
        mihta with a dotted, e over a (C).
250 uta, with n added above a (C).

260 þe ūs eorre gewearð,
meotod mihtum swilc.
licgan on leahtrum;
flēogan ofer foldan—
on æghwylcum,
265 Ne mōt hē þām sāwlum
ēadige of eorþan
Ah ic be hondum mōt
grīpan tō grunde,
Sume sceolon hweorfan
270 and unsibbe
monna mǣgðum
Ic hēr geþolian sceal
bitres nīðæs
sīc and sorhful,
275 þonne ic on heofonum
hwæðer ūs se ēca
on heofona rīce
ēðel tō ǣhte,
Swā gnornedon
280 hāte on helle.
wrāð geworden
Forþon mæg gehycgan,
þæt hē him āfirre
lāðe leahtras,
285 Gemunan symle on mōde
gearwian ūs tōgēnes
ūp tō englum,
and ūs befæðman wile
gif wē þæt on eorðan
290 and ūs tō þām hālgan
Þonne hē ūs nō forlǣteð,
uppe mid englum,
Tǣceð ūs se torhta
beorhte burhweallas.
295 gesǣlige sāwle
þǣr hēo ǣfre forð
cestre and cynestōl.

ēce drihten,
Sceal nū þēos menego hēr
sume on lyft scacan,
fȳr bið ymbūtan
þǣh hē uppe sēo.
þe ðǣr sēcað ūp,
ǣfre gehrīnan.
hæþenre **sceale**
godes andsacan.
geond hæleða land
oft onstyrian
geond middaneard.
þinga ǣghwylces,
beala gnornian,
þæs ic seolfa wēold,
hām staðelode,
ǣfre wille
hām ālēfan,
swā hē ǣr dyde!''
godes andsacan
Him wæs hǣlend god
for womcwidum.
sē ðe his heorte dēah,
frēcne geþōhtas,
lifigendra gehwylc.
meotodes strengðo;
grēne strǣte
þǣr is se ælmihtiga god,
frēobearn godes
ǣr geþencað,
helpe gelēfað.
ah līf syleð
ēadigne drēam.
trumlicne hām,
Beorhte scīnað
sorgum bedǣlde,
wunian mōten
Uton cȳþan þæt!

---

262 **scacan**, with **e** above first **c** (C).
266 **gehrīnan**: MS has **gerinan**, with **h** above **er** (C).
267 **sceale**: MS reads **sceal**.
273 **nīðæs**: MS reads **in ðæs**.
274 **sīc**: MS reads **seoc**, with **o** superscript, **e** changed from **i** (C).
278 **ēðel**: MS reads **eðle**.
290 **gelēfað**: with **a** dotted and **e** above (C).

Dēman wē on eorðan,   ǣrror lifigend,
onlūcan mid listum   locen waldendes,
300   ongeotan gāstlice!   Ūs ongēan cumað
þūsend engla,   gif þider mōton,
and þæt on eorðan   ǣr gewyrcað.
Forþon sē bið ēadig   sē ðe ǣfre wile
mān oferhycgen,   meotode cweman,
305   synne ādwǣscan.   Swā hē sylfa cwæð:
"Sōðfæste men,   sunnan gelīce,
fǣgre gefrætewod   in heora fæder rīce
scīnað in sceldbyrig."   Þǣr sceppend seolf
hēo befæðmeð,   fæder mancynnes,
310   āhefeð holdlice   in heofones lēoht,
þǣr hēo mid wuldorcyninge   wunian mōton
āwa tō aldre
āgan drēama drēam   mid drihtne gode,
ā tō worulde   ā būton ende.

315   Ēalā hwæt! se āwyrgda   wrāðe gebōhte   [VII]
þæt hē heofencyninge   hēran ne wolde,
fæder frēfergendum.   Flōr āttre wēol,
hāt under hæftum;   hrēopan dēofla,
wīde geond wīnsele   wēa cwānedon,
320   mān and morður.   Wæs sēo menego þǣr
swylce onǣled;   wæs þæt eall full strong,
þonne wæs heora aldor,   þe ðǣr ǣrest cōm
forð on fēþan,   fæste gebunden
fȳre and līge.   Þæt wæs fæstlic þrēat.
325   Ēc sceoldon his þegnas   þǣr gewunian
atolan ēðles,   nalles ūp þanon
gehēran in heofonum   hāligne drēam,
þǣr hēo oft fægerne   folgað hæfdon
uppe mid englum.   Wǣron þā alles þæs
330   gōda lēase   nymþe gryndes ādes,
ah wunian mōton   þone wērigan sele

---

308   **seolf**, with two, possibly three, letters erased after **f**.
309   **hēo** in MS is before **sceppend**, l. 308b; **mancynnes**, with **nes** superscript.
310   **in heofenes lēoht**: the **es** of **heofones** is over an erasure, and there is an erasure between **s** and **l**.
315   **Ēalā**: MS reads **ala**, with space left for a capital, and **e** noted in the outer margin.
318   **hrēopan**: MS reads **hreowan**.
319   **wīnsele**, with **d** above, between **ns** (C).
320   **sēo menego**: MS reads **ðær menego ðær**.
330   **lēase** with the **e** added (C); MS reads **ah nymþe**, with the **ah** underlined for cancellation; **ādes** not in MS.
331   **ah**: transposed from 330b, where it is underlined for cancellation; the MS reads "**7 þone werigan sele**."

þǣr is wōm and wōp
and gristbitunge
"Nabbað wē tō hyhte
335 wēan and wītu
dracan and nǣddran
Forðon mihte gehēran,
twelf mīlum nēh,
hlūde and gēomre.
340 hweorfan geond helle
ufan and ūtan
wītum wērige,
drēamum bedǣlde.
þā hēo on heofonum
345 þæt hīe woldon benǣman
rodera rīces,
hīred heofona
Nis nǣnig swā snotor
nē þæs swā glēaw,
350 þæt āsecgan mǣge
hū scīr **sunu** þǣr
meotodes mihte
þǣr habbað englas
sanctas singað:
355 Þonne bēoð þā ēadigan
bringað tō bearme
wyrte wynsume
Þonne hīe befæðmeð
and hīe gesegnað
360 lǣdað tō līhte,
ā tō aldre,
byrhtne burhstyde.
þǣm ðe hǣlende
and wel is þām

365 Wæs þæt encgelcyn
Lūcifer hāten,
on gēardagum

wīde gehēred,
and gnornunge mecga:
nymþe cyle and fȳr,
and wyrma þrēat,
and þone dimman hām."
sē ðe æt hylle wæs
þæt ðǣr wæs tōða gehēaw,
Godes andsacan
hāte onǣled;
him wæs ǣghwǣr wā,
wuldres bescyrede,
Hēofon dēop gehygd,
hām staðelodon,
nergendne Crīst
ah hē on riht gehēold
and þæt hālige seld.
nē swā cræftig,
nymþe god seolfa,
swegles lēoman,
scīneð ymbūtan
geond þæt mǣre cynn,
ēadigne drēam,
þæt is se seolfa god.
þe of eorðan cumað,
blōstman stences,
þæt synd word godes.
fæder mancynnes,
mid his swīðran hond,
þǣr hī līf āgon
ūplicne hām,
Blǣd bið ǣghwǣm
hēran þenceð,
ðe þæt **wyrcan** mōt.

ǣr genemned, [VIII]
lēohtberende,
in godes rīce.

---

339 **hlūde**, with the **h** before and above **l** (C).
351 MS reads **sunnu**.
354 MS reads **þæt is seolfa for god**, with **þæt** an abbreviation modified from **wynn**, and **se** erased before **seolfa**.
357 **wyrte**, with **e** changed to **a** (C or S).
360 **lǣdað**, with **a** changed to **æ**.
362 **byrhtne**, with **eo** above **y**; **styde**, with **e** above **y** (C).
363 **hēran**, with **e** dotted for cancellation and **y** above **e** (C).
364 **wyrcan** not in MS.

Þā hē in wuldre
þæt hē oferhȳda

370 Se Sātānus
þæt hē wolde on heofonum
uppe mid þām ēcan:
yfles ordfruma.
þā hē tō helle

375 and his hīred mid hine,
nergendes nīð;
þæt hī mōsten in þone ēcan
būton ende.
dyne for dēman,

380 bræc and bēgde.
þā hī hælendes
Þonne wæs þām atolan

    *   *

Þā wǣron mid egsan
wīde geond wīnsele

385 "Þis is stronglic.
þegen mid þrēate,
Him beforan fēreð
þonne wē ǣfre ǣr
būton þā wē mid englum

390 Wile nū ūre wītu
eall tōweorpan.
dyne for drihtne;
ungēara nū
Hit is se seolfa

395 engla drihten.
sāwla lǣdan,
þæs yrreweorces
    Hwearf þā tō helle
meotod þurh mihte;

400 fela þūsenda,
ūp tō ēðle.
dyne on dægrēd;
fēond oferfohten.

wrōhte onstalde
āgan wolde.
swearte geþōhte
hēhseld wyrcan
þæt wæs ealdor heora,
Him þæt eft gehrēaw
hnīgan sceolde,
in hȳnðo geglīdan,
and nō seoððan
andwlitan sēon
Þā him egsa becōm,
þā hē duru in helle
Blis wearð monnum
hēafod gesāwon.
þe wē ǣr nemdon

    *   *   *

ealle āfyrhte
wordum mǣndon:
Nū þes storm becōm,
þēoden engla.
fǣgere lēoht
ēagum gesāwon,
uppe wǣron!
þurh his wuldres cræft
Nū ðes egsa cōm,
sceal þes drēorga hēap
atol þrōwian.
sunu waldendes,
Wile uppe heonan
and wē seoððan ā
hēnðo geþoliað."
hæleða bearnum
wolde manna rīm,
forð gelǣdan
Þā cōm engla swēg,
hæfde drihten seolf
Wæs sēo fǣhðe þā gȳt

---

368 **wrōhte**, with final e added; **onstalde**, with e above and between **ta** (C).
370 **Se** not in MS.
373 MS reads **ordfruman**.
375 MS reads **in to geglidan**.
377 **sēon** not in MS.
382-83 a gap in the text, probably one line.
384 **winsele**, with d above, between **ns** (C).
387 **fǣgere**, with final e added by C.
398 **tō helle**, with **tō** added above and before **h** (S).

open on ūhtan

405 Lēt þā ūp faran
Ādāmes cyn,
wlītan in wuldre
"Ic þē æne ābealh,
þā wit Ādām twā

410 þurh næddran nīð,
Gelærde unc se atola
beorneð on bendum,
hāligne hām,
Þā wit ðæs āwærgdan

415 nāmon mid handum
beorhte blæda.
þā wit in þis hāte scræf
and wintra rīm
þūsenda feolo

420 Nū ic þē hālsige,
for þān hīerde
engla þrēatas,
mæge and mōte
And ymb þrēo niht cōm

425 hām tō helle;
wītum wērig,
for onmædlan
Segdest ūs tō sōðe
wolde helwarum

430 Ārās þā ānra gehwylc
hleonade wið handa.
egeslic þūhte,
fægen in firnum
wolde him tō helpe

435 Ræhte þā mid handum
bæd meotod miltse
"Hwæt, þū fram minre dohtor,
in middangeard
Nū is gesēne

440 ēce ordfruma

þā se egsa becōm.
ēadige sāwle,
and ne mōste Ēfe þā gȳt
ær hēo wordum cwæð:
ēce drihten,
eaples þigdon
swā wit nā ne sceoldon.
sē ðe æfre nū
þæt wit blæd āhton,
heofon tō gewalde.
wordum gelȳfdon,
on þām hālgan trēo
Unc þæs bitere forgeald
hweorfan sceoldon,
wunian seoððan
þearle onæled.
heofenrīces weard,
þe ðū hider læddest,
þæt ic ūp heonon
mid mīnre mægðe.
þegen hælendes
is nū hæftum strong,
swylce him wuldorcyning
eorre geworden.
þætte seolfa god
hām gelīhtan.
and wið earm gesæt,
Þēah hylle gryre
wæron ealle þæs
þæt heora frēodrihten
helle gesēcan."
tō heofencyninge,
þurh Marian hād:
drihten, onwōce
mannum tō helpe.
þæt ðū eart sylfa god,
ealra gesceafta."

---

405 sāwle, with e changed to a in MS (C?).
406 Ēfe, with erasure before first e, and after second. It appears that æfre has been changed to Ēfe (S?).
407 hēo, with o added (S).
421 hider, with der over an erasure.
433 frēo not in MS.
435 Ræhte, with æ by Corrector, above i dotted as an error.
437 minre: MS reads mire.
439 god repeated in MS, the repeat dotted for cancellation.
440 7, the abbreviation for and, partly erased before ece.

Lēt þā ūp faran
wuldre hæfde
fēondum oðfæsted,
in þæt neowle genip,
445 þǣr nū Sātānus
earm āglǣca,
wītum wērige.
habban mōton
nē hī edcerres
450 wēnan seoððan.
wrāð geworden;
atole tō ǣhte,
dimne and deorcne
hātne helle grund,
455 Þæt, lā, wæs fǣger,
ūp tō earde
meotod mancynnes
Hōfon hine mid him
wītigan ūp tō ēðle,
460 Hæfde þā drihten seolf
fēond geflēmed,
wītegan sǣdon
Þis wæs on ūhtan
ǣr dægrēde,
465 hlūd of heofonum,
forbræc and forbēgde;
þā hīe swā lēohtne
   Gesæt þā mid þǣre fyrde
sǣde sōðcwidum:
470 ic ēow þurh mīne
Ādām ǣrest
Þā hīe begēton
fēowertig bearna,
middangearde
475 and wintra feola
eorlas on ēðle,
þæt hē **āfyrde** eft
fāh is ǣghwǣr.
   Ic on neorxnawonge

ēce drihten;   [IX]
wītes clomma
and hēo furðor scēaf
nearwe gebēged,
swearte þingað,
and þā atolan mid him,
Nalles wuldres lēoht
ah in helle grund;
ǣfre mōton
Him wæs drihten god
sealde him wītes clom,
and egsan gryre,
dēaðes scuwan,
hinsīðgryre.
þæt se fēða cōm
and se ēca mid him,
in þā mǣran burh.
handum hālige
Abrahames cynn.
dēað oferwunnen,
þæt in fyrndagum
þæt hē **sāwlum** wolde.
eall geworden,
þæt se dyne becōm,
þā hē helle duru
bān weornodon
lēoman gesāwon.
frumbearn godes,
"Snotre gāstas,
mihte geworhte,
and þæt æðele wīf.
on godes willan
þæt forð þonon
menio onwōcon;
wunian mōston,
oððæt eft gelamp
fēond in firenum;
nīwe āsette

---

453   **dimne:** MS reads **dimme.**
454   **hinsīðgryre:** MS reads **in sið gryre.**
461   **fēond,** followed by three or four letters erased; **geflēmed,** with **ge** in the margin (S).
462   **sāwlum:** MS reads **sawla.**
474   **middangearde,** with **e** added (C); **onwōcon:** MS reads **on weocon,** with the **e** dotted for
     cancellation (?C).
477   **āfyrde:** MS reads **afyrhte.**

480   trēow mid telgum,
        æpla bǣron,
        beorhtan blǣda,
        handþegen helle.
        þæs git ofergȳmdon
485   ǣten þā egsan.
        sē inc bām forgeaf
        Þā mē **gehrēaw**
        þæs carcernes
        Næs ðā monna gemet,
490   nē wītegena weorc,
        þæt ēow mihte helpan,
        sē þæt wīte ǣr
        Fērde tō foldan
        ufan from ēðle,
495   **tintregan fela**
        Mē seredon ymb
        dæges and nihtes,
        rīces **rǣd**boran,
        Þā wæs þæs mǣles
500   þæt on worulde wæs
        þrēo and þrītig gēara
        Gemunde ic ðæs mænego
        lange þæs ðe ic of hæftum
        ūp tō earde,
505   drihtnes dōmas
        wuniað in wynnum,
        þūsendmǣlum.
        þā mē on bēame
        gārum on **galgan**.
510   and ic eft up becōm
        tō hāligum drihtne.''

    Swā wuldres weard
    meotod moncynnes
    þæs þe drihten god

þæt ðā tānas ūp
and git ǣton þā
swā inc se balewa hēt,
Hæfdon forþon hātne grund,
hǣlendes word,
Wæs se atola beforan,
balewe geþōhtas.
þæt mīn handgeweorc,
clom ðrōwade!
nē mægen engla,
nē wera snytero,
nimðe hǣlend god,
tō wrece gesette!
þurh fǣmnan hād
and on eorþan gebād
and tēonan micelne.
secgas monige
hū hēo mē dēaðes cwealm,
hrefnan mihten!
mearc āgangen
wintra gerīmes
ǣr ic þrōwode.
on þām minnan hām
hām gelǣdde
þæt hēo āgan **sceolon**
and duguðe þrym;
habbað wuldres blǣd
Ic ēow þingade
beornas sticedon,
Hēow se giunga þǣr,
ēce drēamas

wordum sǣde,   [X]
ǣr on morgen
of dēaðe ārās.

---

487   **gehrēaw**: MS reads **gereaw**; **handgeweorc**, with g partially erased.
488   **þæs** not in MS.
495   **tintregan fela and**: MS reads **and fela**.
498   **rīces rǣdboran**: MS reads **rices boran**.
502   **on**: MS reads **7**; **þām**: MS reads **þa**; **minnan**, with first n above i (C?).
504   **sceolon** not in MS.
509   **galgan**: MS reads **galgum**, with e above first a (C).
512   **Swā**, with **wa** in the MS, a space left for s.
514   **þe** above and before **drihten** (S).

515   Næs nān þæs stronglic   stān gefæstnod
      þēah hē wære mid īrne   eall ymbfangen,
      þæt mihte þām miclan   mægne wiðhabban,
      ah hē ūt ēode,   engla drihten,
      on þæm fæstenne.   And gefatian hēt
520   englas eallbeorhte   **andleofan gingran**;
      and hūru secgan hēt   Sīmon Pētre
      þæt hē mōste in Galilēam   god scēawian,
      ēcne and trumne,   swā hē ær dyde.
      Þā ic gongan gefregn   gingran ætsomne
525   ealle tō Galilēam;   hæfdon gāstes blēd,
      ongeton hāligne   godes sunu.
      Swā hēo gesēgon   hwær sunu meotodes
      þā on upp gestōd,   ēce drihten,
      god in Galilēam.   Tō ðæs gingran þider
530   ealle urnon,   þær se ēca wæs.
      Fēollon on foldan,   and tō fōtum hnigon;
      þanceden þēodne   þæt hit þus gelomp
      þæt hī scēawodon   scyppend engla.
      Þā sōna spræc   Sīmon Pētrus:
535   "Eart þū þis, drihten,   dōme gewurðad?
      Wē ðē gesāwon   æt sumum cyrre;
      þec gelegdon   on lāðne bend
      hæþene mid hondum.   Him þæt gehrēowan mæg
      þonne hēo endestæf   eft gescēawiað."
540   Sume **hit** ne mihton   **mōde** oncnāwan:
      þæt wæs se dēora,   Didimus wæs hāten,
      ær hē mid hondum   hælend genōm
      sylfne be sīdan   þær hē his swāt forlēt;
      fēollon tō foldan   fulwihtes bæðe.
545   Fæger wæs þæt ongin   þæt frēodrihten
      geþrōwode,   þēoden ūre.
      Hē on bēame āstāh   and his blōd āgēat,
      god on galgan,   þurh his gāstes mægen.
      Forþon men sceolon   mæla gehwylce

---

515   stān: MS reads **satan**.
518   ah, with h dotted for cancellation, c above h (C).
519   gefatian: MS reads **gefætian**, with the **æ** from a (C).
520b   The MS reads 7 **leofan gingran winum** (or **sinum?**).
526   ongeton not in MS.
528   þā on: MS reads **þa gingran on**; gestod: ge not in MS.
532   þæt hit written twice, the second time underlined for cancellation.
537   þec, with the c dotted for cancellation.
538   hæþene: MS reads **hæþenne**.
540   hit: MS reads **hie**; mōde: MS reads **mod**.
548   galgan, with e above and before first a (C).

550 secgan drihtne þanc   dǣdum and weorcum,
    þæs ðe hē ūs of hæftum   hām gelǣdde
    ūp tō ēðle,   þǣr wē āgan **sceolon**
    drihtnes dōmas,
    and wē in wynnum   wunian mōton.
555 Ūs is wuldres lēoht
    torht ontȳned,   þām ðe teala þenceð.

    Þā wæs on eorðan   ēce drihten   [XI]
    fēowertig daga   folgad folcum,
    gecȳðed **mancynne**,   ǣr hē in þā mǣran gesceaft,
560 burhlēoda fruma,   bringan wolde
    hāligne gāst   tō heofonrīce.
    Āstāh ūp on heofonum   engla scyppend,
    weoroda waldend.   Þā cōm wolcna swēg,
    hālig of heofonum,   mid wæs hond godes.
565 Onfēng frēodrihten,   and hine forð lǣdde
    tō þām hālgan hām   heofna ealdor.
    Him ymbflugon   engla þrēatas
    þūsendmǣlum.   Þā hit þus gelomp,
    þā gȳt nergende Crīst   **gecwæð** þæt hē þæs
570 ymb **tēne** niht   twelf apostolas
    mid his gāstes gife,   gingran geswīðde.
    Hæfde þā gesette   sāwla unrīm
    god lifigende.   Þā wæs Iūdas of,
    sē ðe ǣr on tīfre   torhtne gesalde,
575 drihten hǣlend;   him sēo dǣd ne geþēah,
    þæs hē bebohte   bearn wealdendes
    on seolfres sinc;   him þæt swearte forgeald
    earm ǣglǣca   innon helle.
            Siteð nū on þā swīðran hond sunu his fæderes;
580 dǣleð dōgra gehwǣm   drihten weoroda
    help and hǣlo   hæleþa bearnum
    geond middangeard.   Þæt is monegum cūð
    þæt hē āna is   ealra gescefta
    wyrhta and waldend   þurh his wuldres cræft.
585 Siteð him on heofnum   hālig encgel
    waldend mid wītegum.   Hafað wuldres bearn
    his seolfes seld   swegl **betolden**.

552 **sceolon** not in MS.
557 **þā**: MS reads **a** with a space left for **þ**.
559 **mancynne**: MS reads **man cynnes**.
569 **gecwæð** not in MS.
570 **tēne**: MS reads **ane**.
572 **gesette**, with a letter erased between **e** and **s**.
587 **betolden**: MS reads **betalden**, with **t** partially erased, **he** above, thus **behealden** (C?).

Leaðað ūs þider tō lēohte   þurh his lǣcedom,
þǣr wē mōton seolfe   sittan mid drihtne
590 uppe mid englum,   habban þæt ilce lēoht,
þǣr his hīred nū   hālig eardað,
wunað in wynnum,   þǣr is wuldres blēd
torht ontȳned.   Uton **teala** hycgan
þæt wē hǣlende   hēran georne,
595 Crīste cwēman.   Þǣr is cūðre līf
þonne wē on eorðan mǣgen   ǣfre gestrēonan.

Hafað nū geþingod tō ūs   bēoden mǣra,   [XII]
ælmihtig god,
on dōmdæge   drihten seolfa.
600 Hāteð hēhenglas   hlūddre stefne
bēman blāwan   ofer burga geseotu
geond foldan scēatas.
Þonne of þisse moldan   men onwecnað:
dēade of dūste ārīsað   þurh drihtnes miht.
605 Þæt bið daga lengust   and **dinna** mǣst
hlūd gehēred,   þonne· hǣlend cymeð,
waldend mid wolcnum   in þās woruld færeð.
Wile þonne gescēawian   wlitige and unclǣne
on twā healfe,   tile and yfle.
610 Him þā sōðfæstan   on þā swīðran hond
mid rodera weard   reste gestīgað.
Þonne bēoð blīðe   þā in burh mōton
gongan in godes rīce,
and hēo gesēnað   mid his swīðran hond,
615 cynincg alwihta   cleopað ofer ealle:
"Gē sind wilcuman!   Gāð in wuldres lēoht
tō heofona rīce,   þǣr gē habbað
ā tō aldre   ēce reste."

---

588   Leaðað, with a dotted e erased before first a (S or C).
591   his, with h added above (S).
593   teala not in MS.
595   cwēman, with an æ changed to a.
599   on written twice.
600   hēhenglas, with an erasure before first h, an a added above between e and h (C), the words separated, thus heah englas.
601   bēman, with y above e (C).
603   onwecnað, with superscript i between n and a (C).
605   dinna: MS reads dimma.
606   gehēred, with y over second e (C).
612   þā in: Corrector adds þe above and between words.
613   gongan: MS reads gangan, with first a from o (C).
618   reste, the first e altered to æ by a cedilla (C).

Þonne stondað þā forworhtan, þā ðe firnedon;

620 bēoð beofigende   hwonne him bearn godes
      dēman wille   þurh his dǣda spēd.
      Wēnað þæt hēo mōten   tō þǣre mǣran byrig
      ūp tō englum   swā ōðre dydon,
      ac him bið **reordende**
625 ēce drihten,   ofer ealle gecwæð:
      "Āstīgað nū, āwyrgde,   in þæt wītehūs
      ofostum miclum.   Nū ic ēow ne con."
      Sōna æfter þǣm wordum   wērige gāstas,
      helle hæftas,   hwyrftum scrīþað
630 þūsendmǣlum,   and þider **leaðað**
      in þæt sceaðena scræf,   scūfað tō grunde
      in þæt nearwe nīð.   And nō seoððan
      þæt hīe ūp þonan   ǣfre mōton,
      ah þǣr geþolian sceolon   **þearlic** wīte,
635 clom and carcern,   and þone caldan grund
      dēopne ādrēogan   and dēofles spellunge:
      hū hīe him on edwīt   oft āsettað
      swarte sūslbonan,   stǣleð **fēondas**
      fǣhðe and **firne**,   þǣr ðe hīe **frēo**drihten
640 ēcne anwaldan,   oft forgēaton,
      þone þe hīe him tō hihte   habban sceoldon.
        Uton, lā, geþencan   geond þās worulde,
      þæt wē hǣlende   hēran onginnen!
      Georne þurh godes gife   gemunan gāstes blēd,
645 hū ēadige þǣr   uppe sittað
      selfe mid **swegletorhtne**   sunu hǣlendes,
      þǣr is geat gylden   gimmum gefrætewod,
      wynnum bewunden,   þǣm þe in wuldres lēoht
      gongan mōten   tō godes rīce,
650 and ymb þā weallas   wlitige scīnað
      engla gāstas   and ēadige sāwla,

---

620   hwonne: MS reads þonne, with þ altered to w and h prefixed above (S).
624   ac, with c from altered h; reordende: MS reads reordiende, with superscript en above an erasure, second r above o and d, two letters erased after the word (C).
625   gecwæð, with æ dotted for cancellation, y above (C).
630   a word, probably he, erased before þider; leaðað: MS reads lædað, with æ from e with a cedilla, an erasure between æ and d, d from altered ð (C).
634   þearlic: MS reads earmlic.
638   fēondas not in MS.
639   firne: MS reads in firne; frēo not in MS.
641   þone: MS reads þonne with first n erased, þe superscript after e (S).
643   hēran, with y above e (C).
646   MS reads selfe mid swegle torht sunu ... ; selfe, with y over first e (C).
647   gylden, with ne erased after.

þā ðe heonon fērað.
Þǣr martiras
and herigað hēhfæder
655   cyning in cestre.
"Þū eart hæleða helm
engla ordfruma,
ūp gelǣddest
Swā wuldres weard
660   þegnas ymb þēoden,
sang æt selde,
ealra aldor,
     Þæt is se drihten
gebrōwode,
665   Swylce hē fæste
metod mancynnes,
Þā gewearð þone wēregan,
of heofonum
þā costode
670   Brōhte him tō bearme
bæd him for hungre
"gif þū swā micle
Þā him andswarode
"Wēndest þū, āwyrgda,
675   nymþe mē ænne..."

    *   *   *   *   *

ac geseted hafast,
lifigendum līht,
on heofenrīce,

    *   *   *   *   *

680   atol þurh edwīt,
herm bealowes gāst,
āsette on dūne
"Lōca nū ful wīde
Ic þē geselle

meotode cwēmað,
hālgum stefnum,
Cweþað ealle þus:
and **heofendēma**,
and eorðan tūdor
tō þissum ēadigan hām."
wordum herigað
þǣr is þrym micel,
is sylf cyning,
in ðǣre ēcan gesceft.
sē ðe dēað for ūs
þēoden engla.
fēowertig daga,
þurh his mildsa spēd.
þe ǣr āworpen wæs
þæt hē in helle gedēaf,
cyning alwihta.
brāde stānas,
hlāfas wyrcan—
mihte hæbbe."
ēce drihten:
þæt āwriten nǣre,

sigores āgend,
lēan būtan ende,
hālige drēamas.

Þā hē mid hondum genōm
and on esle āhōf,
and on beorh āstāh,
drihten hǣlend:
ofer londbēwende.
on þīnes seolfes dōm

---

656   **heofendēma**: MS reads **heofen deman.**
657   **ordfruma**, with **n** erased after **a.**
658   **ūp gelǣddest** not in MS.
662   **aldor**: MS reads **ador**, with **d** from altered ð, **e** superscript before **a**, **l** above **a** (C).
668   **hē** superscript before **in** (S).
675-78   A break in the text. See explanatory notes.
680   **esle**, with **h** above and between **e** and **s** (C).
681   **herm**, with the **m** above **r** (C).
683   **londbēwende**: MS has **w** underlined for cancellation, first **e** erased, and **u** above erasure (C).
684   **on** not in MS; **seolfes dōm**: MS reads **seoferdum.**

685 folc and foldan.
burh and breotone
rodora rīces,
engla and monna,
Þā him andswarode
690 "Gewīt þū, āwyrgda,
Sātānus seolf;
geara tōgegnes,
Ah ic þē hāte
þæt ðū hellwarum
695 ah þū him secgan miht
þæt ðū gemēttes
cyning moncynnes.
Wite þū ēac, āwyrgda,
helheoðo drēorig,
700 Grīp wið þæs grundes;
oððæt þū þone ymbhwyrft
and ǣrest āmet
and hū sīd sēo
Wāst þū þonne þē geornor
705 seoððan þū þonne hafast
hū hēh and dēop
grim græfhūs.
ǣr twā seondon
þæt ðū merced hūs
710 Þā bām wērigan wearð
Sātān seolua ran
earm ægdēce.
wēan and wītu;
lǣhte wið þes lāþan;
715 hæftas in hylle;
ðonne hē on þone atolan
Hæfdon gewunnon

Fōh hider tō mē
bold tō gewealde,
gif þū sēo riht cyning
swā ðū ǣr myntest."
ēce drihten:
in þæt wītescræf,
þē is sūsl weotod
nalles godes rīce.
þurh þā hēhstan miht
hyht ne ābēode,
sorga mǣste,
meotod alwihta,
Cer ðē on bæcling!
hū wīd and sīd
and mid hondum āmet.
gang þonne swā
alne cunne,
ufan tō grunde,
se swarta ēōm.
þæt þū wið god wunne,
handum āmetene
hell inneweard sēo,
Gong ricene tō,
tīda āgongene,
āmeten hæbbe."
wracu getenge.
and on sūsle gefēol,
Hwīlum mid folmum mæt
hwīlum se wonna lǣg
hwīlum hē licgan geseah
hwīlum hrēam āstāg,
ēagum gesāwun.
godes andsacan

* * * * *

686 tō superscript before **gewealde** (C).
692 **geara**: with **o** above second **a** (C).
697 **cer**, with **y** above **e** (C).
703 **sēo** follows **ēðm** in the MS.
708 **seondon**, with **on** superscript after **d** (C).
710 **þā**, with **a** over an erasure; **bām** (MS reads **þa**) with **a** from **e**, **þ** probably from **s**; **wērigan**: MS reads **werga**, with **i** above and between **r** and **g**, **n** above and after **a** (C); **wracu**: MS reads **wrece**, with first **e** altered to **a** , final **e** dotted for cancellation with **u** superscript (C?).
711 **ran**, with **n** above and after **a** (C).
712 **ægdēce**, first **e** with a cedilla, thus **æ** (C).
713 **lǣg**, with **æ** to **e** by erasure (C).
715 **hrēam**, with **h** superscript before **r**; **āstāg**, with **h** above **g**. (Gollancz offers C or ?S.)
717 A break in the text, probably not more than a line or two.

blāc bealowes gāst,
Þā him þūhte
720 tō helleduru
mīla gemearcodes,
þæt þurh synne cræft
Ðā hē gemunde
Lōcade lēas wiht
725 atol mid ēgum,
dēofla mænego
Wordum in wītum
reordian and cweðan:
"Lā, þus bēo nū on yfele!

þæt hē on botme stōd.
þæt þanon wǣre
hund þūsenda
swā hine se mihtiga hēt
sūsle āmǣte.
þæt hē on grunde stōd.
geond þæt lāðe scræf,
oððæt egsan gryre
þonne ūp āstāg.
ongunnon þā wērigan gāstas

Noldæs ǣr teala!"

Finit Liber II.   Amen

---

718 **bealowes,** with **s** superscript (C?).
723 **þæt:** MS reads **þa**.
727 **ongunnon þā:** MS reads **þa on þa**.

EXPLANATORY NOTES

4-6   We might see the ordering of creation suggested in ll. 4-6, particularly ll. 5b and 6a, as influenced by the tradition stemming from *Genesis* 1:6-7, that there were waters above the earth beyond the firmament. The sphericity of the earth, and the universe as a whole, was hypothesized by Aristotle long before the time of Claudius Ptolemy, the popularity of whose writings rendered the hypothesis the common property of educated men through the time of Copernicus. It is accepted by Ambrose, Augustine, Jerome, Isidore and Bede. For the waters above a spherical earth, see Isidore of Seville's *De Natura Rerum*, *PL* 83, cols. 963-1018, particularly chs. 9, 12, 14, and *Etymologiarum*, Liber XIV, caput 1-2, *PL* 82, cols. 495-96; Bede's *De Natura Rerum*, *PL* 90, cols. 187-274, particularly chs. 3, 5-7, and *De Temporum Ratione*, *PL* 90, caput 32, cols. 437-38. On the question of mediaeval beliefs in the earth's shape, see C. W. Jones, "The Flat Earth," *Thought*, 9 (1934), 296-307.

5b   Thomas D. Hill, *PQ*, 48 (1969), understands **sæ** as a reference to the Oceanus of classical mythology which was often identified with the cosmic Jordan of apocryphal cosmography. He suggests that **stream** be construed as a current within the sea "much like the Gulf stream."

6a   **wolcn**: the **n** is syllabic.

7a   **ymblyt**: I assume the MS reading **ybmlyt** is the result of the transposition of **bm** for **mb** and emend accordingly. The emended form **ymblyt** is probably to be derived from the verb **ymbliðan**, "to surround, to circumnavigate," and is analogous in meaning to **ymbhwyrft**. For an exhaustive discussion of the proposed variants see Clubb (*Notes*, pp. 45-47) and Krapp (*Notes*, p. 231). The alliterative pattern of the line is unusual.

10a   **grundas in heofene**: There is no reason to emend **heofene** to **geofene** with Grein, Graz, Cosijn, Clubb and Krapp. The emendation supposes that l. 10a is exactly co-ordinate with, and a substantial restatement of, l. 9b. This is possible, but what I think the poet wanted to describe here is the ability of **godes agen bearn** to look **through** the sea to the foundations of creation, which foundations are set in heaven. Given the cosmography of Isidore and Bede (see note, l. 5 above), such an interpretation is as likely as any proposed in defense of the emendation. Moreover, it accepts the MS reading which is clear at this point, and harmonizes with the closing lines of this introductory section where the poet states that the creator set the regions of the earth up in the heavens (16b).

10b   **godes ägen bearn**: Rather than constituting an artistic blemish, the withholding of the subject of all the transitive verbs in the first ten lines until l. 10b is a successful way of introducing emphatically the poem's main figure, Christ: the audience or reader sees first the basic creation—i.e., earth, water, heaven and heavenly bodies—and only then is the Creator recognized. What follows, through l. 17a, is a statement of this Son's ability to know in intimate detail his creation and, therefore, metaphorically, to control it.

11b   **rægnas:** an as ending for the genitive singular is relatively rare, though possible, in Late West Saxon. See Sievers-Cook, p. 170, 237, n. 1; Grein-Köhler, p. 549.

16a   **dæles:** A form of the nom.-acc. plural in **es** is possible in Late West Saxon. See Sievers-Cook, p. 170, 237, n. 3.

16-17a   Though Clubb's assertion (*Notes,* p. 49) that in these lines "There is little doubt that the poet is referring to the triple creation of earth, heaven, and sea" is appealing, I am not convinced that this is what the poem says. The **eorðan dæles** are emphatically placed **ūp on heofonum:** l. 16b has a specific locative function that calls for careful handling. Further, the only way to have these lines offer a picture of the tripartite creation is to emend not once (Clubb, following Thorpe [note], Ettmüller, Cosijn, and Bright, reads **and ūpheofon** for l. 16b), but twice: Clubb offers **and hēanne holm** for MS **hēanne holme,** 17a. There is a confusion in 17a, since the adjective is not in concord with the noun it modifies, the former accusative, the latter dative, probably with a locative function. But to emend the noun to agree with the adjective supposes a preconception which has already caused the emendation of 16b, and requires for sense the addition to the MS of **and** in l. 17a. If **hēanne** is understood as a mistake for the analogically formed **hēaum** (see *Rdl* #22, l. 19), caused by the similarity of scribal **um** to **nn,** or even the scribe's misreading and picking up the ending of **holme,** an emendation restores matters. The meter requires that **hēaum** be accepted as a disyllable. We should translate ll. 15-17a: "(the creator) planned and set in six days the regions of earth up in the heavens in the high sea." If we assume the **heofonum** to refer here to the elemental sphere beyond that of the earth and its surrounding sphere of water, the lines as they stand make good sense. See note to l. 5b, and, particularly, Bede's *DNR*, ch. 3, *PL* 90, cols. 192-94.

19-20   There are two problems in these lines: **geþeode** in 19b, and the syntax of l. 20 which suggests that Adam was created before the angels. To have any sense from 19b as it stands in the MS, both **duguðe** and **geþeode** must be handled figuratively: Clubb, for example, offers "prosperity," and "tongues" or "peoples" respectively (*Notes,* p. 50). While "prosperity" is a possible, though somewhat remote, reading of **duguðe,** the suggested translation of **geþeode** is as unique as is its collocation with **duguðe** in the surviving poetic corpus. It seems wiser to admit the necessity of an emendation, and accept Bright's suggestion, following Ettmüller, that **geþeode** be replaced by **geoguðe.** Support for this half-line may be found in **Bwf** 160b, 621a, 1674a; **And** 152b, 1122a. I have further accepted Bright's punctuation of the lines, placing a colon after 19b, a comma after 20a. Such punctuation "is intended to suggest the omission of the copula **wæs,** the sense being **Adam wæs ærest,** etc.... This predication **wæs ærest** is made of both subjects, **Adam** and **cyn**" (Bright, 129). The emended lines thus read: "Joys he distributed to old and young: / Adam first, and that noble race...." Joys of any sort could not be distributed to any category of being, human or angelic, until that category was created. Since l. 19 supposes the creation, an event alluded to only in l. 20, the lines form a classic example of hysteron-proteron (see Appendix, pp. 152-53); l. 20 is an inversion, a successful attempt to connect ll. 19 and 20 chiastically. Duguð, particularly when juxtaposed with geoguð, connotes a tried and experienced band of retainers, and is used occasionally to describe the heavenly host. Geoguð connotes that which is young and untried. In context, duguð could refer only to the angels, the æðele cyn of 20b, who, it was generally believed, were created before man; geoguðe, then, would refer to man, whose creation is symbolized in that of Adam. See my note in *PQ*, 49 (1970), 558-59.

22a **þūhte him on mōde**: for similar expressions of Satan's, or the devils', incapacity to judge correctly, see ll. 55a, 59a, 674a. In 622a, a like expression with **wēnan** links the damned souls who, at the judgment, think to follow the blessed to paradise, with the devils: both possess the same type of spiritual myopeia.

29b Kock's interpretation of **hēahgetimbrad** (*Anglia,* 43 [1919], 311-12), as qualifying **heofnum** in contrast to **wælm** and **grund**, 30b and 31b, is correct. Clubb's citation of *Guthlac* ll. 582-85 to establish a reading for this line supposes too close a connection between the poems, and requires an emendation to **hēahgetimbra** as well (*Notes,* p. 53).

30-31 For a discussion of the traditions surrounding the location and description of hell, see above, section III, pp. 42-47.

34a All editors emend MS **cleopad** to **cleopað**, though **cleopade** might be an alternative. The **Cleopað ðonne** establishes a temporal connection between the lament of Satan and the expostulation of the devils, ll. 36b-64, and the expulsion from heaven, ll. 24b-33. These are the first words of Satan and the devils upon finding themselves in hell. **Cleopað** appears to be an example of an historical present whereby the poet brings his audience into the very moment of Satan's first speech, a happy dramatic touch.

Clubb misses this point, arguing that **Cleopað ðonne** introduces in the laments "an action of indefinite date (or possibly even an action many times repeated) at any time between the fall and the New Testament period" (*Notes,* p. 55). Since there is no temporal progression to the laments, Clubb is able to gloss the situation in one in terms of many, or all, of the others: e.g., he construes **heleð** l. 47a to include men as well as angels, citing as evidence ll. 134b-35a, 144b-46, 265-68, 333, all of which presume the fall of man. But we can accept the proposition that the laments take place in eternity without violating the self-contained, essentially autonomous character of each, and without overlooking the dramatic temporal specificity of the first. For the creature, as opposed to the Creator, events, even in eternity, must be described linearly according to a finite perspective.

36a **eisegan**, from **egsa**.

37a MS **ða þe** seems impossible, since **ða** is not in concord with its apparent antecedent **ðrym**. One might emend to **ðone þe**, but a simple omission of the **ða** is preferable, since the relative **þe** carries the sense very well.

38-39a For the fire which gives forth no light as a punishment of hell, see, e.g., Gregory the Great, *Moralium,* Liber IX, caput 66, *PL* 75, cols. 914-15.

40b-43 We may have a reference here to the increased suffering of the devils at the harrowing of hell, or at the final judgment. But I think that the poet is indulging a bit of grim irony by having Satan affirm as "not far off" what in fact is now upon them.

42a wērgu: MS wergum has occasioned much discussion. The most intelligent attitude is that of Sievers (followed by Grein-Köhler and Clubb) who emends to wērgu (*BGDSL,* 37 [1912], 339). Kock (p. 71) offers wēan on wērgum as a possible alternative.

42b wuldres: MS wulres here and in 85b is a scribal oversight, since the poem contains some twenty-eight forms with d.

46-47 Clubb (*Notes,* p. 58) reads æðele and heleð to include both angels and men, thus doing violence to the admittedly tenuous time scheme the poet offers in Part I (see l. 34a and note). To have the souls of men in heaven at this point in the poem is to place Satan's first speech after the ascension of Christ, at which time heaven was thought to be opened to men. Surely this is to put an impossible burden on the lines.

50a For a discussion of the various explanations traditionally associated with the angelic fall, see above, section III, pp. 37-42.

50b The capacity of the eternally damned Satan to hope now and again for an amelioration of suffering seems to be one of the psychological torments of hell. See ll. 272-78.

52b sūsle begrorenne: begrorenne is a word unique in Old English, derived, apparently, from an unrecorded Old English verb begrēosan, "to be terrified" (Grein-Köhler, p. 275).

57b Clubb's reconstruction of this half-line is surely correct (*Notes,* p. 61). MS earm is the result of dittography, where the scribe incorrectly repeated a form of earttu. With the restoration of the erased letters na sum, we have what is probably the original reading.

64 Abbetmeyer (p. 14) was right in suggesting that ll. 63b-64a present a simple inversion, with meotod as subject of wære. Ll. 53-64 detail the progressively more serious and outlandish lies by which Satan suborned the angelic host which followed him to hell. Initially he contended that they should no longer obey "helende," ll. 53-54. Going a step further, ll. 55-60, he maintained that he himself was the creator and promised the angels a part in the control of the kingdom. The final and logical progression of the blasphemous lies is taken in ll. 63-64, where, not content to be deemed creator, Satan asserts that he is the Father of meotod mancynnes, who, in this poem, is identical with scypend, Christ. That the poet considered this to be the final enormity is suggested by the fact that these lines conclude this particular dramatic section. See my note in *The Explicator,* 31 (1972), #10, and above, section II, p. 27.

66b The text is clear here, and MS unreordadon makes good sense. Since, however, such a reading would require the inseparable prefix to carry alliteration and major stress, it seems best to emend slightly, considering on from MS un to be an adverb having the same connotation as un, "against."

67a   The MS reading gives a metrically deficient verse. Clubb's slight emendation to **cearium** (*Notes*, p. 63) improves the metrics and the sense.

67b   For Christ's role in the heavenly rebellion, see above, section III, pp. 38-42.

70a   An example of the poet's irony: there is nothing of the "joyful expectation" connotated by **to hyhte** in **helle floras**.

72b   Sievers' emendation (*BGDSL*, 10 [1885], 453), accepted by Clubb and by Krapp, restores a normal D verse.

76b   As it stands in the MS, this half-line is deficient in alliteration and metrics. Clubb and Krapp, following an emendation in Grein's *Bibliothek*, alter **for worht** to **forht**.

78a   Ettmüller, note, first suggested that MS **sweartade** was a scribal error for **spearcade**. The MS bears out Clubb's (*Notes*, p. 65) assertion that the scribe first wrote **swearcade** and then changed the nonsense word to **sweartade** by altering the **c**. For a discussion of the possible influence of *The Visio Pauli* on *Christ and Satan* in general, on this part of the poem in particular, see above, section III, pp. 45-47. See also T. D. Hill, "Satan's Fiery Speech: 'Christ and Satan' 78-79," *N&Q*, 217 (1972), 2-4, and H. T. Keenan, "Satan Speaks in Sparks... ," *N&Q*, 219 (1974), 283-84.

80b   An emendation of some sort is necessary to restore the metrics. Clubb, following Kock (p. 17), emends to **worde**, while Krapp supplies **wordum**. Both emendations seem exceptional, though type E might be expanded to include them. Bright's suggestion (129) **þa word** provides a normal B verse.

85b   **wuldres**: See note to l. 42b.

89   The line in the MS is hopelessly muddled, and suggestions to restore the reading are as varied as they are ineffective. The reading in the text is Clubb's, accepted by Krapp as "the simplest way of disposing of the confusion in the MS" (Krapp, *Notes*, p. 233).

94b   This is one of the few occasions where the Corrector's addition seems necessary. The **ne** with which he supplies 95a is superfluous.

97b   For the dragons which guard hell, Clubb (*Notes*, p. 67) cites the Jewish Apocrypha, particularly *2 Enoch* 42:1.

98a   **reðre**: the loss of initial **h**, perhaps a diacritic, is not uncommon in the poem: see ll. 206b, 454b, 487a, 715b, and the notes. For a discussion of the phenomenon, see Campbell, pp. 186-88.

100-101a   The inability of Satan and the devils to hide themselves, here obviously from the sight of God, may be another psychological pain of hell. The source is probably Gregory the Great, *Moralium*, Liber II, caput 4, *PL* 75, col. 557. See also l. 169.

102b   **ðis**: most earlier editors emend to **ðes** for concord, but **ðis** is possibly a masculine form. Clubb (*Notes*, p. 68) cites Sievers-Cook, p. 247, 338, n. 4.

105a   **sciman**: an appropriate word for the shadowy character of hell, since, in context, it can connote either "light" or "dark."

106a   All editors but Clubb accept the Corrector's **ic** and emend MS **nu** to **iu**. But surely Satan as a speaker in preceding lines would supply an adequately specific subject for **āhte**, and the burning recollection of past happiness and glories would allow him to express their loss as **nu**. Furthermore, though the temporal frame of Part I is tenuous, this is the second of five laments, but one removed from what I understand to be the first words of Satan and his angels upon finding themselves in hell. The **nu**, therefore, may bear some temporal weight.

109a   **fagum** modifies **me**, l. 108a; **flora** appears to be a variant of the more usual dative form **flore**. See Thorpe's edition of *Aelfric's Catholic Homilies*, vol. 2, p. 56, l. 33; p. 334, l. 35.

111   These half-lines are neither redundant, nor do they require transposition of **flyge** and **flyhte**. Translate: "But I shall to flight and in flying at times / visit the earth."

115-116   The **eard** is qualified here as an **æðel**, a native dwelling place, something uniquely and particularly one's own. It is ironic that Satan should seek an **æðel** such as he possessed in heaven when he is already in possession of hell, the native dwelling place of sinners.

117a   All editors accept the Corrector's **ecne**. But such a reading makes **ecne onwald** co-ordinate with **eard** and **æðel** as things which the devils, particularly Satan, once possessed in heaven. That they never had **ecne onwald** is indicated by their present condition. If a period is placed after 116b, and the Corrector's **ecne** is dispensed with, then **ēce onwald** is seen to be co-ordinate with 118b **waldendes sunu** as subject of **āh**, 117b, and with **wuldorcyning** l. 114b. The punctuation of the MS, with a *punctus versus* or semicolon (;) after **dyde**, l. 116b, and after **sunu** l. 118b, seems to support this reading. Whoever was responsible for the punctuation apparently wished to set these lines off, and has used the semicolon to do it. Although "power" is more often an attribute of the Father or the undifferentiated divinity—God—in Patristic commentaries and the liturgy, it is not unknown as a denomination of Christ: see, e.g., M. A. Cassiodorus, *Expositio in Psalmum xciv, PL* 70, col. 672, where we find: "Rex est magnus omnipotens Christus."

119a   The Corrector's **sceal** improves the sense.

127b   Clubb (*Notes*, p. 70) believes that this line refers to Satan sparking when speaking, and so makes it parallel to ll. 78 and 161. But in such lines the poet is quite specific about the matter, and the lack of such specificity here ought give pause. It may be that the **fyrleoma** is the general miasmic atmosphere of hell which provides the background for Satan's speech.

131a   For the extremes of temperature as a punishment of hell, see above, section III, pp. 44-45. See also the *Book of the Secrets of Enoch A*, 10:2. There is no reason to follow early critics and find here a pagan Teutonic influence.

132b   **hellescealcas**: This unique word probably refers to the devils and to men who are inhabitants of hell. It seems fair to assume that men were in hell by the time of this lament. See ll. 134b-135a and 144b-148.

134b-135a   These lines may require an emendation. As Clubb (*Notes*, p. 71) remarks, the grammatical arrangement forces either of the following translations: "naked men fight around (or 'over') serpents"; "serpents fight around (or 'over') naked men." Of the two, I lean towards the former, since the poet might have been attempting to depict an eternally internacine conflict in hell where, even in the midst of torment, here symbolized by the serpents, the damned battle each other. Clubb resolves the problem by emending **winnaδ** to **windaδ**. One might also change **ymb** to **wiδ**.

140-142a   The memory of heaven is a psychological torment that contributes to the pains of hell. See above, section III, p. 44. **wyrsa**: Unless a scribal error, this seems a variant of **wyrse**, the nsm. comparative of the adjective **yfel**.

142b-143a   The **eadigne** of the MS may be kept if one assumes, with Ettmüller, that it modifies **sunu meotodes** as object of **habbaδ**. Krapp and Clubb, following Bouterwek (*Notes*), emend to **eadige**, assuming that it modifies **bearn**. Although the MS arrangement is a bit strained, it makes good sense and is metrically unobjectionable, and so I have kept it. We have here a picture like that in ll. 231-234a where angelic devotion to the Son takes the form of a song. Clubb (*Notes*, p. 72) construes **bearn** to include angels and men, citing as support ll. 46b and 265-266. But it is problematic whether one can gloss 46b to include men (see note to this line) and, in as much as ll. 265-266 are drawn from a different lament, it is questionable whether the situation there described bears any necessary relation to what we have here. That men are in hell is certain from l. 134b; but, since heaven proper was not opened to mankind until after the ascension, and since there is nothing to indicate that such an event has yet taken place, I am loath to gloss the lines with Clubb.

Clubb is no doubt aided in his interpretation by l. 146a **þe of eorδan cumaδ** of his text, which he supplied from 355b, emending slightly a suggestion by Barnouw (p. 104) to fill a gap in the MS. Such a line forces us to conclude that men are now in heaven as well as in hell. But without the line, the context could be construed as suggesting Satan's knowledge of the limitation of his power, and even, perhaps, as constituting a subtle psychological torment in that Satan is able to harm only those souls God wills not to have himself.

My interpretation assumes some foreknowledge on Satan's part. At the harrowing a number of souls will be released from hell, to be taken to heaven with Christ at the ascension. Those who are left, and those who choose hell after heaven is open, will be those to whom hell is a **hām**. Not all men who inhabit hell before the harrowing and ascension are permanent residents; many are, quite simply, not at home there. I think Satan realizes this, as the poet's audience surely did, and sorrows over it here. For the justification of independent half-lines in Old English, see A. J. Bliss, "Single Half-Lines in Old English Poetry," *N&Q*, 216 (1971), 442-49, where an analogy is drawn between the **ljoδahattr** meter of Old Norse gnomic poetry and Old English verse. There are a number of such lines in the Junius XI, and quite a few, excluding the one under discussion, in *Christ and Satan*: 224, 312, 478, 511, 553, 555, 598, 602, 613, 624, 652, 679(?), 728.

146b   **āgan**: The MS **tō āgan** is accepted by Clubb, who reads it as a "simple inflected infinitive" (*Notes*, p. 73), citing Sievers-Cook, p. 267, 363, n. 3. But Sievers, in a note to Cosijn's "Anglosoxonica III," *BGDSL*, 21 (1896), 23, suggests that this tō is a scribal anticipation of the tō in tō hæftum. This seems a more reasonable explanation, and I have emended accordingly.

151b swēg: an addition which completes the sense and meter of the line, first proposed by Grein (*Bibliothek*), rejected by Wülker (*Bibliothek*), but accepted by most editors.

152b bearne: Kock's emendation (p. 69) of bearn to bearne is preferable to the MS reading which would make bearn the subject of brōhton. For an idiom similar to brōhton tō bearme, see ll. 356a and 670a.

154b leomu: Clubb correctly rejects Bouterwek's emendation of leomu to leoðu. Lim "was commonly used . . . to denote beings who were subordinate to one head, hence 'servants'" (*Notes*, p. 74). Leomu is in apposition with we, l. 153a; lofsonga word is the object of both hōfan and sædon.

159 There is an outside possibility of retaining the MS reading of cwidum or cwide and herede, translating: "then yet often with word(s) of evil, the miserable outcast praised out of (from) hell. . . ." But the direct ironic thrust seems too strong for the allusive technique of the poet, and the meter of the first half-line would remain faulty. The emendation to cwiðde, first proposed by Rieger (*Alt- und angelsächsisches Lesebuch* [Giessen, 1861]) and to herede, first proposed by Grein (*Germania*, 10 [1865], 419) restores meter and improves sense.

161 See note to l. 78.

163-174a For the rhetoric of these lines, see Appendix, pp. 154-57.

169 I assume that this refers to Satan's inability to see heaven while he himself is constantly in the sight of God. See note to ll. 100-101a.

175 The alliteration is carried by ic and āgan.

178b in ðæm: the antecedent is hām in 177b. The line makes good sense, though its alliterative pattern is peculiar.

179b Bouterwek's emendation of MS mid to nið has been accepted universally. If, however, one assumes that the nasal mid could alliterate in this instance with neowle, the alliterative pattern would be acceptable, and neither sense nor meter would demand a change.

180a worulde: This refers to the heaven from which Satan and his angels were expelled by Christ. It cannot include the earth, the habitat of man, since the devils are said to be active there.

183b þæsmorðres: Thorpe's emendation (note) of MS morðre to morðres gives a genitive with a causative function. Translate: "I shall because of the crime suffer. . . ." This catches the sense of the lines better than Kock's emendation (p. 70) that makes þæt morðor parallel to wēan, wītu and wrace.

188b siðas: MS sidas is a scribal error for siðas. All editors so emend.

189-192 These lines introduce the poem's first long hortatory-homiletic section. As such, they sum up what has gone before, though they bear no close temporal or logical connection with the lines immediately preceding.

191b **hīg**: This is the form almost universally adopted by scholars. Junius offers **hie**, while Clubb maintains the MS reading **hē**. It is just possible that Clubb is correct in assuming the existence of such a form as an accusative plural, but the support he offers, Sievers-Cook, p. 244, 334, n. 3, marks the form with a question (**hē?**).

194a **ābælige**: We may either assume a weak infinitive **ābæligan** for this form, or, with Clubb (*Notes*, p. 77), consider it a graphic variant of **ābelge** from **ābelgan**.

198a **uppe**: All editors accept MS **upne** except Clubb and Krapp who emend to **uppe**, the adjective **upne** being improbable. Clubb (*Notes*, p. 78) believes the **ne** of **upne** a scribal dittograph for the **ne** of **ecne** in the same line.

199a **gecȳdde**: A normal late assimilation of ðd to **dd**. See Campbell, p. 194.

199b **mægencræft**: A number of editors omit the **mægen** to regularize the line. Clubb (*Notes*, p. 78) theorizes that the scribe's copy of the poem had **mægen** as a gloss for **cræft**, and that the scribe took the two together as a conflate reading.

201a There is irony here in the statement that the devils were driven from the high throne. It was from the high throne that Satan attempted to drive Christ (see ll. 85ff.). There may be a pun as well, since **hēan** may connote "wretched" and "miserable," just the condition in which the devils found themselves when they were driven out of heaven.

202-203 These lines have often been rewritten. I follow the suggestion of J. C. Pope (*The Rhythm of Beowulf*, p. 103) though, as Bliss remarks (447), the position of **ceosan** is questionable. Krapp offers: **ecne in wuldre mid alra gescefta ealdre; / ceosan us eard in wuldre mid ealra cyninga cyninge, / se is Crist genemned**. Clubb reads: **ecne mid alla gescefta ceosan us eard in wuldre / mid ealra cyninga Cyninge, se is Crist genemned**.

206b The MS **nigan** seems a scribal error for **hnigan**, which form is required for alliteration.

209b **wlite** is instrumental. Translate: "that he himself shine in countenance." The beauty of the saved is a Patristic commonplace. Here it is used metaphorically to indicate a sinless life.

211a **fægere**: The Annotator's **mycle**, accepted by earlier editors and critics, is rejected by Clubb and Krapp, who emend to the comparative form required by sense and meter.

212a The Annotator's **þær** improves the sense.

214a **hyhtlicra**: A comparative degree of the adjective modifying **ham**.

215a **gecwēmra**: The genitive plural of the adjective **gecwēme**, used as a noun.

215b Clubb (*Notes*, p. 81) is correct in rejecting the Corrector's emendation of **uta cerran** to **uton acerran**, the loss of a final **n** in the subjunctive being a common event (see Campbell, p. 189).

216a **sit**: A contraction for **siteð**.

219b **eadigre**: The normal form of this genitive plural would be in **ra**, but **re** appears a possible variant: see l. 267b where **hæþenre** is also genitive plural. There is no doubt that in the picture of heaven given in this homiletic-hortatory section **eadig** refers to the blessed souls of men who have merited the heavenly reward.

222   This line has an almost formulaic cast to it by reason of its repeated use in many of the vernacular homilies, and is thus properly used here to conclude the first homiletic section of the poem.

223a   The **ic**, of course, is the poet, or perhaps his **persona**, who is directly responsible for the hortatory comments.

223b   MS **feonda** is unacceptable on all counts. If we emend with Bouterwek to **feondas** we achieve syntactic and metrical regularity.

224-225   I follow here the suggestion of A. J. Bliss (446). See note to ll. 142-143.

228-278   There is some confusion as to the speaker(s) of these lines, but the text affords much help. The **we** of l. 228b is surely the **feondas** of l. 223b, which probably includes Satan. These **feondas** continue the discourse through l. 244, including a most affecting recollection of an almost liturgical ceremony in heaven (ll. 236b-242a). Such a painful memory provides the dramatic background for Satan to come forward, and his personal musings and recollections continue from ll. 245a-278b. Ll. 248a-253b are Satan's recapitulation of the speech by which he brought the angels into rebellion with him, and it is properly delivered in the historical present. With l. 254a Satan re-establishes the time-frame of the lament, and assumes the *pluralis majestatis*. Having established a division of demonic labour in ll. 262b-271b, he differentiates himself from his followers to assume the personal **ic** through l. 278.

231a   The Corrector's **in** improves the sense.

229b-230   It appears that the devils are aware of the eternally hopeless nature of their struggle against God. The richly ambiguous character of l. 230b allows one to assume that the struggle is hopeless because of the Lord's might, and that such a hopeless struggle is undertaken and persisted in as a punishment dictated precisely by such might. This recognition adds poignancy to Satan's remarks in ll. 261b-271, in which he details the devils' activity against man. Even here there is the implicit recognition of divine control: Satan can grip to hell only God's enemies (l. 268), thereby becoming an instrument of God's justice. See ll. 144b-148 for a similar sentiment, and ll. 424-429, where Judas becomes God's messenger in hell (see above, section III, pp. 44 and 51.

236b-242a   The problem here is syntactic and thematic. The identification of the Son in l. 241b as **his**, that is, different from and in some sense belonging to and dependent upon that **Byrhtword** (236b) who is at once **engla ordfruma**, **sigetorht**, and **ece drihten**, suggests that the referent of these appellations, and the one blessing the **bilewitne heap**, is the Father. The line **his se deora sunu** appears almost as an afterthought, and the activity in which he engages is redundant, since the only verb available to indicate the action of ''sunu'' is the same ''gebletsode'' which also governs the activity of **Byrhtword/sigetorht** (238b).

A thematic problem intrudes as well. Parts II and III of *Christ and Satan* are clearly the province of the Son; the action is his to the exclusion of other members of the Trinity. Indeed, so Christocentric is the poem that the spirit which descends upon the apostles at Pentecost is not an independent person of the Trinity, the Holy Ghost, but rather the spirit of Christ (see ll. 568b-571). And though the Christocentricity of Part I is not as overt as that of Parts II and III, it is nevertheless clear (see above, section II, pp. 26-29). Further, and particular to l. 237a, the two other times in *Christ and Satan* that **ordfruma** is used to refer to the deity, its referent is Christ: ll. 440, 657.

The problem, then, is clear. In a poem that has a consistent Christocentric bias, a syntactic pattern which gives unique and prominent place to the activity of the Father is suspect.

I emend **his** of l. 241b to **þes**, the nominative singular masculine demonstrative pronoun. With a colon after 241a, and the copulative **wæs** understood before **se**, the emended line would identify **byrhtword** and **sigetorht** as **sunu**, thus bringing the lines into conformity with the poem's Christocentric bias. It is noteworthy, too, that the emendation would constitute the figure "prolepsis," a figure of which the poet of *XSt* is reasonably fond (see Appendix, pp. 152-53).

The kennings **Byrhtword** and **Sigetorht** are unique in the Anglo-Saxon corpus: both are felicitous, in that the **byrht** element of the one, the **torht** of the other, carry on the contrast between light and darkness which is of the very fabric of the poem. **Sigetorht** is additionally happy, because the implied anachronism of having the fiends in the collective recollection of their heavenly home refer to Christ as one "bright in victories" is in reality a stroke of psychological realism: the devils have experienced Christ in a remarkably painful way in the expulsion from heaven, and this colours their remembrance of things past. Again, from the audiences' point of view, Christ is brightly victorious in all things, and through him, as the poem demonstrates, man may be too.

Sigetorht, then, may be explained within the economy of the poem; that is, the explanation of the kenning may be found in the actions, characters, and themes with which the poem deals, and its points of reference are all included within the artistic frame. Not so, or rather, not necessarily so, with **Byrhtword**. (My reading of the line precludes the possibility of construing **byrhtword** as either **voce clarus** [Grein-Köhler, *Sprachschatz,* p. 48] or "bright of word, clear of voice or speech" [Bosworth-Toller, *Dictionary,* p. 140].) Though **Byrht** carries through the light/dark contrast of *XSt,* **word** suggests something that is merely alluded to in the poem's initial eighteen lines, the creative agency of Christ. The justification of this kenning is not to be found in the action of the poem in the same manner as the justification of **sigetorht**. Rather **Byrhtword** goes beyond the artistic frame and seems to speak to the **lux** and **verbum** of the *Gospel of John* 1:1-12; it thus brings to bear on these lines the theological doctrine and explication associated with John, and throws into relief the incongruity of having the fiends, who have already rejected their Light and Creator, recollect him as just that: **byrhtword**. (The concept of Christ as the Creating Word becomes a commonplace among the Latin Fathers. Augustine combines the notion of light and creating word in his commentary on the "lux" and "verbum" of John, *In Joannis Evangelium,* tractati i-ii, *PL* 35, cols. 1379-95. Gregory the Great, quoting *John* 8:12 "ego sum lux mundi," discourses on Christ as Light in *Moralium,* Liber IV, caput 32, *PL* 75, col. 672.) The action of the devils in the heavenly rebellion is analogous to the action, or lack of action, of those spiritually blind souls who, in John's gospel, failed to see the light. See Hill's note on "Byrht word" in *ELN*, 8 (1970), 6-9, and my "Three Notes on the Junius XI *Christ and Satan*," *MP*, 72 (1974), 177-79.

With the emendation, then, and the commentary on **Byrhtword** in mind, the lines would translate thus:

> The Bright-Word arose,
> the Prince of Angels, and to that noble one
> the saints knelt; the one glorious in victory arose,
> the eternal Lord; [He] stood above us
> and blessed the guiltless host
> every day: and this [was] the dear Son,
> the Creator of Spirits.

242b-244 Although I have included these lines in the quotation ascribed to the devils, Clubb (*Notes*, p. 83) is certainly correct in asserting that there is a dramatic inconsistency here. The poet has included lines that can only refer to the welcome in heaven afforded to those men who have proved themselves worthy on earth in a section which comprises the devils' recollection of their blissful situation in heaven before the fall. If we recall that no one was allowed to enter heaven proper until the ascension of Christ, then the measure of confusion is large indeed.

245a Grein's addition of **me** after **þa** (*Bibliothek*) would clarify the thought, but I think the **ic** in l. 246b sufficiently specific to carry the sense.

248b **langsumne ræd**: The positive connotations of this half-line provide an excellent example of ironic manipulation: it is this very **ræd** which causes the devils to lose heaven. See, e.g., *Exodus*, l. 6, *Chr.* l. 44, *Gu* l. 794.

252b-253 **īdel gylp**: With the connotation "empty ostentation," "vain glory," "arrogance," indicates Satan's apprehension of God's power, which apprehension occasioned the heavenly rebellion. I thus follow Thorpe, Bouterwek, Grein, Wülker and Krapp by including the lines within Satan's speech of recollection. Clubb prefers an interpretation which takes the lines as Satan's comment upon the unsuccessful rebellion—i.e., that in its defeat it is seen as an **idel gylp** (*Notes*, p. 84). But ll. 254ff. continue a cryptic narration of the events subsequent to the rebellion, culminating in the fine reticence of ll. 256b-259a: **cūð is wide . . . rice haldeð**. These lines become a bit anticlimactic if Satan already in l. 252b admits that his activity is an **idel gylp**. Further, there is a good measure of irony in having Satan give as a cause of the rebellion that God's conduct was "empty ostentation" when in fact it is demonstrably his own that is such.

257a Grein and Wülker add **we** as subject of **mōton** after **þæt**. Since neither **wreclāstas** nor **grundas** would make sense as subject of **mōton**, the **we** may be supplied by context.

259 This line lacks normal alliteration, though the staves may be bound together by the "h" of **haldeð** and **Hē**. Grein and Wülker overcame this difficulty by a re-arrangement:

| 260 | grimme grundas | god seolfa him rice haldeð |
| 261 | he is ana cyning | þe us eorre gewearð, ece drihten . . . |

This is desperate. Should one wish to follow Graz (18) and substitute **riht** for **ana**, the difficulty would disappear; Clubb adds **riht** after **ana**, but the problem persists. Krapp follows the manuscript. Since the lines make excellent sense, and non-alliterating lines, though an anomaly, are not few in number in our poem (see, e.g., 296, 334, 450, 484, 634, 712, 717, 723, 726, the list compiled by Krapp, *Notes,* p. 237), I have let the MS reading stand.

261a   Clubb's defense of **swilc** (*Notes,* p. 85) is sound; there is no reason to emend to **swīð.**

263b-264.   For this peculiar detail, see Bede, *Super Divi Jacobi Epistolam,* caput 3, *PL* 93, col. 27.

265-266   This recalls early Gnostic beliefs that the soul passes through various heavenly spheres, each under the control of a demon or demons, on its way to its heavenly reward after death. In fact, given the cosmography of the poem, with heaven *up,* hell *down,* earth in the *middle,* the devils, in their capacity as "Powers of the Air," might well attempt to intercept the blessed soul as he passes by. For a picture of the evil spirit successfully holding back the sinful souls as they attempt to rise to heaven, but being unsuccessful in so thwarting the just, see *Vita S. Antonii, versio Evagrii, PG* 26, cols. 936-37, and H. T. Keenan, "Satan Speaks in Sparks . . . ," *N&Q,* 219 (1974).

265a   **hē** refers to one of the devils mentioned in ll. 262b-264.

267b   The addition of an **e** to **sceal** is the most economical way of rendering the line intelligible. **Sceale,** then, with the sense of "throng," "band," from **scolu/scalu** (see Club, *Notes,* p. 86).

273a   Krapp's note on the line is instructive (*Notes,* p. 237). He supposes the MS **in ðæs** to be a scribal error for **niðæs** and assumes **beala** to be the object of **gebolian,** with **þinga æghwylces** and **niðæs** as dependent genitives. This seems to be as close to the original reading as we are likely to get.

278a   **eðel:** All editors, following Thorpe (note), so emend MS **eðle.**

279-314   These lines comprise the second large homiletic section of the poem. Perhaps the *punctus versus* after l. 278b is intended to set this section off, as division [IV] sets off the first homiletic section.

286b   **grēne strǣte:** Hugh Keenan ("Exodus 312: 'The Green Street of Paradise,'" *NM,* 71 [1970], 455-60) investigates the use of **grene** here, in *Exodus* 312a, and Psalm 141:1a of the *Paris Psalter.* Citing Cassiodorus' commentary on Psalm 141 (*PL* 70, col. 1006) and the relevant section of the *Glossa Ordinaria* (*PL* 113, col. 1065), and noting that **grene** is associated with the perdurable foundation of the castle which stands for Mary as the protector of the faithful in the *Cursor Mundi* (R. Morris, ed., Part II, EETS 59 [London, 1875], p. 574) and with the way of salvation in *Poema Morale* (R. Morris, ed., *Old English Homilies,* Part II, EETS 34 [London, 1868], p. 179: ". . . þene narewe wei and þene wei grene"), Keenan concludes that there was a well established tradition in Anglo-Saxon times which saw the way to Paradise as **green.**

296   This line has no alliteration. Clubb, following Grein (*Bibliothek*) emends **æfre forð** to **wide ferð** to restore matters. But see the note to l. 259.

298-300   Kock's suggestion (p. 70), accepted by Clubb and Krapp, that the **on** ending of MS **lifigendon** (l. 298b) in fact belongs to **lucan** (l. 299b), thus **onlūcan**, clarifies the sense of these lines. The sense is improved, too, if we assume that **dēman** has the connotation "consider" or "think of" with **þæt** of l. 297b, which refers to the description of heaven and the way to achieve salvation (ll. 282-297a), as **dēman**'s actual, though not grammatical, object. The play on the words **onlūcan** and **locen**, l. 299, is particularly felicitous, the **locen waldendes** understood as those secrets of God the knowledge of which allows one to obtain salvation: a metaphor, surely, for the wisdom to lead a good life.

300a **ongeotan gāstlice**: ll. 297b-300a are quite like *Exodus* ll. 519b-530a in the emphasis on reading or seeing with the spirit. Particularly striking in *Exodus* is the veritable call for an allegorical reading of the poem contained in ll. 523ff.: "... gif onlucan wile lifes wealhstod, / beorht in breostum, banhuses weard, / ginfæstes god gastes cægon."

300b-302 This recalls *Christ II,* ll. 545a-546, wherein Christ and the holy souls are met in their ascent to heaven by angels.

306-308a See *Matthew* 13:43.

309 This line presents a problem. Grein, followed by Krapp, adds **friðe** before **befæðmeð**; Holthausen, followed by Clubb, transfers **heo** of 308b to 309a before **befæðmeð**. While A. J. Bliss makes a case for treating l. 309 as an independent half-line, the line's similarity to l. 358a gives some textual support to Holthausen's emendation.

314 These half-lines have something of a formulaic cast to them by reason of their repeated use in closing petitions of prose homilies.

315-347 These lines are a narrative recapitulation of essentially the same material that had been brought forward in the dramatic monologues and dialogues of Part I; ll. 348-364 give a picture of heaven and the saved to balance the description of hell and the damned. Such a knitting together seems a proper ending of the poem's first main movement.

318b MS **hreowan** is most often used impersonally, and, as Clubb notes (p. 90), is probably a mistake for **hrēopan, p** and **wynn** being quite similar in OE script. I have followed most recent editors in emending to **hrēopan**, though the **hreowan** may be an isolated case of a personal use with np **deofla** as subject.

319a The MS **winsele** ought be kept, despite the Corrector's superscript **d** which gives **windsele**. Here, and again in l. 384a, it seems that the Corrector has missed the poet's ironic intention in terming hell a **winsele**. See my "Two Notes on MS Junius XI," *PQ*, 49 (1970).

319b Clubb retains the MS **wēa** as the Northern equivalent of **wēan**, parallel to **mān** and **morðor** as objects of **cwānedon**. Earlier editors offered **weacwanedon**, but Clubb and Krapp, following Bouterwek and Holthausen, separate the word. Krapp, following Kock (p. 71), emends **wea** to **wean**.

320b Thorpe's suggestion (note) that the first **þær** of this line is an error for **sēo** affords a smoother reading.

330 The second half-line requires something in addition to **gryndes** and, accepting either **ād** with Clubb or Grein's (*Bibliothek*) **bealu**, that addition ought be in

the genitive case, parallel grammatically to **gōda lēase**. With **ādes** I translate: "they were bereft of all goods, except of the fire of the pit . . . ."

331 If the **ah** which heads 330b be transposed to head 331a, then Thorpe's addition of **ne** to 331b, accepted by Clubb, Krapp, Grein and Wülker is unnecessary. Translate: "but they must inhabit the wretched hall."

333 See *Matthew* 8:12. There is insufficient reason to emend **gristbitunge** and **gnornunge**, though Clubb terms them "metrically suspicious" (*Notes*, p. 91), and accepts Cosijn's emendation (24) to **gristbitungc** and **gnornungc**. So too Krapp.

334-336 There is nothing in the sense of these lines that requires emendation. The **wē** of l. 334a indicates that either the devils collectively (**mecgas** of l. 333b) or Satan, having been graced with the "imperial plural," are being used by the poet to exemplify the **gristbitunge and gnornunge** of l. 333. That this section is but three lines long should offer no special difficulty: See, e.g., ll. 616-618, 626-627, 672. L. 334, however, is defective in alliteration, a not uncommon failing in the poem. One might follow Clubb, who follows Cosijn (24), and emend to **hat and cyle**.

343b-344b Clubb's translation is possible, though it does not follow the text literally: "They lamented the deep plot, contrived while they were in heaven" (*Notes*, p. 92). But l. 344b is quite specific, and, if translated literally, would offer: "They lamented the deep plot by which they established a home in heaven." This is close enough to *Isaiah* 14:13-14 to give pause. What we have here is an allusion to the devils' attempt to establish a throne in heaven to counter God's. The following lines support this suggestion, since it may be generally assumed that the successful establishment of a rival throne, or the usurpation of the one throne, would bring with it exactly what the devils are said to have intended: **woldon benǣman nergende Crīst**.

348-349b A common rhetorical form. See, e.g., *Christ* ll. 219-223.

351-354 With slight emendation these lines make elegant sense. Cosijn's suggestion (24) that l. 351a be emended to read **hū scīr sunu þǣr** ought be accepted: MS **sunnu** is a dittographic error for **sunu**, which refers to Christ whose shining countenance was a Patristic commonplace. **Meotodes**, l. 352a, in this instance alludes to God the Father. Such an interpretation makes sense of the **þæt** of l. 354b, which otherwise has as a referent the **meotodes** who makes the sun shine, an insufficient reason, I think, for the emphatic strength of l. 354b. Moreover, the necessary emendation of l. 354b is itself clarified. The MS reading **þæt is (se** erased) **seolfa for god** is impossible. But if **þæt** be understood to refer to **sunu** in l. 351a, an emendation such as Clubb's **þæt is se seolfa god** becomes an affirmation of the divinity of the Son.

356a Translate "offer." See l. 152a.

356-357 This recalls the *Phoenix* with the bird, variously a symbol for Christ and the holy soul, building its nest from sweet-smelling herbs and flowers, symbols of good deeds. Clubb (*Notes*, pp. 94-95) offers the following sections for comparison: *Phx* ll. 526-530, 583-586, 658-661.

364b Dietrich's addition of **wyrcan** before **mot** fulfills sense, metrical and alliterative requirements.

365ff.   For a discussion of the relationship of Part II to the *Gospel of Nicodemus, Blickling Homily #7*, the *Book of Cerne*, and the *Mercian Martyrology*, see above, section III, pp. 49-55.

365-378a   A brief recapitulation of the main points of the angelic rebellion, most of which have been treated at length in ll. 1-364.

365a   **encgelcyn**: Refers either to the angelic order of which Lucifer was the head, or to Lucifer himself. The actual number of the angelic orders was not fixed in Patristic times. If we conflate the enumeration of the angelic hierarchies in Paul's epistles (*Ephesians* 1:21 and *Colossians* 1:16) we arrive at seven. Augustine, while in one place (*Enchiridion*, c. 58-59, *PL* 40, cols. 259-60) acknowledging Paul's list, speaks in another (*Collatio cum Maximino Arianorum Episcipo*, c. 9, *PL* 42, col. 727) of eight orders. Pseudo-Dionysius (*De Cael. Hier.*, c. 3, *PG* 3, cols. 163-78) notes nine, disposed in three hierarchies. Gregory the Great also accepts nine (*XL Hom. in Evang.*, #34, 6-7, *PL* 76, cols. 1249-50), as does Isidore of Seville (*Etymologiarum*, Liber VII, caput 5, *PL* 82, col. 272). Aelfric, in "Sermo de Initio Creaturae" (Thorpe, *Homilies of Aelfric*, 2, p. 10) notes ten, of which one order rebelled. The name of the chief of this rebellious group was "Leohtberend," a translation, surely, of Lucifer. Further, Aelfric (ibid., p. 12) believes that man was created to fill the void in heaven left by the expulsion of the rebellious host. In this he follows the likes of Augustine (*De Civitate Dei*, Liber XXII, caput 1, *PL* 41, col. 752; *Enchiridion*, c. 29, *PL* 40, col. 246) and Hilary of Poitiers (*In Matth.*, c. 18, *PL* 9, col. 1020). If the poet is thinking here of the angelic order which followed Satan in rebellion, rather than of Satan himself, it is a proper and logical extension to denote such an order by the name of its chief.

365b   **ær genemned**: parallel to **hāten**, l. 366a: "named before." L. 367a further specifies the temporal sense of 365b.

366a   **Lucifer**: P. E. Dustoor ("Legends of Lucifer in Early English and Milton," *Anglia*, 54 [1930], 229) notes that it is rare to find the devil identified by the name Lucifer before the eleventh century: "But by the time of Anselm and Peter Comestor the name Lucifer had become almost synonymous with Satan, with commonly just this distinction that Lucifer was rather the glorious Angel's name and Satan the fallen devil's." We seem to have here the only occurrence of the name Lucifer in the surviving Anglo-Saxon poetic corpus.

368a   **in wuldre**: Cosijn (24) interprets "in caelo." Clubb (*Notes*, p. 97) remarks that it may also allude to Satan's beauty or glory.

369a   **oferhȳda**: With Clubb (*Notes*, p. 97), we might take "prides" metaphorically as those trappings of divinity Lucifer intended to possess in his rebellion. Since the rebellion itself was motivated, as the commentators and our poet maintain, by "pride," and since that sin was generally considered to be the premier and the foundation of the seven deadlies, it is appropriate that it should be associated with both the cause and the object of Lucifer's revolt. See M. W. Bloomfield, *The Seven Deadly Sins* (East Lansing, Michigan, 1952).

370a   The line is metrically irregular. Clubb and Krapp, following a suggestion by Bright (130), add **þa** before **Satanus**. But this sets up a clumsy temporàl/causal relationship with the **þā** in l. 368a. Bright suggested **se** or **þæt** as alternatives to ḇā, and either would be preferable. There is elegance in the shifting of names: Lucifer, having given way to pride, becomes of a sudden Satan.

372b-373a These lines break the continuity of the passage and are anticlimactic. If they are relocated between l. 378a and b, the sense would be greatly improved. The **heora** would then have as referent **hīred** (375a) and **hī** (377a) rather than a referent supplied either from Part I, the reader's general knowledge of sacred history, or some sense of **encgelcyn** (365a). Further, the lines would provide a climactic statement about Satan's actions, and his relationship to those who followed him.

375b **in hȳnðo geglīdan**: The MS reads **in to geglidan**, a clear impossibility. I accept Clubb's reconstruction, as emended slightly by Krapp. Clubb (*Notes*, p. 98) reasons that "the scribe, even though he copied the accent, thought the repetition of **in** in the reading of his copy (i.e., **in inðo**) was a mere dittography."

377b **andwlitan sēon**: Clubb, following a suggestion by Holthausen (233), adds **sēon** to complete meter and sense. Bright (130) transfers **mosten** of l. 377a to after **andwlitan**, thus **andwlitan mosten**. But Clubb correctly questions the assumption that **andwlitan** is a verb (Bright treats the form as an infinitive) and notes that such a line would be metrically abnormal.

378b-380a See *The Acts of Pilate*: Part II, *The Descent into Hell*, sometimes called *The Gospel of Nicodemus*, in *The Apocryphal New Testament*, trans. M. R. James. The Latin "B" version, II (XVIII), pp. 123-24: "And there was heard the voice of the Son of the most high Father, as it were the voice of a great thundering, and it proclaimed aloud and began: Draw back, O princes, your gates, remove the everlasting doors: Christ the Lord the king of glory approacheth to enter."

381b **hēafod gesawon**: T. D. Hill ("*Byrht Word* and *Hælendes Heafod*: Christological Allusion in the Old English *Christ and Satan*," *ELN*, 8 [1970-71], 6-9) argues, citing Paul's first *Epistle to the Corinthians* 11:3 and Gregory the Great's thirty-third homily in *XL Homiliarum in Evangelia*, Liber II, *PL* 76, col. 1243) that the head of Christ was understood by exegetes as a symbol of the divine aspect of his nature.

382 Something has been lost after this line. Ettmüller supplies **fagum folce forht geworden**, Grein (*Bibliothek*) offers **fagum folce ferhð geaclod**.

384a **winsele**: See note to l. 319.

387-389 See James, *The Descent into Hell*, Part II of *The Gospel of Nicodemus*, the Latin "B" version, II (XVIII), p. 123: "... suddenly there shone upon us a great light, and hell did tremble, and the gates of death." The Latin "A" version of II (XVIII), pp. 123-24, emphasizes the "light" more than the "B" version: "... on a sudden there came a golden heat of the sun and a purple and royal light shining upon us. And ... the father of the whole race of men, ... rejoiced, saying: This light is the beginning (author) of everlasting light which did promise to send unto us his co-eternal light." The punctuation of ll. 385-389 attempts to catch the growing terror of the devils as they realize the character of Christ and the implication for them of his visit. The *punctus versus* after l. 389b indicates, I think, the moment of felt recognition, when they implicitly contrast the conditions they had in heaven **mid englum** with the current chaos of hell.

387b **fægere**: The comparative is required by sense and meter.

390   James, *The Descent into Hell,* Part II of *The Gospel of Nicodemus,* the Latin "B" version, IV (XX), p. 127: "But our holy father Adam made answer to Satan thus: O prince of death, wherefore fearest thou and tremblest? Behold the Lord cometh which shall destroy all thy creatures, and thou shalt be taken captive of him and be bound, world without end."

390a **witu**: This appears to refer to the torments that the devils inflict on the souls in their charge. Grein notes a similar use of the term in *Jul* 211.

392a **dyne for drihtne**: Thus the devils apprehend the coming of Christ. To the holy souls, this **dyne** is **engla swēg** (l. 401b-402a).

397   We might with Clubb, who follows Graz (21), read **hereweorces** for alliteration. But the **h** of **hēnðo** may be a diacritic, and the alliteration would then be carried by the vowels of **yrreweorces** and **(h)ēnðo**.

401a **eðle**: The poet here, and in the use of **earde**, ll. 456a, 504a, and **burh**, l. 457b, seems to suggest that the souls of the just who were released from bondage at the harrowing went immediately to heaven. The position that has come to be accepted as orthodox, based for the most part on the speculations of Aquinas, Bellarmine and Suarez, asserts that the just remained in limbo, having been given the supernatural happiness of the Beatific Vision with the arrival of Christ at the harrowing, until the Saviour's ascension reopened for them the gates of heaven. Ideas on this head, though, were quite fluid in the early centuries of the church, and much speculation on the disposition of the deceased Old Testament saints between the time of the harrowing and the last judgment, and the disposition of the just who died after the harrowing, was influenced by chiliastic and millenarian expectations. Still, were we to think that the habitation of the saints between the time of the harrowing and the ascension, a period of something more than forty days, posed a problem to the poet or his contemporaries, we might assume them to have understood **eðel, eard** and **burh** to refer not to the heaven of God, but to that Paraidse promised the Good Thief by Christ, thought by some to be identical with the Paradise whence Adam and Eve were driven and to which Enoch and Elijah were translated, sometimes designated by the term "Bosom of Abraham." *The Descent into Hell,* Latin "A" and Greek versions, IX (XXV)-X (XXVI), follow this tradition. The saints meet the Good Thief, Enoch and Elijah in Paradise, and each relates the story of his coming thither. This Paradise is called "Eden" in the Greek version, and mention is made of the "flaming sword" whom the Thief asks to bring him to Eden's gate, a clear metaphor for the angel guardian of the gate of Paradise. In the Latin "A" version, the Thief recounts that he explained his arrival to "the angel that keepeth paradise." Early speculation placed this Paradise on earth, in the east, but later it was thought to be located in one of the heavens. That the Anglo-Saxons were aware of a division of the heavenly realms is apparent from, e.g., Aelfric's remark in *Sermo in Ascensione Domini* (Thorpe, 1, p. 308) that Elijah and Enoch were taken to an aerial heaven, not an ethereal: **lyftenre heofenan, no to roderlicere.**

402a dægrēd: This emphasis on dawn is striking. See ll. 404, 463-464.

406b and: Thorpe (note), followed by Bouterwek, Ettmüller and Krapp, emends the abbreviation 7 to ac; Eve: The choice of Eve as spokeswoman here is logical and sympathetic: logical because it was through her that Satan conquered; sympathetic because of the maternal connection Eve has with all mankind, and the plea to maternal connection she can thus make through Mary with Christ. Since Mary was Christ's mother, it can be allowed that Eve was his grandmother at many removes. Such cannot be adduced for a projected Fatherhood of Adam, and this, in addition to the fact that the Mother-Son relationship is the richer emotionally, may account for the exclusion of Adam from a speaking role in the harrowing, a role that he has in all other analogues. Only in *XSt* is Eve the exclusive speaker.

From quite early times Eve was considered a type of the Church: as she was brought forth from the side of the sleeping Adam, so the Church was brought from the side of the crucified Christ in the form of blood and water. (Isidore succinctly remarks: *Eva designat Ecclesiam factam per mysterium lavacri, quae de latere in cruce morientis Christi fluxit, sicut Eva de costa hominis dormientis. Allegoriae Quaedam Scripturae Sacrae,* ex veteri testamento. *PL* 83, col. 99.) It might be argued, too, that the saints who await Christ in hell constitute a Church *in potentia*: thus Eve in her typological capacity becomes appropriate to her immediate context. Again, the Virgin upon whom Eve based her successful plea to Christ was herself a type of the Church in her character of Mother of God and Mother of all men. Such references to Eve and Mary are felicitous poetic and emotive choices, but in a typological sense also function as links in the apparently episodic action of Part II: Eve pleading through Mary to Christ is a typological iteration of the activity of the Church, and a forevision of the proper founding of the church at Pentecost, ll. 557-573. For Eve as a type of the Church, see: Augustine, *De Genesi Contra Manichaeos,* Liber II, caput 24, *PL* 34, cols. 215-16; *Enarratio in Psalmum xl, PL* 36, col. 461; *Enarratio in Psalmum cxxvi, PL* 37, col. 1673. For the equation of Eve and Mary, see Ambrose, *Expositio in Psalmum cxviii,* sermo secundus, *PL* 15, col. 1276; *Liber de Institutione Virginis,* caput 5, *PL* 16, col. 328. For Mary as a type of the Church, see: Ambrose, *Expositionis in Lucam,* Liber II, *PL* 15, col. 1635; Augustine, *PL* 38, *Sermo cxcii,* cols. 1011-13; *Sermo clxxxviii,* cols. 1003-1005; *Sermo cxcv,* cols. 1017-19; Venerable Bede, *In Lucae Evangelium Expositio,* Liber I, *PL* 92, cols. 330, 342. See my "Three Notes on the Junius XI *Christ and Satan*," *MP,* 72 (1974), 180-81.

408-434 Compare this account of the fall of man with ll. 469b-486; cf. *Genesis B* ll. 491-723a; *Juliana* ll. 494-505; *Christ* ll. 1379-1418; *Guthlac* ll. 819-893.

410a næddran: The serpent of *Genesis* 3 and Satan were early identified by commentators.

411a se atola: The Satan næddran of l. 410a.

419b þearle onæled: What was the disposition of the souls of the just as they awaited the coming of Christ? In the parable of Dives and Lazarus, *Luke* 16:22ff., we find Dives in torment, Lazarus in repose in "Abraham's Bosom";

they are in sight of each other, but separated by an unbridgeable gap. From this parable, and, perhaps, from the speculation of Jewish writers on the nature and construction of *sheol,* most Patristic commentators deduced that the just and the saints awaited the coming of Christ in a place of repose, variously termed "Abraham's Bosom," "Bosom of the Patriarchs," later "Limbo of the Fathers," located in the vicinity of the hell of the damned, but separate from it. Here the deceased saints suffered only that spiritual longing which was to be fulfilled by the Beatific Vision. So, e.g., Augustine, *De Anima et ejus origine,* Liber IV, c. 14-15, *PL* 44, cols. 537-38; Gregory the Great, *XL Hom. in Evang.,* #40, *PL* 76, cols. 1302-1304; *Moralium,* Liber XII, c. 9; Liber XIII, c. 44, *PL* 75, cols. 993, 1038. (By an extension of the metaphor, "Abraham's Bosom" was occasionally used to denominate heaven and its Beatific delights properly so-called. So, e.g., Augustine, *Quaestionum Evangeliorum,* Liber II, c. 38, *PL* 35, col. 1350.) Another, though minor, tradition held that the saints did in fact suffer some form of pain while awaiting Christ: so, e.g., Bede, *Liber Retractationis in Act. Apost.,* c. 2, *PL* 92, col. 1001. It is not surprising, then, to note that the Anglo-Saxons document both beliefs. Clubb (*Notes,* p. 103) cites, in addition to this section of *XSt,* Vercelli homily 19 (folio 107a) and an Old English homily dealing with a version of the *Gospel of Nicodemus* (W. H. Hulme, "The Old English Gospel of Nicodemus," *MP,* 1 [1903-04], 606) for the more rigorous view, Aelfric (*Homilies,* 1, p. 94; 2, p. 80) and Cynewulf (*Chr.* 146-47) for the less. It is, of course, much more dramatic to have Christ release the souls of the just from pain and torment than to afford them the Beatific Vision, and this may have been a factor in the poet's choice of tradition here.

420-423   *Blickling Homily* #7, p. 89, for a similar prayer. It is not found in the *Descent into Hell,* Part II of the *Nicodemus.*

423   Some verb such as **gan** must be understood here.

424a   **ymb**: With the sense of "ago." Thus "and about three nights ago . . . ."

424b   **þegen**: This must be Judas Iscariot who hung himself on the Thursday-Friday of Easter Week. Since it was generally assumed, on the basis of *Matthew* 12:40, that Christ was in "hell" from the moment of his death until the resurrection, the harrowing may be placed between late Good Friday and dawn on Easter Day. In this admittedly vague temporal frame, Eve's **ymb þreo niht** would be approximately correct. See above, section III, p. 51. Cf. *The Descent into Hell* of the *Exeter Book,* where John the Baptist is the predecessor of Christ in hell. But neither John nor the Good Thief fit the circumstances of **þegn hælendes** in *Christ and Satan.*

428-429   Eve apparently addresses these lines to **þegen hælendes.**

430b   So *Beowulf* l. 749b as Beowulf grapples Grendel.

433b   **heora freodrihten**: The MS **heora drihten** is defective in alliteration, and I follow Ettmüller's emendation to restore matters. Krapp, following Clubb, who follows Holthausen (233), has **freadrihten.** Clubb (*Notes,* p. 105) defends the emendation as a "loftier term than the more intimate **heora drihten.**" Just so, but the ambience here, with Eve as spokeswoman, is intended to be intimate; indeed, to secure such intimacy is the function of the elegant little stage direction in ll. 435-436 (see above, section II, p. 31). The combination of the intimate and the lofty, the personal and the transcendent, was what the poet was working towards. That a scribe should retain **heora** but drop inadvertently the similar **frea/freo** is not remarkable.

435-436 See note to l. 433b. For the possible connection between *Blickling Homily* #7, the *Mercian Martyrology,* and this appeal, see above, section III, pp. 53-55.

442a **wuldre**: Instrumental.

442b **clomma**: Accusative plural variant; for the ending, see Sievers-Cook, p. 170, 237, n. 3. But Thorpe (note) already suggested an emendation to **clommas**.

442-447a See *The Descent into Hell,* the Latin "B" version, VIII (XXIV): "And behold, the Lord Jesus Christ coming in the glory of the light of the height, in meekness, great and yet humble, bearing a chain in his hands bound therewith the neck of Satan, and also, binding his hands behind his back, cast him backwards into Tartarus, and set his holy foot upon his throat...."

449-451a The MS pointing, as Krapp remarks (*Notes*, p. 241), is wrong here: **ne he ed cerreš. æfre moton wenan. Seoððan him wæs drihten god wrað geworden.** The reading he proposes, with a metrical point after **moton**, is the one I follow, even though it leaves l. 451 defective in alliteration (see note to l. 259). One might omit **god** and add **weroda** before **drihten**, a change that would make the line unexceptionable. Clubb points the line as an expanded verse, omitting **god**: **Seoððan him wæs Drihten wrað geworden, sealde him wites clom** ....

452a **atole**: Here probably an adverb. Clubb modifies to **atol**, "a neuter adjective used substantively in either the inst. sing. or acc. pl." He also suggests a "weak adjective... modifying clom" (*Notes,* p. 107).

453a **dimne**: Thorpe (note) suggests this form instead of the MS **dimme**.

454b **hinsiðgryre**: Although initial **h**, construed as a diacritic, might allow the line vocalic alliteration, it is safer to read MS **in sið gryre** as **hinsiðgryre** with Grein, Wülker, and Krapp.

455-459 See *The Descent into Hell,* the Latin "A" version, VIII (XXIV): "And the Lord stretched forth his hand and made the sign of the cross over Adam and over all the saints, and he took the right hand of Adam and went up out of hell, and all the saints followed him."

456a See note to l. 401a.

458-459 The prophets take the Lord with them **tō eðle.** Clubb is right to remark something amiss (*Notes,* p. 108), since almost all accounts of the harrowing depict Christ leading the host from hell, holding Adam by the hand. But in some early Jewish-Christian works, it is interesting to note, Christ is borne up in a combination resurrection/ascension by others: by "two young men," obviously angels, in *The Gospel of Peter* (36-40); by "the angel of the Holy Spirit, and Michael, the chief of the holy angels" in *The Ascension of Isaiah* (3:16-20). Clubb's reconstruction is astute:

hōf hī[e] mid him	handum hālige
wītegan up to eðle,	Abrahames cynn.

462b   sāwlum: The MS sawla is impossible, and Grein, Wülker, and Clubb read swa la; Krapp, following Bouterwek (*Notes*), reads swa. We might emend to sawlum, however, a form closer to that in the MS, and achieve good sense. Translate: "Then had the Lord himself overcome death, defeated the fiend, which in former days the prophets said he would [do] for (on behalf of) souls." The infinitive to complete the action suggested in wolde is omitted.

466b   bān: An effective image. Clubb (*Notes,* p. 109) defends the reading by asserting that the poet is using scriptural phraseology. He cites *Ps.* 101:4; *Prov.* 17:22; *Ezch.* 37:11; *Nicod.* 1:7.

471   Cf. l. 20.

473a   fēowertig bearna: The number of Adam's children is variously attested: in the *Vita Adae et Evae* 24:2, thirty sons and thirty daughters, plus Cain, Abel and Seth to make sixty-three. In the *Book of Jubilees* 4:1-12, nine sons, plus Cain, Abel, Seth, and the daughters Awan and Azura for a total of fourteen. I have nowhere found a source for precisely forty children. It may be that the number was used because of its associations in the Old and New Testaments: the forty days Moses spent on Mt. Zion, the forty years the Israelites wandered in the desert, the forty days Elias and Christ fasted in the desert. According to Augustine (*De Doctrina Christiana,* Liber II, c. 16, #25, *PL* 34, col. 47-48) the spiritual symbolism of "40" indicates the knowledge of all things involved in time, finite time being suggested by "4," infinity by "10." The proper relationship between Creator and creature is further adumbrated by "40." See also Isidore of Seville, *Liber Numerorum qui in Sanctis Scripturis Occurrunt,* caput 23, *PL* 83, cols. 197-98.

Of more moment here, however, is the peculiar chronology which, in ll. 472-477, suggests that the fall occurred after Adam and Eve had had these forty children. Now we have a document which places Satan's fall after the creation of Adam, and makes the heavenly rebellion contingent upon Satan's refusal to worship Adam as God's image (*Vita Adae et Evae,* 12-17), and we have some early commentators who assume that Satan's fall was contemporaneous, or nearly so, with his temptation of Adam and Eve: e.g., Justin Martyr, *Dialogus cum Tryphone,* c. 124, *PG* 6, col. 765; Irenaeus, *Contra Haereses,* Liber III, *PG* 7, c. 23, col. 965; Tertullian, *Adversus Marcionem,* Liber II, caput 10, *PL* 2, cols. 296-97. But there is no indication of a tradition that Adam and Eve had children before their fall. Had there been such a tradition, surely a commentator somewhere would have mentioned it: the theological problems posed by the lack of culpability of the children, already in Paradise at the time of the hypothetical fall of their parents, in the development of the doctrine of original inherited sin would have merited the closest attention.

Krapp (*Notes,* p. 241) suggests that these lines are unskillfully done. Clubb (*Notes,* pp. 109-10), having placed the lines in a parenthesis as interrupting the direct discourse, explains that the poet is elucidating the common doctrine that man might have remained in Paradise had the fall not taken place. Eorlas he assumes to be a generic term for men, the men who might have lived "in innocency" had Adam and Eve remained faithful. Thus l. 475b wunian mōston has a conditional quality: "might have dwelt." Though I am loath to disregard the disturbing specificity of the lines, in the absence of any viable alternative I accept Clubb's interpretation. Cf. *Gen* B 784b-88a.

474a **middangearde**: The Corrector's final **e** gives a dative /locative case. Ettmüller's addition of **on** before **middangearde**, accepted by most editors but Wülker, is unnecessary.

477 The MS reading **þæt he afyrhte eft/feond in firenum** is dubious. The **eft** suggests that this is not the unique fall of man, a most curious position. It is probably a dittograph for **eft** in l. 476b. **He** may be construed as a Northern variant of the nom.-acc. plural, its referent Adam and Eve, l. 471. The **afyrhte** just might be kept, but the weight of opinion (Bouterwek, Clubb, Dietrich, Ettmüller, Grein, Krapp, Wülker) is for a form like **afyrde**, which makes better sense: one might assume that Satan **drove** Adam and Eve **in firenum**, but it is difficult to accept that he **frightened** them there.

481a **æpla**: A possible variant of **æplas**. See Sievers-Cook, p. 170, 273, n. 3, and **clomma**, l. 442b.

484a **ofergȳmdon**: Clubb emends to **oferhygdon** to secure alliteration. But see note to l. 259.

485a **egsan**: In so far as the apple brought spiritual degradation and physical death it is most properly termed **egsa**. Klaeber (*Anglia,* 37 [1913], 541) compares with *Genesis* B 717-18, *Genesis* A 936-38. Clubb (*Notes,* p. 112) cites *Guthlac* 868-69, 982-93, *Genesis A* 893. For a like metaphor see *Andreas* 1532a, where death by flood is a bitter **beorþegu** to the Mermedonians.

487-492 The *punctus versus* after **ðrowade**, l. 488b, and after **gesette**, l. 492b, plus the repetition of **ne** in ll. 489b-490, sets off the discourse of ll. 487-492. Christ affirms his concern for man's suffering, and emphasizes that the remedy was his alone who initially set the punishment. My punctuation tries to catch the emphasis.

487-488 Cf. *Christ,* ll. 1414-18.

487a **gehreaw**: for MS **gereaw**, thus securing the alliteration. So Dietrich and Grein (*Bibliothek*).

488a **þæs**: Ettmüller, followed by Clubb and Krapp, supplies **þæs** to complete the line.

495a The MS reads **tintregan and fela**. Thorpe transposes the **and**, and so all later editors.

498a **rices rǣdboran**: The MS **rices boran** has been so emended by Krapp and Clubb, following Sievers (*BGDSL,* 10 [1885], 454), Holthausen (233), and Graz (23). Clubb (*Notes,* p. 113) remarks that **bora** is "never found alone save in the MS reading of this line," whereas it frequently occurs as the second member of a compound.

498b **hrefnan**: It may be that the initial **h** is a diacritic, and that the alliteration is on the consonant following, the **r**. The *punctus versus* after **mihten** serves to emphasize the enormity of the offense they committed who sought to kill Christ.

501a   **gēara:** If this be kept, the line is expanded. Graz (23) and Cosijn (24) omit, Cosijn citing *Andreas* l. 157 as an analogue.

502b-503   The MS reads: **7 þa minan ham / lange þæs þe ic of hæftum / ham gelǣdde.** The lines have been variously rewritten and punctuated. I follow Clubb and Krapp. Graz (23) emended **7 þa minan ham** to **in þam minnan ham,** and omitted **lange.** But **lange** is third sing. subj. of the impersonal **langian,** with **þǣs mænego** l. 502a as object. The **þæt** to introduce the **langian** clause has been omitted from the MS. **þæs þe** usually translates as "because," but here it seems to have the sense "that," and introduces the clause headed by **gelǣdde.** Clubb (*Notes,* p. 114) translates: "I was mindful that this company in this wretched home were longing that I should lead them from their bonds [to their heavenly] home."

504b   **sceolon:** Added to the MS by Clubb and Krapp, who follow Holthausen (*Indog. Forsch.,* 4 [1894], 383) and Graz (23) who propose **sculon.**

506   **wuniaδ . . . habbaδ:** This appears to be a present to indicate the future. But according to ll. 455-467, the souls to whom Christ addresses this speech may in fact be already in possession of bliss and glory.

509a   **galgan:** The MS **galgum** is probably owing to the influence of the preceding **garum,** or to the scribe's miscopying the MS before him, or to a mistake therein. As Clubb remarks (*Notes,* p. 114), **galgum** is never used of the cross. Cf. l. 548.

509b-511a   These lines mean that Christ rose to heaven, to the Father, immediately after his death on the cross. I have been able to find no support for this assertion (neither was Clubb successful in his search). The orthodox position is that Christ ascended to heaven forty days after the resurrection: cf. ll. 557-558.

512-514   These lines place the dialogue between Christ and the souls at some time before Easter Sunday morning.

515-519a   For one whom we have seen recently break the doors of hell (l. 308a), the grave, surely, would prove no obstacle.

515b   **stān:** The MS **satan** is clearly an error. Grein and all later editors read **stan.**

520b-521a   These lines in the MS read: **7 leofan gingran winum (sinum?). 7 huru secgan het. . . .** I follow Clubb and Krapp, who follow Holthausen (233), Graz (23) and Cosijn (25) in omitting **winum** as metrically obtuse, and construe **7 leofan** as **andleofan,** "eleven." In the New Testament, the angels at the tomb give their message to the three Marys who transmit it to the apostles. The change in tradition here may be due to the poet's wish to emphasize the establishment of the church, and, consequently, the role of Peter. See the notes to ll. 534b, 544.

526   The line is metrically defective but makes good sense if we assume **hāligne godes sunu** to be in apposition with **gāstes blēd.** The line, though, is different from the other independent half-lines in the poem, and is not included in Bliss's list of them. Although it just might be kept unemended, it seems safer to follow Grein (*Bibliothek*) and add **ongeton** before **haligne.** As Krapp remarks (*Notes,* p. 243),

"*bled* . . . ends a line in the MS, and it may be that something dropped out in passing from one line to the next."

528 The MS reads þa gingran on upp stod ece drihten. Clubb, whose reconstruction is by far the best of the many offered for this confused section, suggests omitting gingran as an anticipation of gingran in l. 529b, following Grein (*Bibliothek*). He accepts Holthausen's (*Indog. Forsch.*, 4 [1894], 383) gestod for MS stod as metrically necessary, thus giving the lines as they are in the text.

534b Note the emphatic position of Peter, here engaged in a conversation with Christ for which there is no biblical warrant. There may be a connection, though at some removes, with *John* 21:1ff., wherein, among other events, the primacy of Peter is noted.

538a hǣþene: Grein's emendation (*Bibliothek*) of MS hæþenne has been accepted by all editors.

540a Clubb finds ll. 540-544 "both syntactically and logically incoherent" (*Notes*, p. 118). But by accepting Bouterwek's, Grein's and Wülker's emendation of hie to hit, the hit referring specifically to the appearance of the risen Christ to Peter, and to the resurrection generally, and either emending mod to mode with Thorpe, Bouterwek and Holthausen (233), or assuming elision of the final e before a vowel, good sense and acceptable syntax are obtained. For the syllepses thus formed, see Appendix, p. 155.

541a se dēora: Surely a proper appellation for the disciple whose doubt, as Gregory remarks in *XL Homiliarum in Evangelia*, #26, *PL* 76, col. 1201, was divinely ordained that our doubts of the resurrection might be dispelled. Further, in John Cassian's *Liber de Incarnatione Christi*, Liber III, caput 14-15, *PL* 50, cols. 69-73, the affirmations of Peter and Thomas concerning the resurrection are connected with the faith of the whole church in that event.

544b bæðe: nom. pl., perhaps "a scribal blunder for *baðu* or *baðe*, or . . . a somewhat unusual form of the same" (Clubb, *Notes*, p. 120). The water and blood which the spear brought forth from the side of Christ (*John* 19:38) were from early times given sacramental significances: either simple baptism, or baptism and the eucharist. Clubb (*Notes*, p. 119) remarks another tradition which regards the passion itself as a second baptism—the first, that which took place at John's hands in the Jordan. But the citations Clubb offers to suggest that such a tradition of interpretation was available to our poet are not compelling: Ogilvy can find no knowledge of the writings of Cyril of Jerusalem (whose *Catecheses*, Liber III, De Baptismo, *PG* 33, col. 439, Clubb cites) or of Euthymius Zigabenus (whose *Commentaria in Joannem*, *PG* 129, col. 1474, Clubb cites). The other two commentators Clubb mentions were known to the Anglo-Saxons, but of the works he cites, Tertullian's *De Pudicitia*, *PL* 2, cols. 1029-84 has left no trace, while Rufinus' *Commentaria in Symbolum Apostolorum*, *PL* 21, cols. 335-86, is known only in MS Harley 3065, probably from the tenth century. Since baptism is the sacrament that admits the recipient into the mystical body of the church, and since the foundation of the *ecclesia* is of central concern to this middle section of Part II, it is appropriate to see in l. 544a reference to that first of sacraments. See notes to ll. 520b, 534b. The flow of water and blood from the side of Christ was also considered to be a type of the founding of the Church. In this capacity, it serves to link the ecclesiastical typology of Eve's action in ll. 406ff. with the emphasis on the activity of Peter, the rock upon which the church was built. See note to l. 406a.

547-548 The crucifixion is so described to emphasize the agency of Christ: this event happened because he willed it so. Cf. *Dream of the Rood,* 34, 40; *Christ* 727, 1172.

550b **weorcum:** Dietrich, Grein, and Wülker emend to **wordum,** taking account of **secgan,** l. 550a.

552b **sceolan:** Holthausen's addition of **sculon** (*Indog. Forsch.,* 4 [1894], 383), changed slightly by Clubb to harmonize with other occurrences of the term in the poem, completes the sense of the line.

553 An independent half-line. Clubb, following Bouterwek, adds **and duguðe þrym** to complete.

555 An independent half-line. Clubb, following Bouterwek, Grein and Wülker, reads ll. 554 **and we...** 555 **wuldres leoht** as one line. He offers, among analogues, *Andreas* ll. 1611-12: **Eow is wuldres leoht torht ontyned, gif ge teala hycgað.** The likeness is remarkable, and we may have here a formulaic system composed of three half-lines.

557-558 The duration of Christ's stay on earth between the resurrection and the ascension is forty days. Clubb, following a suggestion by Grein (note), inverts the half-lines of l. 558 to secure normal alliteration.

559a **mancynne:** The MS **mancynnes,** a gen. sing. after **gecyðed,** is strained. Grein's emendation improves matters.

561a **hāligne gāst:** Clearly the "holy spirit" of Christ. We have here an allusion to the ascension, not to Pentecost.

562-568 Cf. *Christ,* ll. 458-532; *Guðlac* 1314-16.

564b Early iconographical representations of the Father depict but a hand coming out of a cloud. See A. Didron, *Christian Iconography,* vol. 1, p. 201.

569b **gecwæð:** The addition to the line is Krapp's. It completes the sense and is metrically unexceptionable.

570a **tēne:** The MS **ane** is a mistake. Since Pentecost occurred ten days after the ascension, there is a substantive, as well as a formal alliterative, reason to accept Bright's emendation (130), as modified by Clubb: **tȳn-tēne.**

570b **twelf:** Holthausen (233) had proposed to emend to **andleofan** to restore the alliteration. But the place of Judas had been taken by Matthias before the descent of the Holy Ghost, so that **twelf** is substantively correct. See *Acts of the Apostles* 1:16ff. Further, as Bright notes, the poet has here used the term *apostolas* for the disciples, indicating, perhaps, the specific influence of *Acts* 1:26 (the only other use of the term *apostolas* is in *Men.* l. 122).

571a **his:** So strong is the Christocentricity of this poem that the Holy Ghost is here replaced, as it were, by the proper spirit of Christ. So we must conclude, unless we assume **his** to be a blunder for the demonstrative pronoun.

573b-578   It is not inappropriate for the poet to recall the situation of Judas who, had he remained faithful, would have received the gift of the spirit and become a charter member of the church.

585b   **hālig encgel**: For this somewhat peculiar denomination of Christ, see: Augustine, *Sermo #125, PL* 38, col. 691; Eucherius, *Liber Formularum Spiritalis Intelligentiae,* caput 3, *PL* 50, col. 739. There is nothing in this usage to suggest the heresy of Marcion or the Gnostics, which identified Christ with an angel properly so-called. But it is interesting to note that the representation of the Lord, and sometimes of the Holy Ghost, by the figure of a higher angel seems to be a trait proper to early Jewish Christianity: *Ascension of Isaiah* 8:23, 9:35, 11:33; *2 Enoch* 22:6, 24:1. J. Daniélou, *A History of Early Christian Doctrine before the Council of Nicea,* Volume I: *The Theology of Jewish Christianity,* trans. A. Baker (London, 1964), p. 117, notes that the term *angel* was a common appellation for Christ up to the fourth century. But Wülker emends to **encgla** with Dietrich, which, with **waldend**, disposes of any difficulty of interpretation.

587b   **swegl**: Clubb (*Notes,* p. 125) construes this form as an uninflected instrumental. Krapp (*Notes,* p. 244) proposes **swegle**.

593b   **teala**: Dietrich, Grein, Clubb and Krapp so add to regularize meter and alliteration.

597-662   This section of Part II comprises details of the last judgment. Cf. *Christ,* ll. 868ff.; *þe Domes Dæge; The Dream of the Rood* ll. 103-21; *Elene* ll. 1277ff. for similar descriptions.

598   All early editors assume a loss after **god**. But there is no break in the sense, and, as Krapp notes (following Stoddard, *Anglia,* 10 [1887], 162), there is no indication of a break in the MS, the repeat of the last word of page 226, **on**, as the first word of page 227 suggesting the contrary. We have here an independent half-line.

602   Another independent half-line. Clubb, following Grein and Holthausen (*Indog. Forsch,* 4 [1894], 383) adds **þa feower** after **geond** to complete the metrics.

607   Cf. *Revelations* 1:7; *Matthew* 24:30.

608a   The MS reading makes good sense, though it is strained metrically. **gescēawian** has here the sense of "show forth," "exhibit." Clubb, following Grein (*Bibliothek*), offers **gescearian** (but Grein reverted to the MS reading in *Germania,* 10 [1865], 420) to translate the Latin *separabit,* the poet here following the judgment scene as depicted in *Matthew* 25:31ff. Krapp, following Thorpe (note), Bouterwek and Graz (25), offers **gesceaden**.

613   Another independent half-line.

616-618   Cf. *Matthew* 25:34.

619a   **forworhtan**: A difficult decision. Alliteration and meter justify an emendation to **forhtan** (cf. l. 76b), following Graz (26) and Clubb. But, as Krapp remarks, "it is doubtful if the metrical gain compensates for the weakening of the sense" (*Notes,* p. 245).

624   **reordende:** The original reading, before the activity of the Corrector. We have another independent half-line.

626-627   *Matthew* 25:41.

625b   **gecwæð:** The Corrector emends to **gecwyð,** the present which the context requires. But **gecwæð** may be a Northern equivalent (see Sievers-Cook, p. 294, 391, n. 5) and so I leave it unchanged.

628-632a   Clubb (*Notes,* p. 127) finds parallels in MS B of the *Ethiopic Book of Enoch* 62:11; the fifteenth *Vercelli Homily;* MS CCCC 41, an O. E. homiletic version of *Nicodemus* (Hulme, *MP,* 1 [1903-04], 613); *Matthew* 13:49-50. We need not conclude, however, with Clubb, that "the poet was not drawing on his [own] invention" for the scene.

630b   **leaðað:** The Corrector's emendation to **lædað** seems an error. When compared with l. 588a, the similarity of the terms underscores the contrast between the places to which the blessed and damned are called.

634b   **þearlic:** Grein's emendation of **earmlic** remedies defective alliteration.

638b   **stæleð fēondas:** Clubb (*Notes,* pp. 128-29) proposes **feondas** to complete the line. As he remarks, the scribe in this section is obviously hurrying—thus the cramped writing—and it is quite likely that something has dropped out. Kock (*Anglia,* 27 [1903], 229-33) suggests that **(ge) stælan hwæt on hwone** is an idiom translating "lay something to someone's charge," thus accuse someone of something. Incorporating Cosijn's emendation (25) of MS **in firne** (l. 639a) to **firne,** Kock reads **Satanas stæleð / fæhðe and firne.** Clubb, however, supposes **stæleð** a form of the plural in **e** (see Sievers-Cook, p. 264, 360, n. 2; Campbell, pp. 301-302), believing it unlikely that the discourse **āsettað-stæleð** would be deranged by a change in the subject number. With Clubb's **feondas,** then, rather than a form of **Satan** as proposed by Grein, Holthausen (*Indog. Forsch.,* 4) and Kock, as subject of **stæleð,** the lines are restored.

639b   **frēodrihten:** Clubb and Krapp, following Grein, add **frēo** to MS **drihten** for alliteration. Cf. l. 433b for a similar scribal error.

641b   The *punctus versus* after **sceoldon** marks a significant shift in point of view, and thus I begin a new paragraph after it.

645-646   Clubb, followed by Krapp, assumes **sunu** (l. 646b) to be subject of **sittað,** with **eadige** and **selfe** in apposition. MS **swegle·torht** Clubb treats as an error for simple **swegle,** even though he remarks that **swegletorht** might stand for "a northern uninflected acc. masc. modifying *sunu.*" But it is likely that the MS reading is a mistake for **swegeltorhtne,** as Grein (note) proposed, which would suggest that **sunu** is an acc. sing. referring to Christ. Clubb justifies his cancellation by assuming that the scribe inserted **torht** between **swegle** and **sunu** "owing to the influence of the common phrase, *swegltorht.*" But since the MS page is remarkably crabbed and hurried, I rather believe that the scribe would drop an ending than add a word. On a different head, a homiletic charge to remember that the blessed ones are **mid swegle,** "in the clouds, the ether" is less striking than an assertion that they are **mid swegltorhtne sunu hǣlendes,** "with the heaven-bright son of the healer."

658a **ūp gelǣddest**: Unlike the instances of independent half-lines in the poem, there is clearly something lacking in l. 658. The addition of l. 658a is Grein's, accepted by Clubb and Krapp.

663-669 Transitional lines which serve to connect Part III with what has gone before. The **þæt** of l. 663a has as a specific referent the **self cyning** / **ealra aldor** of ll. 661b-662a; more generally, it refers to the Christ that has been revealed in Parts I and II. It may be that another section, [XIII], ought be indicated here. There is a brief summing up and a change in perspective similar to what we find in the first twelve lines of section [VIII], the poem's second major division. Page 228 which contains these lines shows every indication of a desire to save space: a sectional division might have been overlooked for the sake of economy, or in haste. Further, section [XII], ll. 597-729, is the largest division of *Christ and Satan* by some forty lines. A break at l. 663 would balance section [XII] and the hypothesized section [XIII] with other units of the work.

665-729 The poet follows the broad outlines of the temptation in the desert as found in *Matthew* 4:1-11. The second temptation is omitted, perhaps lost in one of the transcriptions antecedent to our MS. For a discussion of Part III in relation to Patristic tradition, see above, section II, pp. 33-36.

668a **of heofonum**: Sievers (*BGDSL*, 10 [1885], 514) offers **heah of heofonum**, Graz (26) **of heofonrice** to regularize the meter.

670b **brāde**: Clubb's note is worth quoting: "The qualification of *stānas* by *brāde* here was probably inspired by the fact that this adjective was used in a technical sense with *hlāf*, to signify *paximatium* (the overdone bread which served as part of the provisions on sea-voyages and military campaigns). Hence Satan is said to bring Christ broad, flat stones shaped like bread" (*Notes*, p. 131).

675-678 There appears to be a considerable gap in the MS at this point, and it is by no means certain that l. 675a is correctly placed. The lines which immediately follow, ll. 676-678, are clearly misplaced. Clubb correctly remarks that they would fit well after l. 658, if **ac** were emended to **and**. We can only assume the most glaring of scribal lapses either in the scribe responsible for this section of our MS, or in the scribe responsible for our manuscript's ancestor.

679 Bouterwek, Grein and Wülker read ll. 678-679 as one line. Graz (27) adds **halig scyppend**, Clubb **hæleða scyppend** as l. 679b. We may have an independent half-line here, but the condition of the text makes any judgment problematical.

684b **seolfes dom**: So all editors but Junius and Thorpe, who maintain MS **seoferdum**. Grein supplies **on** before **þines**, and so Wülker, Clubb and Krapp.

687b **gif**: The emendation to **þæt** in Grein and Wülker masks the conditional nature of what Satan believes to be Christ's power. If Christ is to be lord of angels and men, he must, according to Satan, receive that power from him. Have we here an echo of ll. 53-64 where, in another context, Satan arrogates to himself the paternity of Christ?

698b **hū wid and sīd**: Some form of the verb *to be* is understood.

699a **helheoðo**: A compound form, otherwise unattested, of **hel(l)** + **heoðu**, "hell-hall." Clubb emends to **heorodreorig**.

703   The MS reads: **and hu sid se swarta eðm seo**. Cosijn (25) transposes the **seo** after **sid**, and so Clubb and Krapp.

706b   The sense is clear, but the metrical pattern is peculiar. Sievers (*BGDSL*, 10 [1885], 515) and Graz (27) delete the **ward** of **inneward**. Cosijn (25) transposes **seo** after **deop**; Sievers (ibid., note) would place **seo** after **hu**.

708b   **tida**: Surely Clubb (*Notes,* pp. 134-35) is correct in rejecting Kock's suggestion (14) that this be glossed "years." The whole thrust of the closing lines is that Satan is defeated by Christ and made to do his will, and some poetic license ought be allowed in this demonstration: a Satan speedily measuring his torments at Christ's command is a properly degrading and ludicrous spectacle.

709a   **merced**: Clubb (*Notes*, p. 135) argues that there is no evidence of a verb **mercian** or **myrcian** from the adjective **myrce**, "dark," "murky," and so construes the form to be derived from **mercian**, "mark," "design," "appoint." Perhaps, and I have so treated it in the glossary. But it was common practice to derive weak verbs from adjectives, and what we may have here is a nonce formation on the adjective base.

710a   **wērigan**: So all editors but Junius and Clubb, who accept MS **werga**. Clubb construes this as dat. sing. masc. weak adj., equivalent to **wergan**.

710b   **wracu**: So all editors but Junius and Clubb, who accept MS **wrece**, which Clubb construes as equivalent to **wracu**.

712   This line is defective in alliteration. **æglēce** is a Northern variant of nom. sing. See Sievers-Cook, p. 201, 276, n. 5; Campbell, p. 249.

716a   **hē**: Nom. plural.

717   There is a gap, probably slight, after this line. The line is defective in alliteration.

720   Cf. ll. 97a, 379b, 465.

722a   **synne**: Clubb accepts Grein's emendation (*Germania,* 10 [1865], 420) to **sinne**, a possible reading if the line is understood to refer to Christ. But if it refers to Satan, then the MS reading ought be kept, since Satan is then commanded to measure sufferings "because of (þurh) sinful craft," a perfectly proper reason for Christ's condemnation: we have seen the arrogance of sin in the temptation.

723   The line is defective in alliteration: Grein (*Bibliothek*) offers **þæt he gaste gemunde**, Holthausen (*Indog. Forsch.,* 4 [1894], 383) suggests **gemde** for **gemunde**, **þæt** for the second **þa**. I accept, with Krapp, the substitution of **þæt** for **þa** as rendering the sense more exactly.

724-729   These lines present insuperable metrical and alliterative problems. They make good sense, however, and so I print them as in the MS.

725b-726   There are two ways to read these lines. Either **gryre** is the nom. subj. of **āstāg** with **mænego** as a dependent gen., or the latter is the subj. of **āstāg** with the former as an instrumental. I lean towards the first choice, with Krapp (*Notes,* p. 247).

727a   The MS reads **inwitum**. I follow Grein (*Bibliothek*), Clubb and Krapp, rather than read the half-line as an adverbial phrase.

727b   The MS reads **ongunnon þa on þa**, the **on þa** apparently a repetition of the two preceding syllables.

FINIT LIBER II   If we assume that *Christ and Satan* alone composed Liber II, then Liber I would consist of *Genesis, Exodus* and *Daniel*. The original plan of the MS may have called for other works in this hypothetical Liber I, or in Liber II for that matter, but the manuscript evidence, with page 212, the last page of the *Daniel*, forming the left-hand leaf of which page 229, the last page of *Christ and Satan*, is the right, suggests that whoever was responsible for the inclusion of our poem in the MS intended it as an integral part of the whole. Gollancz (p. lxxxix) and Krapp (p. xii) believe that the *Daniel* is incomplete, and that the rubric *Finit Liber I*, or some other such indication, was thus lost. (But see the two articles by Robert T. Farrel, "The Unity of the Old English *Daniel*," *RES* (ns), 18 [1967], 117-35, and "The Structure of Old English *Daniel*," *NM*, 69 [1968], 533-59, which argue for the essential completeness of the work.)

THE GLOSSARY

The glossary records and identifies all forms used in the poem. æ follows ad, þ and ð follow t. ę, ȝ and ƿ have been transcribed here as well as in the text by æ, g and w. Verbs are listed initially in the infinitive; when tense and mood are not indicated, supply "present indicative." All forms of the verb "to be" are found under **wesan**. Nouns are listed initially under "nominative singular," adjectives under "nominative singular masculine." Separable prefixes are considered part of the form: **gemunan** will be found under **g**, not **m**. Forms marked * are found in the poetic corpus only in *Christ and Satan*.

A

ā, adv., ever, for ever, always: 314(2), 361, 396, 618.

ābelgan, III, anger, offend, provoke: pret. 1s. ābealh, 408; opt. 3s. ābælige, 194.

ābēodan, II, offer, announce: opt. 2s. ābēode, 694.

Abraham, pr. n.: gs. Abrahames, 459.

ac, see ah.

ād, m., flame, fire: gs. 330.

Ādām, pr. n.: ns. 20, 409; gs. Ādāmes, 406; as. Adām, 471.

ādrēogan, II, bear, suffer, endure: inf. 636.

ādrīfan, I, drive, expel: pret. 3s. ādrāf, 200; inf. 173, 186, 255.

ādwǣscan, WI., extinguish, quench: inf. 305.

æfre, adv., ever, for ever, always: 50, 115, 139, 141, 170, 229, 266, 276, 296, 303, 388, 411, 449, 596, 633.

æfter, prep., w. dat., after: 26, 628.

æghwā, pron., every one: ds. æghwǣm, 362.

æghwǣr, adv., everywhere: 341, 478.

æghwylc, pron., each, every (one or thing): ns. 193; gs. æghwylces, 272; dsm. æghwylcum, 264.

æglǣca, m., wretch, demon, fiend: ns. 160, 578; āglǣca, 446; ægléce, 712; np. æglécan, 73.

ǣht, f., possession: ds. 87, 116, 252, 278, 452.

ælmihtig, adj., almighty: nsm. 598; nsm. wk. ælmihtiga, 287.

ǣne, adv., once: 408.

ǣnig, pron., any: dsf. ǣnigum, 145.

æpl, m., apple: gs. eaples, 409; ap. æpla, 481.

ǣr, adv., before, formerly, previously, beforehand: 74, 116, 122, 244, 253, 278, 289, 302, 365, 382, 388, 492, 513, 523, 574, 667, 688, 729; comp. ǣrror, 150, 298; sup. ǣrest, first: 20, 322, 471, 702.

ǣr, prep., w. dat., before: 464.

ǣr, conj., before: 407, 501, 542, 559, 708.

æt, prep., w. dat., at, by, near: 97, 337, 536, 661.

ætsomne, adv., together: 41, 126, 524.

æðele, adj., noble, excellent, glorious: dsm. wk. æþelan, 237; nsn. wk. 20; asn. wk. 471; npm. æðele, 46.

āfirran, WI., remove, put away, expel: pret. 3s, āfirde, 67; āfyrde, 477; opt. 3s. āfirre, 283.

āfyllan, WI., fill: pp. āfylled, 99.

āfyrhtan, WI., frighten, terrify: pp. npm. āfyrhte, 383.

āgan, prp., have, possess, own, get possession of, obtain: 3s, āh, 117; 3p. āgon, 360; pret. ls. āhte, 106; 2s. āhtest, 55, 59; opt. pret. lp. āhton, 412; inf. 86, 95, 121, 146, 173, 175, 251, 313, 369, 504, 552. Negative: nāgan: lp. 100.

āgangan, red., go by, pass: pp. āgangen, 499; npf. āgongene, 708.

āgen, adj., own: nsn. 10.

agēn, adv., again, anew: 76.

āgend, m., possessor, Lord: ns. 676.

āgēotan, II, pour out, shed: pret. 3s. āgēat, 547.

ah, conj., but: 267, 291, 331, 346, 448, 518, 634, 693, 695; ac: 30, 111, 124, 406, 624, 676.

āhebban, VI, raise, lift: 3s. āhefeð, 310; pret. 3s. āhōf, 680.

ālǣdan, WI., lead out: pp. ālǣded, 177.

ald, adj., old, ancient: nsm. wk. alda, 34.

aldor, n., age, life (ā tō aldre, for ever): ds. aldre, 312, 361, 618.

aldor, m., chief, prince: ns. 76, 322, 662; ealdor, 372, 566.

aldorðægn, m., chief, prince: as. 66.

ālēfan, WI, grant: inf. 115, 277.

alwihte, fp., all creatures, all created things: gp. alwihta, 615, 669, 696.

āmetan, V, measure: opt. 3s. āmǣte, 722; imp. 2s. āmet, 699, 702; pp. āmeten, 709; asn. āmetene, 705.

ān, num., one, a certain, alone, only: nsm. 26; dsm. ānum, 55; asm. ænne, 675; gpm. ānra, 430; dpf. ānum, 146; wk. nsm. āna, 32, 247, 259, 583.

and, and (as 7 in the MS): 2, 4, 5, 6, 8, 11, 15, 19, 20, 32, 42, 48(2), 49, 52, 56, 60, 79, 83, 87, 104, 111, 112, 118, 119, 131, 151, 173, 174, 184(2), 191, 205, 207, 218, 219, 221, 225, 233, 237, 240, 241, 244, 246, 247, 270, 274, 288, 290, 297, 302, 320, 324, 333(2), 334, 335(2), 336(2), 339, 341, 347, 359, 364, 375, 376, 380, 396, 406, 418, 423, 424, 430, 443, 446, 452, 453, 456, 466, 471, 475, 481, 494, 495, 497, 501, 505, 510, 519, 521, 523, 531, 547, 550, 554, 565, 581, 584, 605, 608, 609, 614, 630, 632, 635(2), 636, 639, 650, 651, 654, 656, 657, 680, 681, 685, 686, 688, 698, 699, 702, 703, 706, 711.

andfeng, m. guardian: ns. 243.

andleofan, num., eleven: 520.

andsaca, m., adversary, enemy: ns. 190; np. andsacan, 279, 339, 717; ap. andsacan, 268.

andswarian, W2, answer, reply: pret. 3s. andswarode, 673, 689; 3p. andsweradan, 51.

andwlita, m., countenance: as. andwlitan, 377.

ānforlǣtan, red., abandon, forsake: pp. ānforlǣten, 226.

anwalda, m., ruler, sovereign: asm. anwaldan, 207, 640.

apostol, m., apostle: ap. apostolas, 570.

ār, f., favour, mercy, grace: gp. āra, 207.
āriman, WI., count: inf. 11.
ārīsan, I arise, rise: 3p. ārīsað, 604; pret. 3s. ārās, 236, 238, 430, 514.
āscēadan, red., separate, exclude, cut off: pp. āscēaden, 176.
āsecgan, W3., declare: inf. 350.
*āsellan, WI., expel: pp. āseald, 89.
āsettan, WI., set, set down, plant: 3p. āsettað, 637; pret. ls. āsette, 479; 3s. 682.
āstīgan, I, arise, ascend, mount; descend: pret. 3s. āstāh, 547, 562, 681; āstāg, 715, 726; imp. 2p. āstīgað, 626.
atol, adj., dire, fierce, horrible, loathsome; as substantive: devil, fiend: nsm. 160, 680, 725; wk. atola, 95, 411, 485; nsf. atol, 61; gsm. wk. atolan, 326; dsm. wk. 107; asm. wk. 716; asn. wk. atole, 26, 73, 128; npm. atole, 51; wk. atolan, 446; dpm. wk. 382.
atol, n., terror, horror: as. 393; is. atole, 136, 452(? is. or dat. sing. used adverbially).
āttor, n., poison: ds. āttre, 162; is. 40, 128, 317; ātre, 79.
āwa, adv., for ever: 312.
āweorpan, III, cast out, expel: pp. āworpen, 180, 667.
āwrītan, I, write: pp. āwriten, 674.
āwyrged, adj., accursed: nsm. wk. āwyrgda, 315; gsm. wk. āwærgdan, 414; vsm. āwyrgda, 674, 690, 698; vpm. āwyrgde, 626.

B

bæc, n., back: ds. bæce, 157.
bæcling, adv., only used with on: back, backwards, behind: 697.
bættra, see gōd.
bæð, n., bath: np. bæðe, 544.
balu, adj., baleful, wicked, pernicious: nsm. wk. balewa, 482; apm. balewe, 486.
bān, n., bone: np. 466.
be, prep., w. dat. and instr., by, with: 267, 543.
bealo, n., bale, woe, evil: gs. bealowes, 681, 718; as. 71; ap. beala, 273.
bēam, m., tree, cross: ds. bēame, 508, 547.
bearm, m., lap: ds. bearme, 152, 356, 670.
bearn, n., child, son: ns. 10, 586, 620; ds. 152; as. 86, 194, 576; np. 143; gp. bearna, 473; dp. bearnum, 398, 581.
bebycgan, WI, sell: pret. 3s. bebohte, 576.
becuman, IV, come, arrive: pret. ls. becōm, 510, becwōm, 178; 3s. becōm, 243, 378, 385, 404, 464.
bedǣlan, WI., deprive, free: pret. 3s. bedēlde, 68; pp. bedǣled, 185; bedēled, 121; npm. bedǣlde, 343; npf. 295.
bedrīfan, I, drive, force: pret. 3s. bedrāf, 191.
befæðman, WI., embrace: 3s. befæðmeð, 309, 358; inf. 288.
beforan, adv., before, present before: 485.
beforan, prep., w. dat., before: 387.
bēgan, WI., bend, bend down: pret. 3s. bēgde, 380.
bēgen, num., both: d. bām, 486.
begitan, V, beget, bring forth: pret. 3p. begēton, 472.
*begrēosan, II, render fearful, horrify: pp. npm. begrorenne, 52.
behōfian, W2, need: 3s. behōfað, 208.

bēme, f., trumpet: gs. bēman, 171, 236; ap. bēman, 601.
benǽman, WI., deprive: inf. 345; pp. benēmed, 120.
bend, m., bond, fetter: as. 537; dp. bendum, 49, 412.
beofian, W2., tremble: pres. p. beofigende, 620.
beoran, IV, bear: opt. lp. beoran, 204; pret. 3p. bǽron, 481; inf. 157.
beorh, m., mountain: as. 681.
beorht, adj., bright, splendid, glorious, beautiful, clear: asm. byrhtne, 362; asf. wk. beorhtan, 138; apm. beorhte, 294; apf. beorhte, 416; wk. beorhtan, 482; sup. gsf. wk. byrhtestan, 171.
beorhte, adv. brightly: 213, 294.
beorn, m., soldier: np. beornas, 508.
beornan, III, burn: 3s. beorneð, 412; pres. p. beornende, 71, 157.
bescyrian, WI., deprive, cut off from: pp. npm. bescyrede, 342.
beteldan, III, cover: pp. betolden, 587.
bewindan, III, encircle: pp. bewunden, 648.
bīdan, I, abide, dwell, endure: inf. 27, 49.
biddan, V, ask, pray for, bid: pret. 3s bæd, 436, 671; inf. 207.
bilewit, adj., guileless: asm. bilewitne, 240.
biter, adj., bitter, dire: gsm. bitres, 273; asm. wk. biteran, 148.
bitere, adv., bitterly, cruelly: 416.
blāc, adj., black, pale, livid: nsm. blāc, 718; npm. blāce, 71; wk. blācan, 195.
blǽd, m., blessedness, joy, honour: ns. 362; blēd, 592; as. blǽd, 42, 412, 506; blēd, 525, 644.
blǽd, f., fruit: ap. blǽda, 416, 482.
blāwan, red., blow, sound: inf., 601.
blis, f., bliss, exultation, joy: ns. 380.
blīðe, adj., happy: npm. 612; apm. 204.
blōd, n., blood: as. 547.
blōstma, m., flower, blossom: gs. blōstman, 356.
bold, n., home, palace: ds. bolde, 148; gp. bolda, 138; ap. bold, 686.
botm, m., bottom: ds. botme, 718.
brād, adj., broad, flat: nsm. wk. brāde, 213; apm. brāde, 670.
brecan, IV, break, burst through: pret. 3s. bræc, 380.
brēost, n., breast: dp. brēostum, 204.
***breoton**, adj., spacious: apn. breotone, 686.
bringan, WI., bring, carry: 3p. bringað, 356; pret. 3s. brōhte, 670; lp. brōhton, 152; inf. 148, 560.
brūcan, II, possess, enjoy: inf. 137.
brynewelm, m., burning heat or surge: is. brynewelme, 27.
brytta, m., lord: ns. 123; np. brytan, 23.
burh, f., city, citadel: ds. byrig, 622; as. burh, 457, 612, 686; gp. burga, 86, 138, 601; dp. burgum, 213.
burhlēod, m., citizen: gp. burhlēoda, 560.
burhstyde, m., city, citadel: as. 362.
burhweall, m., city-wall: ap. burhweallas, 294.
būtan, prep., w. dat., without: 146, 677; būton, 314, 378.
būton, conj., except, save: 389.
***byrhtword**, n. (substantive), Brightword = the Son, Christ: n. 236.
bysen, f., example: ds. bysne, 195.

C

cald, adj., cold: asm. wk. caldan, 635.

carcern, n., prison: gs. carcernes, 488; as. 635.

ceald, n., cold: ns. 131.

cearig, adj., sorrowful: dpm. cearium, 67.

cēosan, II, choose: lp. cēosan, 202.

cerran, WI., turn, direct one's course: imp. 2s. cer. 697; inf. 215.

cester, f., city: ds. cestre, 256, 655; as. cestre, 297.

clēne, adv., wholly, entirely, altogether: 7, 18.

cleopian, W2., cry: 3s. cleopað, 34, 615.

clom, m., bond, chain, bondage: ns. 102; as. 156, 451, 488, 635; ap. clomma, 442.

costian, W2., tempt: pret. 3s. costode, 669.

cræft, m., power, might, cunning: as. 390, 584, 722.

cræftig, adj., ingenious: nsm. 348.

Crīst, pr. n., Christ: ns. 67, 203, 569; ds. Crīste, 215, 595; as. 345.

cuman, IV, come: 3s. cymeð, 606; 3p. cumað, 300, 355; pret. ls. cōm, 109; 3s. cōm, 36, 322, 391, 401, 424, 455, 563.

cunnan, prp., know, understand, can: ls. can, 248; con. 627; pret. ls. cūðe, 141; opt. 2s. cunne, 701; 3s. cunne, 17.

cūð, adj., known, evident, safe, nsn. 256, 582; comp. nsn. cūðre, 595.

cwānian, W2, bewail, lament: pret. 3p. cwānedon, 319.

cwealm, m., death, torment, pain: as. 497.

cwēman, WI., please, serve: 3p. cwēmað 653; opt. lp. cwēman, 595; inf. 183, 304.

cweðan, V, say, speak: 3p. cweþað, 655; pret. 3p. cwædon, 227; pret. 3s. cwæð, 305, 407; inf. 728.

cwide, m., phrase, words: dp. cwidum, 67.

cwīðan, WI., lament: pret. 3s. cwīðde, 159.

cyle, m., cold: as. 334.

cyn, n., race, people, kin: ns. 20; cynn, 459; as. 406; cynn, 133, 352.

cynestōl, m., royal city or throne: as. 297.

cyning, m., king: ns. 259, 661, 687; cynincg, 615; gp. cyninga, 203; ds. cyninge, 203; as. 256, 655, 669, 697.

cyrr, m., occasion, time: ds. cyrre, 536.

cȳðan, WI., make known, proclaim: inf. cȳþan, 297.

D

dǣd, f., deed: ns. 575; gp. dǣda, 621; ip. dǣdum, 155, 550.

dæg, m., day: ns. 104; gs. dæges, 497; vs. 165; gp. daga, 12, 558, 605, 665; dp. dagum, 15.

dægrēd, n., dawn, daybreak: ds. dægrēde, 464; as. 402.

dǣl, m., portion, region, quarter: ap. dǣles, 16.

dǣlan, WI., portion out, distribute: 3s. dǣleð, 580.

dēad, adj., dead: npm. dēade, 604.

dēað, m., death: gs. dēaðes, 453, 497; ds. dēaðe, 514; as. 460, 663.

dēma, m., judge: ds. dēman, 379.

dēman, WI., judge, proclaim: opt. lp. dēman, 298; inf. 108, 621.

dēofol, n., devil: gs. dēofles, 636; np. dēofla, 318; gp. dēofla, 110, 726.

dēop, adj., deep: nsf. dēop, 706; asm. dēopne, 7, 636; wk. dēopan, 30; asn. dēop, 343.

deorc, adj., dark, gloomy: asm. deorcne, 453; npm. deorce, 104.
dēore, adj., dear, beloved: nsm. 82; wk. dēora, 241, 541; dsm. wk. dēoran, 217, 255.
Didimus, pr. n.: ns. 541.
dim, adj., dim: dsm. wk. dimman, 110; asm. dimne, 453; wk. dimman, 336; npm. dimme, 104.
dōgor, m., day: gp. dōgra, 241, 580.
dohtor, f., daughter: ds. dohtor, 437.
dōm, m., glory, majesty, dignity: as. 684, is. dōme, 535; ap. dōmas, 505, 553.
dōmdæg, m., doomsday, judgment day: ds. dōmdæge, 599.
dōmlēas, adj., inglorious: asn. wk. dōmlēase, 230.
dōn, anv., do: pret. 3s. dyde, 116, 278, 523; 3p. dydon, 190, 623.
draca, m., dragon: np. dracan, 97; ap. dracan, 336.
drēam, m., joy, bliss, rapture; melody, music: ns. 79, 93, gs. drēames, 167, 173; drēamas, 181; as. 82, 121, 292, 313, 327, 353; vs. 165; gp. drēama, 313; ap. drēamas, 19, 44, 510, 678; ip. drēamum, 68, 343.
drēogan, II, do, bear, endure: pret. lp. drugon, 253; 3p. 74; inf. 184, 230.
drēorig, adj., mournful: nsm. wk. drēorga, 392, nsf., 699.
driht, f., multitude: ds. 176.
drihten, m., lord: ns. 108, 217, 239, 260, 395, 402, 441, 450, 460, 514, 518, 528, 557, 580, 599, 625, 663, 673, 689; gs. drihtnes, 230, 505, 553, 604; drihtenes, 163; dryhtnes, 68; ds. drihtne, 155, 313, 392, 511, 550, 589; dryhtene, 44, 82; as. drihten, 47, 173, 186, 197, 201, 220, 255, 575, 682; vs. drihten, 408, 437, 535.
dropa, m., drop: gp. dropena, 12.
dugan, prp., be good, virtuous: pret. 3s. dēah, 282.
duguð, f., men, host, glory: gs. duguðe, 505; ds. duguðe, 19; gp. duguða, 163; ip. duguðum, 121.
dūn, f., mountain: as. dūne, 682.
duru, f., door, gate: ds. 97; ap. 379, 465.
dūst, n., dust: ds. dūste, 604.
dyne, m., din: ns. 379, 392, 402, 464; gp. dinna, 605.

E

ēac, adv., also, furthermore: 698; ēc, 325.
ēadig, adj., happy, blessed, prosperous: nsm. 303; gsm. ēadiges, 92; dsm. wk. ēadigan, 658; asm. ēadigne, 143, 292, 353; npm. ēadige, 645; wk. ēadigan, 355; npf. ēadige, 266, 651; gpm. ēadigre, 219; apf. ēadige, 405.
ēage, n., eye: ip. ēagum, 139, 169, 388, 716; ēgum, 725.
ēalā, interj., O, alas: 163(2), 164(2), 165(2), 166(2), 167, 315.
eall, adj., all, everything, wholly: nsm. 136, 516; nsn. 224, 321, 463; gsn. ealles, 106, 167; alles, 55, 117, 181, 329; asm. alne, 8, 701; asf. ealle, 253; asn. eall, 87, 252; npm. ealle, 149, 153, 196, 383, 432, 530, 655; alle, 61; npn. ealle, 143; gpm. ealra, 203; gpf. ealra, 222, 440, 583; alra, 202; gpn. ealra, 662; alra, 60; dpm. eallum, 243, 247; apm. ealle, 525, 615, 625; alle, 92; apn. ealle, 126; eall, 391.
eallbeorht, adj., all-bright: apm. eallbeorhte, 520.
eard, m., land, country, home, fatherland: ds. earde, 92, 229, 456, 504; as. 115, 202; gp. earda, 112.

eardian, W2, dwell: 3s. eardað, 591; 3p. eardigað, 97.

ēare, n., ear: ip. ēarum, 170.

earfoðe, n., affliction, trouble: ap. earfoðo, 126.

earm, m., arm: as. 430.

earm, adj., miserable, wretched, wicked: nsm. 119, 446, 578, 712; wk. earme, 87; npm. earme, 73.

ēce, adj., eternal, everlasting: nsm. 18, 117, 239, 260, 440, 441, 528, 557, 625, 673, 689; wk. ēca, 276, 456, 530; gsm. wk. ēcan, 167, 181; dsm. wk. ēcan, 372; dsf. ēcan, 662; asm. ēcne, 198, 202, 523, 640; wk. ēcan, 46, 377; asf. ēce, 618; vsm. 408; apm. 510.

ēce, adv., eternally, perpetually: æce, 97.

edcerr, m., return: gs. edcerres, 449.

edwīt, n., reproach, scorn, mockery: as. 637, 680.

Ēfe, pr. n., Eve: n. 406.

eft, adv., again, afterwards, hereafter: 21, 75, 210, 227, 373, 476, 477, 510, 539.

egeslic, adj., terrible: nsm. 432.

egsa, m., terror, torment: ns. 378, 391, 404; gs. egsan, 452, 725; is. egsan, 383; ap. egsan, 485.

*eisig, adj., terrible, dreadful: isf. wk. eisegan, 36.

encgelcyn, n., order of angels: ns. 365.

ende, m., end, period: ns. 40; ds. 314, 378, 677.

*enderīm, n., number, final total: as. 12.

endestæf, m., end: as. 539.

engel, m., angel: ns. ængel, 81; encgel, 585; np. englas, 60, 353; gp. ængla, 94; engla, 21, 36, 166, 198, 219, 237, 301, 386, 395, 401, 422, 489, 518, 533, 562, 567, 651, 657, 664, 688; dp. ænglum, 122; englum, 141, 247, 287, 292, 329, 389, 590, 623; ap. englas, 520.

eorl, m., man: np. eorlas, 476.

eorre, adj., angry, fierce: nsm. 260, 427.

eorðbūende, mp., dp. eorðbūendum, 1.

eorðe, f., earth: gs. eorðan, 16, 56, 657; ds. eorðan, 244, 266, 289, 298, 302, 355, 494, 557, 596; as. eorðan, 5.

esl, f., shoulder: as. esle, 680.

etan, V, eat: pret. 2p. æton, 481; æten, 485.

ēðel, m., hereditary home, country, land: gs. ēðles, 326; ds. ēðle, 401, 459, 476, 494, 552; æðele, 107; as. ēðel, 278; æðel, 107, 116.

ēðm, m., vapour: ns. 703.

F

fācne, adj., wicked, factious: ip. fācnum, 65.

fæder, m., father: ns. 309, 358; gs. 307; fæderes, 579; ds. fæder, 317.

fægen, adj., glad, elated: npm. fægen, 433.

fæger, adj., fair, beautiful, sweet: nsm. 79; nsn. 455, 545; asm. fægerne, 328; comp. nsn. fægere, 387; asn. fægere, 211.

fægre, adv., beautifully, elegantly: 307.

fæhðe, f., feud, hostility, enmity: ns. 403; as. 639.

fæmne, f., virgin: gs. fæmnan, 493.

fæst, adj., fast, firmly fastened: ipm. fæstum, 39.

fæstan, WI., to fast: pret. 3s. fæste, 665.
fæste, adv., fast, firmly: 323; feste, 58, 103.
fæsten, n., prison, sepulchre; ds. fæstenne, 519.
fæstlic, adj., firm, perpetual: nsm. 324.
fāh, adj., guilty, hostile: nsm. 96, 127, 155, 185, 478; dsm. fāgum, 109.
fāh, adj., stained, spotted: nsm. 179.
faran, VI, go, proceed, come: 3s. færeð, 607; inf. 405, 441.
feallan, red., fall, fall down: pret. 3p. feollon, 531, 544.
fela, n. indecl., many, much: 400, 495; feola, 475; feolo, 419; adverbial: feola, 159.
feond, m., fiend, devil: ns. 477; as. 403, 461; np. 103, 195; feondas, 638; gp. feonda, 76; ap. feondas, 223; dp. feondum, 443.
feor, adv., far away, distant: 40.
feowertig, num., forty: 473, 558, 665.
feran, WI., go, journey: 3s. fereð, 387; 3p. feraò, 652; pret. 3s. ferde, 493; inf. 109.
feða, m., band, host, company: ns. 455; ds. feþan, 323; np. feðan, 219.
firen, f., sin, crime, iniquity, torment: as. firne, 639; gp. firna, 159; dp. firenum, 477; firnum, 433; fyrnum, 127.
firenfull, adj., sinful, wicked; npm. firenfulle, 65.
firnian, W2, sin: pret. 3p. firnedon, 619.
fleogan, II, fly: pret. 3s. fleah, 161; inf. 263.
flōr, m., floor, ground: ns. 39, 317; ds. flōra, 109; ap. flōras, 70.
flyge, m., flight: ds. 111.
flyht, m., flight: ds. flyhte, 111.
folc, n., people, multitude: as. folc, 685; ip. folcum, 558.
folde, f., earth, ground: ns. 211; gs. foldan, 3, 602; ds. foldan, 493, 544, as. foldan, 263, 531, 685.
folgað, m., service: as. 328.
folgian, W2., follow, attend: pp. folgad, 558.
folm, palm, hand: ip. folmum, 712.
fōn, red., receive: imp. 2s. fōh, 685.
for, prep., w. dat., before, in the presence of, for, because of, through, by: 44, 50, 62, 69, 74, 83, 105, 196, 226, 281, 379, 392, 421, 427, 663, 671.
forbēgan, WI., bend, crush: pret. 3s. forbēgde, 466.
forbrecan, IV, break, break in pieces, destroy: pret. 3s. forbræc, 466.
forgifan, V, give: pret. 3s. forgeaf, 486.
forgildan, III, pay back, requite: pret. 3s. forgeald, 416, 577.
forgitan, V, forget: pret. 3p. forgēaton, 640.
forht, adj., fearful, terrified: nsm. 76.
forlǣtan, red., let go, send forth, forsake, abandon, lose: 3s. forlǣteð, 291; pret. 3s. forlēt, 543; pp. forlēton, 69.
forscrīfan, I, proscribe, condemn: pp. forscrifen, 33.
forscyppan, VI, transform, disfigure: pp. npm. forscepene, 72.
forð, adv., out, forth, forward, thenceforth: 246, 296, 323, 400, 473, 565.
forðon, adv., wherefore, therefore, hence: 119, 337; forþon, 282, 303, 483, 549; forþan, 193.
forweorðan, III, be destroyed, perish: pret. 3s. forwarð, 21; 3p. forwurdon, 196.

forworhta, m., evildoer, malefactor: np. 619.
forwundian, W2, wound grievously: pp. forwundod, 130.
fōt, m., foot: dp. fōtum, 531.
fram, prep., w. dat., from: 176, 177, 437; from, 494.
frēcne, adj., bold, wicked: apm. 283.
frēferian, W2., comfort, console: pres. p. ds. frēfergendum, 317.
frēobearn, n., noble child: ns. 288.
frēodrihten, m., noble lord: ns. 433, 545; as. 565, 639.
fruma, m., ruler, prince: ns. 560.
frumbearn, n., first-born child: ns. 468.
ful, adv., full, very: 151, 224, 683; full, 321.
fulwiht, m. or n., baptism: gs. fulwihtes, 544.
furðor, adv., further: 223, 443.
fyllan, WI., fill: pp. gefylled, 136.
fȳr, n., fire: ns. 263; is. fȳre, 79, 96, 324; as. 334.
*__fȳrclom__, m., fiery chain: ip. fȳrclommum, 39.
fyrd, f., army, host: ds. fyrde, 468.
*__fȳrlēoma__, m., fiery light or radiance: ns. 127.
*__fȳrloca__, m., fiery cell or dungeon: ds. fȳrlocan, 58.
fyrndagas, mp., olden days: d. fyrndagum, 461.

G

galga, m., gibbet, cross: ds. galgan, 509, 548.
Galilēa, pr. n., Galilee: ds. Galilēam, 522, 525, 529.
gān, anv., go: pret. 3s. ēode, 518; imp. 2p. gāð, 616.
gār, m., spear: ip. gārum, 509.
gāst, m., spirit, soul: ns. 125, 681, 718; gs. gāstes, 525, 548, 571, 644; as. 14, 561; np. gāstas, 51, 628, 651, 727; gp. gāsta, 242; vp. gāstas, 469.
gāstlice, adv., spiritually: 300.
gēar, n., year: gp. gēara, 501.
geara, adj., prepared, ready: nsf(n?). geara, 692.
gēardagas, mp., the olden days, days of yore: dp. gēardagum, 367.
gearwian, W2., make ready, prepare: opt. lp. gearwian, 286.
geat, n., gate: ns. 647.
gebēgan, WI., depress, abase, crush: pp. gebēged, 444.
gebīdan, I, abide, await, endure: pret. ls. gebād, 494; inf. 107.
gebindan, III, bind, fasten, secure: pp. gebunden, 38, 58, 103, 323.
geblētsian, W2., bless: pret. 3s. geblētsode, 240.
geblondan, red., mingle, mix: pp. geblonden, 128.
gecwēme, adj., pleasing, acceptable: gpm. gecwēmra, 215.
gecweðan, V, speak, say: pres. (?) 3s. gecwæð, 625; pret. ls. gecwæð, 122, 3s. 569.
gecȳðan, WI., reveal, show, prove: pret. 3s. gecȳdde, 199; pp. gecȳðed, 559.
gedēlan, WI., distribute, allot, give out: pret. 3s. gedēlde, 19.
gedūfan, II, dive, plunge, sink: pret. 3s. gedēaf, 668; inf. 30.
gefæstnian, W2., fix, set firmly, establish: pret. 3s. gefestnade, 3; pp. gefæstnod, 515.
gefatian, WI., fetch, summon: inf. 519.
gefēa, m., joy: as. gefēan, 198.

gefeallan, red., fall, plunge: pret. 3s. gefēol, 711.
gefēlan, WI., feel: pret. 3s. gefēlde, 77.
gefēran, WI., fare: pp. gefēred, 62.
geferian, WI., carry, lead, bring: inf. 147; pp. gefærde, 91.
geflēman, WI., put to flight: pp. geflēmed, 461.
gefrætwian, W2., adorn, ornament; pp. gefrætewod, 307, 647.
gefrignan, III, learn, hear: pret. 1s. gefregn, 524; gefregen, 223.
*geglīdan, I, slip, fall: inf. 375.
gehealdan, red., keep, retain possession of: pret. 3s. gehēold, 346.
*gehēaw, n., gnashing: ns. 338.
gehēnan, WI., humble, overthrow: pp. gehēned, 189.
gehēran, WI., hear: 1s. gehēre, 132; pret. 1p. gehērdon, 235; inf. 170, 327, 337, pp. gehēred, 332, 606.
gehrēowan, red., grieve, cause to rue or repent: pret. 3s. gehrēaw, 373, 487; inf. 538.
gehrīnan, I, touch, lay hold of: inf. 266.
gehwā, pron., each, every: ism, gehwæm, 580.
gehwylc, pron., each, every, every one: nsm. 284, 430 (ānra gehwylc, every one, all); asm. gehwilcne, 241; gehwelcne, 12; isn. gehwylce, 549.
gehycgan, W3., consider, be mindful, take heed, conceive, understand: inf. 193, 282; gehicgan, 178.
gehȳdan, WI., hide, conceal: inf., 100.
gehygd, n., thought, plan: as. 343.
gelædan, WI., lead: pret. 2s. gelæddest, 658; 3s. gelædde, 551; opt. pret. 1s. gelædde, 503; inf. 400; pp. gelēdde, 88.
gelǣran, WI., persuade: pret. 2s. gelærdæst, 53; 3s. gelærde, 411.
gelecgan, WI., lay, put: pret. 3p. gelegdon, 537.
gelēfan, WI., believe, believe in, trust: 1p. gelēfað, 290; pret. 3s. gelēfde, 244; 1p. gelȳfdon, 414; inf. 249.
gelīc, adj., like: npm. gelīce, 306; sup. nsn. gelīcost, 162.
*gelīhtan, WI., descend to, approach, come: inf. 429.
gelimpan, III, happen, befall, come to pass: pret. 3s. gelamp, 24, 174, 476; gelomp, 124, 532, 568.
*gelūtian, W2., hide: inf. 129.
gemercian, W2., mark out, measure: pp. gsn. gemearcodes, 721.
gemet, n., strength: ns. 489.
gemētan, WI., meet, come across: pret. 2s. gemēttes, 696.
gemunan, prp., remember, be mindful of, muse, ponder: pret. 1s. gemunde, 502; 3s. gemunde, 723; opt. 1p. gemunan, 201, 205, 285, 644(inf.?).
geniman, IV, take hold of, seize: pret. 3s. genōm, 542, 679.
genip, n., mist, darkness: ds. genipe, 101; as. 179, 444.
geoguþ, f., youth, young man: ds. geoguðe, 19.
gēomor, adj., mournful: nsn. wk. gēomre, 339.
geond, prep., w. accus., through, over, about, throughout, among: 73, 128, 222, 269, 271, 319, 340, 352, 384, 582, 602, 642, 724.
geondwlītan, I, look or see through: inf. 9.
georne, adv., eagerly, earnestly, gladly, well: 594, 644; comp. geornor, 704.
gerǣcan, WI., reach: inf. 168.
gerīm, n., number: gs. gerīmes, 500.

gesǣlig, adj., blessed, happy: npf. gesǣlige, 295.

gesceaft, f., creation, the heavenly kingdom, creature: ds. gesceft, 662; as. gesceaft, 559; gescæft, 138; gp. gesceafta, 440; gescefta, 202, 583.

gescēawian, W2, behold, see, show forth, exhibit: 3p. gescēawiaδ, 539; inf. 608.

gesēcan, WI., seek, go to, approach, visit: 3s. gesēceδ, 210; inf. 434.

gesegnian, W2., bless, sign with the cross: 3s. gesegnaδ, 359; gesēnaδ, 614.

gesellan, WI., give, betray, sell: 1s. geselle, 684; pret. 3s. gesalde, 574.

gesēne, adj., seen, evident, clear: nsn. 228, 439.

gesēon, V, see, behold: pret. 3s. geseah, 714; 1p. gesāwon, 388, 536; 3p. gesāwon, 381, 467; gesāwun, 716; gesēgon, 527.

geset, n., seat, dwelling, habitation: ap. geseotu, 601.

gesettan, WI., set, fix, establish, appoint, decree: pret. 3s. gesette, 4, 13, 492; pp. geseted, 676; gesette, 572.

gesittan, V, sit, lean: pret. 3s. gesæt, 430, 468.

gestigan, I, ascend to, mount up to: 3p. gestīgaδ, 611.

gestondan, VI, stand: pret. 3s. gestōd, 239, 528.

gestrēonan, WI., obtain: inf. 596.

geswīδan, WI., strengthen: pret. 3s. geswīδde, 571 (subj.?).

getenge, adj., near, at hand: nsf. 710.

geþencan, WI., be mindful of, consider, reflect upon, resolve: 1p. geþencaδ, 289; pret. 1s. geþōhte, 186; 3s. geþōhte, 315, 370; inf. 642.

geþēon, I, thrive, profit: pret. 3s. geþēah, 575.

geþingian, W2., promise, agree: pp. geþingod, 597.

geþōht, m., thought: ap. geþōhtas, 204, 283, 486.

geþolian, W2., w. acc., suffer, endure, bear: 1p. geþoliaδ, 397; inf. 634, w. gen., suffer loss of, forfeit: inf. 272.

geþrōwian, W2., suffer: pret. 3s. geþrōwode, 546, 664.

gewald, n., power, control, dominion, possession: ds. gewalde, 413; gewealde, 686; as. 55, 86, 106, 117, 173.

geweorδan, III, to be, become, happen, be agreeable: pret. 3s. gewearδ, 254, 260, 667.

gewinn, n., struggle, war: as. 230.

gewītan, I, depart: imp. 2s. gewīt, 690.

gewunian, W2., dwell in, inhabit: inf. 325; pp. npm. gewunade, 102.

gewyrcan, W1., make, create, earn, deserve: 1p. gewyrcaδ, 302; pret. 1s. geworhte, 470.

gif, conj., if: 249, 289, 301, 672, 687.

gīfre, adj., greedy, rapacious: npm. 32, 191.

gifu, f., gift, grace: as. gife, 644; is. gife, 571.

gim, m., gem, jewel: ip. gimmum, 647.

gingra, m., vassal, follower, disciple: np. gingran, 190, 529; ap. gingran, 520, 524, 571.

giunga, adj., young: nsm. wk. giunga, 509.

glēaw, adj., sagacious, discerning: nsm. 349.

gnornian, W2., grieve, bewail, lament, murmur: pret. 3p. gnornedon, 279; inf. 273; pres. p. apm. gnornende, 133.

gnornung, f., wailing, lamentation: np. 333.

god, m., God: ns. 18, 32, 56, 108, 191, 242, 258, 280, 287, 349, 354, 428, 439, 450, 491, 514, 529, 548, 573, 598; gs. godes 10, 165, 190, 268, 279, 288, 339, 357,

367, 468, 472, 526, 564, 613, 620, 644, 649, 692, 717; ds. gode, 82, 232, 313; as. 96, 522, 704.

gōd, adj., good: comp. asm. bettran, 49; ipf. sēlrum, 45.

gōd, n., good, blessing, benefit: gp. gōda, 185, 330.

gongan, red., go: imp. 2s. gong, 707; gang, 700; inf. 524, 613, 649.

grǣdig, adj., greedy: npm. grǣdige, 191; grēdige, 32.

***grǣfhūs**, n., house of the dead: ns. 707.

grēne, adj., green: asf. 286.

grim, adj., grim, dire, horrible: nsn. 707; apm. grimme, 258.

grīpan, I, seize, take hold of: imp. 2s. grīp, 700; inf. 268.

gristbitung, f., gnashing of teeth: np. 333.

grund, m., bottom, deep, depth, abyss: gs. grundes, 700; ds. grunde, 268, 631, 702, 723; as. 31, 90, 148, 448, 454, 483, 635; ap. grundas, 10, 133, 258.

***grynde**, n., abyss: gs. gryndes, 330.

gryre, m., terror: ns. 431, 725; as. 452.

gylden, adj., golden: nsn. 647.

gylp, n., pride, vaunt, boasting: ns. 252.

gȳt, adv., yet, still, yet again: 159, 403, 406, 569; gēt, 223.

H

habban, W3., have, possess, hold, keep, get: 1s. hebbe, 88, 91; 2s. hafast, 676, 705; hafus, 64; 3s. hafað, 586, 597; 1p. habbað, 61; 2p. habbað, 617; 3p. habbað, 143, 353, 506; pret. 1s. hefde, 82; 3s. hæfde, 2, 199, 402, 442, 460, 572; hefde, 33; 1p. hæfdon, 150; hefdon, 44; 2p. hæfdon, 483; 3p. hæfdan, 68; hæfdon, 70, 225, 328, 525, 717; opt. 2s. hæbbe, 672, 709; inf. 29, 37, 43, 448, 590, 641. Negative: 1p. nabbað, 334.

hād, m., nature, condition, relation: as. 436, 493.

hæft, m., captive, servant: np. hæftas, 629; dp. hæftum, 318; ap. hæftas, 201, 715.

hæft, m., bond, fetter, captivity: dp. hæftum, 91, 147, 503, 551; ip. hæftum, 425.

hǣlend, m., Saviour: ns. 217, 280, 491, 606; gs. hǣlendes, 152, 381, 424, 484, 646; hēlendes, 86; ds. hǣlende, 363, 594, 643; hēlende, 54; as. 542, 575, 682.

hæleð, m., man, hero, warrior: np. heleð, 47; gp. hæleða, 193, 269, 398, 656; hæleþa, 581.

hǣlo, f., health, well-being, salvation: as. 581.

hǣðen, adj., heathen: npm. hæþene, 538; gpm. hæþenre, 267.

haldan, red., hold, keep, retain: 3s. haldeð, 259.

hālig, adj., holy: nsm. 56, 81, 564, 585, 591; dsm. hāligum, 511; wk. hālgan, 232, 290, 566; dsn. wk. hālgan, 415; asm. hāligne, 327, 413, 526, 561; wk. hālgan, 201; asn. wk. hālige, 347; npm. 220, 458; apm. hālige, 678; ipf. hālgum, 654.

hālsian, W2., beseech, adjure: 1s. hālsige, 420.

hām, m., home, abode, dwelling: ns. 38, 95, 99, 214; gs. hāmes, 137; ds. hām, 110, 217, 255, 502, 566, 658; as. 25, 49, 177, 275, 277, 293, 336, 344, 361, 413; adverbial accus. hām, 88, 91, 147, 425, 429, 503, 551.

handgeweorc, n., work of the hands, handiwork: ns. 487.

***handþegen**, m., servant: ns. 483.

hāt, adj., hot: nsm. 158, 318; asm. hātne, 454, 483; asn. wk. hāte, 192, 417; npm. hāte, 98, 280.

hāt, n., heat: ns. 131.

hātan, red., bid, command, name: 1s. hāte, 693; 3s. hāteð, 600; pret. 3s. hēt, 482, 519, 521, 721; pp. hāten, 366, 541.

hāte, adv., hotly: 340.

hē, pron., he: nsm. 3, 4, 9, 11, 13, 19, 33, 77, 78(2), 80, 116, 146, 162, 189, 194, 199(2), 200, 210, 216, 259, 264, 265, 278, 283, 291, 305, 316, 346, 368, 369, 371, 374, 379, 462, 465, 516, 518, 522, 523, 542, 543, 547, 551, 559, 569, 576, 583, 665, 668, 679, 714, 718, 723(2); nsf. hēo, 407; nsn. hit, 22, 124, 394, 532, 568; gsm. his, 6, 13, 14, 126, 190, 282, 325, 359, 375, 390, 543, 547, 548, 571, 579, 584, 587, 588, 591, 614, 621, 666; dsm. him, 51, 117, 124, 195, 209, 233, 238, 258, 283, 373, 387, 426, 446, 567, 575, 577, 585, 610, 670, 671, 673, 689, 719; asm. hine, 153, 244, 375, 458, 565, 721; asn., hit, 540; np. hīe, 23, 74, 345, 467, 472, 633, 637, 639, 641; hī, 360, 377, 381, 449, 533; hēo, 25, 27, 98, 296, 311, 328, 344, 497, 504, 527, 539, 622; hē, 716; gp. heora, 66, 221, 307, 322, 372, 433; dp. him, 22, 24, 224, 247, 280, 341, 378, 434, 450, 451, 456, 458, 538, 620, 624, 637, 641, 695; hym, 70; ap. hīe, 358, 359; hēo, 67, 309, 443, 614; hē, 477; hīg, 191.

hēafod, n., head: as. 381.

hēah, adj., high, deep: nsf. hēh, 706; dsn. wk. hēan, 201; dsm. hēaum, 17; sup. asf. hēhstan, 693.

hēahgetimbrad, adj., formed of p.p. of **timbrian**, to build, construct, and **hēah**: hēahgetimbrad, 29.

healf, f., side: ap. healfe, 609.

hēan, adj., depressed, miserable: nsn. 119.

hēap, m., company, band, host: ns. 87, 392; as. 240.

hēawan, red., strike, cut: pret. 3s. hēow, 509.

hebban, VI, raise, lift, bear up: pret. 1p. hōfan, 153; 3p. hōfon, 458.

hēhengel, m., archangel: ap. hēhenglas, 600.

hēhfæder, m., patriarch: np. 654.

hēhseld, n., throne, lofty hall: ds. hēhselde, 206; as. 47, 371; gp. hēhselda, 43.

hēhsetl, n., throne: as. 218.

***helheoðu**, f., hell-hall, room: ns. 699.

hell, hyll, f., hell: ns. hell, 706; hel, 192; gs. helle, 70, 97, 454, 465, 483, 629; hylle, 431; ds. helle, 34, 88, 158, 160, 189, 280, 374, 379, 398, 425, 448, 578; hylle, 337, 715; as. helle, 25, 340, 434, 668.

helleduru, f., hell-gate: ds. 720.

***hellescealc**, m., retainer of hell, devil: ap. hellescealcas, 132.

hellwaran, mp., the inhabitants of hell: d. hellwarum, 694; helwarum, 429.

helm, m., helmet, protector: ns. 656; as. 250; vs. 163.

help, f., help, aid, support: ds. helpe, 434, 438; as. helpe, 290; help, 581.

helpan, III, help: inf. 98, 491.

hēnðo, f., humiliation, disgrace: as. 397; hȳnðo, 375.

hēofan, II, lament, bewail: pret. 3p. hēofon, 343.

heofencyning, m., king of heaven: ds. heofencyninge, 182, 316, 435.

***heofendēma**, m., heavenly judge: ns. 656.

***heofenþrēat**, m., heavenly band: np. heofenþrēatas, 220.

heofon, m., heaven: gs. heofones, 310; heofnes, 56; ds. heofene, 10; as. 168, 413; gp. heofona, 277, 347, 617; heofna, 566; dp. heofonum, 16, 150, 275, 327, 344, 371, 465, 562, 564, 668; heofnum, 29, 37, 43, 81, 585.

heofonrīce, n., kingdom of heaven: gs. heofenrīces, 420; ds. heofonrīce, 214, 561, 678.

heolstor, n., place of concealment, retreat: gs. heolstres, 100.
heonon, adv., hence: 422, 652; heonan, 395.
heorte, f., heart: ns. 282.
hēr, adv., here: 92, 104, 131, 208, 261, 272; hǣr, 101.
hēran, WI., obey: opt. 1p. hēran, 594; inf. 54, 182, 232, 316, 363, 643.
herde, m., keeper, lord: ns. 159.
herian, WI., praise: 3p. herigað, 47, 220, 654, 659.
herm, adj., malicious: nsm. 681.
hider, adv., hither: 421, 685.
*__hinsīðgryre__, m., terror of death: as. 454.
hīred, m., household, company, train: ns. 375, 591; ds. hīrede, 421; as. 347.
hlāf, m., loaf: ap. hlāfas, 671.
hleonian, W2., lean, recline: pret. 3s. hleonade, 431.
hlūd, adj., loud: nsm. 465, 606; nsn. wk. hlūde, 339; isf. hlūddre, 600.
hnīgan, I, bend, bow down, sink: pret. 3p. hnigan, 238, hnigon, 531; inf. 206, 374.
hof, n., hall, dwelling: as. 192.
holdlice, adv., graciously, kindly: 310.
holm, m., sea: ds. holme, 17.
hond, f., hand: ns. 564; ds. handa, 431; as. 579, 610; is. hond, 359, 614; ip.
　　hondum, 267, 458, 538, 542, 679, 699; handum, 168, 415, 435, 705.
hraðe, adv., immediately, quickly, straightaway: 227.
hrēam, m., cry, clamour: ns. hrēam, 715.
hreðer, m., breast, interior: ds. reðre, 98.
hrōpan, red., cry out, scream: pret. 3p. hrēopan, 318.
hū, conj., how: 33, 178, 195, 351, 497, 637, 645, 698, 703, 706.
hund, n., hundred: ns. 720.
hungor, m., hunger: ds. hungre, 671.
hūru, adv., even, especially: 170, 521.
hūs, n., house: as. 709.
hwā, pron., who, what: nsm. hwā, 17; asn. hwæt, 108.
hwǣr, conj., adv., where, whither: 36, 527.
hwæt, interj., lo: 44, 131, 231, 315, 437.
hwæðer, conj., whether, 276.
hwearfian, W2., wander about: pret. 3p. hwearfedon, 72.
hweorfan, III, turn, depart, go, wander or roam about: pret. 3s. hwearf, 189, 398;
　　3p. hworfon, 71; hweorfan, 340; inf. 119, 269, 417.
hwīl, f., time: as. hwīle, 253; ip. hwīlum, as. adv., sometimes: 131; correlative,
　　sometimes... sometimes, now... now: 132, 134, 712, 713, 714, 715.
hwīt, adj., white: npm. hwīte, 218.
hwonne, conj., when: 620.
hwyrft, m., course: ip. hwyrftum, 629 (? wheeling, circling).
hycgan, W3., think, take heed, purpose: pret. 1s. hogade, 84; inf. 593.
hyht, m., hope, expectation, joy: ds. hyhte, 70, 334; hihte, 175, 641; as. hyht,
　　694.
hyhtlic, adj., joyous: comp. nsm. hyhtlicra, 214; gsm. hihtlicran, 137.
*__hyhtwilla__, m., hope of joy: gs. hyhtwillan, 158.

I

ic, pron., I: ns. 48, 81, 84, 85, 88, 89, 91, 96, 107, 109, 111, 119, 122, 123, 129(2),
　　132, 137, 139, 140, 144, 147, 155, 167, 168, 172, 175, 176, 178(2), 180, 183, 186,

223, 246, 248, 267, 272, 274, 275, 408, 420, 422, 470, 479, 501, 502, 503, 507, 510, 524, 627, 684, 693; ds. mē, 49, 82, 86, 108, 140, 173, 174, 497, 685; as. mē, 487, 496, 508, 675; np. wē, 37, 41, 44, 54, 60, 61, 94, 100(2), 114, 149, 150, 153, 201, 206, 228, 231, 232, 234, 253, 254, 289, 298, 334, 382, 388, 389, 396, 536, 552, 554, 589, 594, 596, 643; dp. ūs, 63, 98, 114, 197, 202, 239, 251, 260, 276, 293, 300, 428, 555, 597, 663; ūsic, 254; ap. ūs, 53, 100, 286, 288, 290, 291, 551, 588; dual n. wit, 409, 410, 412, 414, 417; d. unc, 416; a. unc, 411.

īdel, adj., empty, vain: nsn. 252.

ilca, pron., same, very: asn. ilce, 590.

in, prep., w. dat., in, within, on: 10, 29, 43, 48, 49, 58, 80, 81, 84, 101, 107, 127, 150, 157, 178, 202, 214, 217, 231, 307, 308, 327, 367, 368, 379, 407, 433, 448, 461, 477, 506, 522, 529, 554, 592, 655, 662, 715, 727; w. accus., in, into, to: 25, 26, 30, 31, 90, 148, 177, 179, 192, 310, 375, 377, 417, 438, 444, 457, 559, 607, 612, 613, 616, 626, 631, 632, 648, 668, 690.

*indrīfan, I, utter: pret. 3s. indrāf, 80.

inneweard, adj., inside, within: 136, 706.

innon, prep., w. dat., in, within: 578.

īren, n., iron: is. īrne, 516.

irnan, III, run: pret. 3s. ran, 711; 3p. urnon, 530.

irreweorces, n., a work undertaken in anger, gs. yrreweorces, 397.

iū, adv., formerly, once: 44, 81, 150.

iūdǣd, m., former deed: ip. iūdǣdum, 185.

Iūdas, pr. n., Judas: ns. 573.

L

lā, interj., oh, ah, indeed: 455, 642, 729.

*lǣcan, WI., spring or flare up: pret. 3s. lǣhte, 714.

lǣcedōm, m., healing: as. 588.

lǣdan, WI., lead: 3s. lǣdaδ, 360; pret. 2s. lǣddest, 421; 3s. lǣdde, 565; inf. 396.

lǣran, WI., teach, show, give: inf. 248.

lǣtan, red., let, suffer; regard as: pret. 3s. lēt, 405, 441; opt. 3s. lǣte, 195.

land, see lond.

lang, adj., long: sup. nsm. lengust, 605.

langian, W2. (impersonal), long for, desire: opt. 3s. lange, 503.

langsum, adj., enduring, sound: asm. langsumne, 248.

lāδ, adj., evil, grievous, hateful, loathed, loathsome, hostile: gsm. wk. lāþan, 714; asm. lāδne, 537; wk. lāδan, 177; asn. wk. lāδe, 724; apm. lāδe, 284.

lāδian, W2., invite, call: 3s. leaδaδ, 588; 3p., 630.

leahtor, m., sin, disgrace, infamy: dp. leahtrum, 262; ap. leahtras, 284.

lēan, n., reward: as. 677.

lēas, adj., destitute of, deprived of, false, perfidious: nsm. 158, 167, 181; nsf. 724; npm. lēase, 330.

lēasung, f., lie, lying: dp. lēasungum, 62.

lēof, adj., dear, beloved: asm. lēofne, 154.

lēoht, līht, n., light: ns. lēoht, 105, 387, 555; ds. lēohte, 177, 588; līhte, 360; as. lēoht, 28, 140, 251, 310, 447, 590, 616, 648; līht, 68, 677.

lēoht, adj., bright, brilliant: asm. lēohtne, 467; vsm. wk. lēohta, 165.

*lēohtberende, m., light-bearer: ns. 366.

lēoma, m., light, radiance, splendour: as. lēoman, 85, 350, 467.

licgan, V, lie: inf. 262, 714.
līf, n., life: ns. 595; as. 210, 291, 360.
lifian, W3., live: pres. p. ns. lifigende, 573; npm. as. subst. lifigend, 298; gp. lifigendra, 284; dp. lifigendum, 677.
līg, m., flame: ns. lǣg, 713; is. līge, 324.
lim, n., limb, member: np. leomu, 154.
***limwæstm**, m., size of limb, stature: ip. limwæstmum, 129.
list, m., f., art, skill: ip. listum, 299.
***locen**, n., secret, mystery: as. 299.
lōcian, W2., look, gaze: pret. 3s. lōcade, 724; imp. 2s. lōca, 683; inf. 169.
lofsong, m., song of praise, hymn: gp. lofsonga, 154.
lond, n., land: ns. 213; as. land, 211, 269.
londbēwende, m., inhabitant of earth: ap. 683.
***Lucifer**, pr. n., ns. 366.
lyft, m., air: as. 262.
lyge, m., lie, deceit: as. 53.
lȳhtan, WI., give light: 3s. lȳhteð, 104.
lȳðre, adv., miserably, wretchedly: 62.

M

mā, n., more: n. 112.
mā, adv., more, again: 139.
mægen, n., might, strength, power: ns. 489; ds. mægne, 517; as. mægen, 548.
mægencræft, m., great power or might: as. 199.
mægð, f., race, progeny, tribe: ds. mægðe, 423; dp. mægðum, 271.
mæl, n., time, appointed time: gs. mæles, 499; gp. mæla, 549.
mænan, WI., lament, mourn: pret. 3p. mændon, 384; inf. 133.
mære, adj., great, illustrious, noble, splendid: nsm. wk. mæra, 597; dsf. wk. mæran, 622; asf. wk. mæran, 457, 559; asn. wk. mære, 352.
magan, prp., can, be able, may: 1s. mæg, 129, 168, 178; 2s. miht, 695; 3s. mæg, 9, 11, 282, 538; 1p. mægon, 100; 3p. magon, 98; pret. 3s. mihte, 337, 491, 517; 3p. mihton, 540; opt. 1s. mæge, 423; 3s. mæge, 350; 1p. mægen, 596; pret. 3s. mihte, 22; 3p. mihten, 498.
mān, n., sin, crime, guilt, punishment, pain: as. 304, 320.
Maria, pr. n., Mary: gs. Marian, 436.
martire, m., martyr: np. martiras, 653.
mearc, f., limit, period: ns. 499.
mecg, m., man: gp. mecga, 333.
mencgan, WI., mingle: 3p. mencgað, 131.
menego, f., indecl., multitude: n. 83, 261, 320; g. mænego, 726; menio, 474; a. mænego, 200, 502; i. menego, 110.
meotod, m., Creator, God, Christ: ns. 2, 8, 64, 261, 399, 457, 513; metod, 666; gs. meotodes, 142, 164, 172, 285, 352, 527; ds. meotode, 83, 183, 304, 653; as. 436, 696.
mercian, W2., design, appoint: pp. merced, 709.
metan, V, measure: pret. 3s. mæt, 712.
micel, adj., great: nsm. 660; dsn. wk. miclan, 517; asm. micelne, 83, 495; wk. micclan, 250; ipf. miclum, 627; apf. miccle, 200, micle, 672; comp. asn. māre, 64; sup. nsm. mǣst, 605; asf. mǣste, 695.

mid, prep., w. dat., with, together with, along with: 82, 122, 141, 203, 222, 292, 311, 313, 329, 372, 386, 389, 423, 446, 456, 458, 468, 480, 586, 589, 590, 607; w. accus., with, together with: 60, 375, 611, 646; w. instr., with, by, through: 144, 156, 168, 169, 170, 299, 359, 383, 415, 435, 516, 538, 542, 571, 614, 679, 699, 712, 725.

mid, adv., in the midst, midst: 564.

middangeard, eard, m., earth, world: as. middangeard, 8, 438, 582; middaneard, 271; vs. middaneard, 164; ds. middangearde, 474.

miht, f., might, power: ds. mihte, 249; as. 2, 6, 13, 604, 693; is. mihte, 352; vs. 164; dp. mihtum, 8; ap. mihte, 399, 470, 672; mihta, 200; ip. mihtum, 230, 261.

mihtig, adj., mighty, powerful: nsm. wk. mihtiga, 721.

***mil**, f., mile: gp. mīla, 721; ip. mīlum, 338.

milds, f., mercy, favour, kindness: gs. miltse, 436; gp. mildsa, 666.

mīn, poss. pron., my: nsn. 487; dsf. mīnre, 249, 423, 437; dsn. mīnum, 84, 157; apf. mīne, 470.

min, adj., mean, wretched: dsm. wk. minnan, 502.

mōd, n., mind, heart: ds. mōde, 22, 84, 285; is. mōde, 540.

molde, f., earth: ds. moldan, 603.

mon, m., man: np. men, 134, 306, 549, 603; gp. monna, 271, 489, 688; manna, 399; dp. monnum, 380; mannum, 438.

mōna, m., moon: as. mōnan, 4.

moncyn, n., mankind: gs. moncynnes, 64, 513, 697; mancynnes, 309, 358, 457, 666; ds. mancynne, 559.

monig, adj., many: npm. monige, 496; dp. monegum, 582.

morgen, m., morning: as. 513.

morður, n., sin, crime, torment: gs. morðres, 183; as. 320.

mōtan, anv., may, must: 1s. mōt, 137, 139, 144, 147, 169, 267; 3s. mōt, 265, 364; 1p. mōton, 257, 301, 554, 589; mōten, 95; 3p. mōton, 311, 448, 449, 612, 633; mōten, 296, 331, 649; pret. 1s. mōste, 107, 175; 3s. mōste, 406, 522; 1p. mōston, 231; 3p. mōston, 475; mōsten, 377; opt. 1s. mōte, 423; 3p. mōten, 622.

myntan, WI., think, intend: pret. 2s. myntest, 688.

N

nā, nō, adv., not, never: nā, 410; nō, 291, 376, 632.

nacod, adj., naked: npm. nacode, 134.

næddre, f., serpent, snake: gs. næddran, 410; nēdran, 101; ap. næddran, 336.

nænig, pron., none, no: nsm. 348; asm. nænigne, 121.

nalles, adv., not, by no means: 42, 326, 447, 692; nales, 28.

nama, m., name: ns. 192.

nān, adj., no: nsm. 515.

ne, adv., not: 50, 54, 79, 98, 104, 114, 129, 137, 139, 144, 168, 169, 170, 178, 182, 194, 265, 316, 406, 410, 540, 575, 627, 694; nē, conj., nor: 93, 94(2), 138(2), 144, 169, 170, 348, 349, 449, 489, 490(2).

nearu, adj., narrow, close, oppressive: asn. nearwe, 632.

nearwe, adv., closely, oppressively: 444.

nēh, adv., near: 338.

nemnan, WI., name, call: pret. 1p. nemdon, 382; pp. genemned, 203, 365.

neorxnawong, m., paradise: ds. neorxnawonge, 479.

nēosan, WI., seek, visit: inf. 112.

neowol, adj., deep, profound: dsn. wk. neowlan, 101; asm. wk. neowlan, 31, 90; asn. wk. neowle, 179, 444.

nergan, WI., save: pres. p. nsm. nergende, 569; asm. nergendne, 345.

nergend, m., Saviour: gs. nergendes, 376.

ness, m., ground, earth, chasm: dp. næssum, 134; ap. nessas, 31, 90.

niht, f., night: gs. nihtes, 497; ap. 424, 570.

niman, IV, take, choose: pret. 1p. nāmon, 415; opt. 1p. neoman, 197.

nīð, m., enmity, hatred, spite, malice, affliction, tribulation: gs. 273; as. 376, 410, 632.

niðer, adv., down: 90, 134, niðær, 31.

*nīðsyn, f., grievous sin: ip. nīðsynnum, 179.

nīwe, adj., new: asn. 479.

nū, adv., now, just now, but now, immediately, now henceforth: 40, 46, 57, 64, 91, 106, 140, 155, 156, 176, 180, 187, 228, 229, 261, 390, 393, 411, 420, 425, 439, 445, 579, 591, 597, 626, 627, 683, 729.

nū, conj., now that, since: 109, 385, 391.

nymðe, conj., except, save: 18; nimðe, 491; nymþe, 330, 334, 349, 675.

O

of, prep., w. dat., of, from, out of: 34, 92, 160, 172, 180, 186, 201, 255, 256, 266, 355, 465, 503, 514, 551, 564, 603, 604, 668.

of, adv., off, absent: 573.

ofer, prep., w. dat., over, above: 213, 239; w. accus., over, above, 263, 601, 615, 625, 683.

oferfeohtan, III, conquer, vanquish: pp. oferfohten, 403.

ofergīman, WI, neglect, disregard: pret. 2p. ofergȳmdon, 484.

oferhycgan, W3., condemn, scorn, renounce: inf. 250; oferhycgen, 304.

oferhygd, n., pride: gs. oferhȳdes, 113; dp. oferhygdum, 50, 69, 196; oferhigdum, 226; ap. oferhȳda, 369.

oferwinnan, III, overcome, vanquish: pp. oferwunnen, 460.

ofost, f., haste: ip. ofostum, 627.

oft, adv., oft, often: 151, 270, 328, 637, 640.

ofþyncan, WI., mislike, displease, be an offence to: pret. 3s. ofþūhte, 245.

on, prep., w. dat., on, in, into, for, from: 5, 8, 15, 16, 22, 37, 39, 45, 67, 98, 109, 111(2), 130, 142, 158, 204, 229, 235, 244, 262, 264, 275, 277, 280, 285, 289, 298, 302, 323, 344, 367, 371, 412, 415, 476, 479, 494, 500, 502, 508, 509, 519, 547, 548, 557, 562, 574, 585, 596, 599, 678, 711, 718, 723, 729; w. acc., on, upon, into, to, by, for: 89, 138, 262, 346, 402, 404, 463, 472, 513, 531, 537, 577, 579, 609, 610, 637, 680, 681, 682, 684, 697, 716.

on (= ms. un), adv., to, against: 66.

on, adv., w. hwǽr forming a rel. adv., whereon, where: 528.

onǽlan, WI., kindle, burn, heat: pp. onǽled, 40, 96, 321, 340, 419.

oncnāwan, red., recognize, understand, believe: inf. 540.

ondetan, WI., confess: inf. 223.

onfōn, red., receive: pret. 3s. onfēng, 565.

ongēan, prep., w. dat., towards, to meet: 300.

ongeotan, V, perceive, understand, conceive: opt. 1p. ongeotan, 300; pret. 3p. ongeton, 526.

ongin, n., action, undertaking: ns. 545.

onginnan, III, begin: pret. 3s. ongan, 78, 246; 3p. ongunnon, 727; opt. lp. onginnen, 643.

onlūcan, II, unlock, disclose, reveal: opt, lp. onlūcan, 299.

onmēdla, m., pride, presumption: ds. onmǣdlan, 427; anmēdlan, 74.

onsēon, f., sight, appearance; ns. 61.

onstellan, WI., institute, be the author of: pret. 3s. onstalde, 368; 2p. onstaldon, 113.

onstyrian, W2., stir up: inf. 270.

ontȳnan, WI., disclose, reveal: pp. ontȳned, 556, 593.

onwacan, onwæcan: VI, arise, spring, be born: pret. 2s. onwōce, 437; 3p. onwōcon, 474.

onwald, m., power: ns. 117; as. 60.

onwecnan, WI., awake: 3p. onwecnað, 603.

open, adj., revealed, opened: nsf. 404.

ord, m., beginning: as. 113.

ordfruma, m., source, author, creator, prince, chief: ns. 237, 373, 440, 657; np. ordfruman, 21.

orðonc, n., art, skill, invention: as. 18.

ōðer, pron., other, another, second: asn. 210; ism. ōðre, 75; isn. ōðre, 227; npm. ōðre, 623, dpm. ōðrum, 26.

oðfæstan, WI., fasten on: pp. oðfæsted, 443.

oððæt, conj., until: 476, 701, 725.

P

Pētrus, pr. n., Peter: ns. 534, ds. Pētre, 521.

R

rǣcan, WI., reach: pret. 3s. rǣhte, 435.

rǣd, m., advice, counsel: as. 248.

rǣdbora, m., counselor: np. rǣdboran, 498.

rægn, m., rain: gs. rægnas, 11.

refnan, WI., carry out, bring to pass: inf. hrefnan, 498.

reord, f., speech, language: is. reorde, 35.

reordian, W2., speak: pret. 3s. reordade, 75; 3p. reordadon, 66; inf. 728, pres. p. nsm. reordende 624.

rest, f., rest, place of rest: as. reste, 611, 618.

rēðe, adj., fierce, savage: npm. 103.

rīce, n., rule, dominion, kingdom: ns. 692; gs. rīces, 346, 498, 687; ds. 277, 307, 367, 617, 649; as. 259, 613.

ricene, adv., quickly, straightaway: 707.

riht, n., justice, right: as. 205, 346.

riht, adj., regular, true, real: nsm., 687.

rīm, n., number, multitude: as. 399, 418.

rodor, m., heaven: gp. rodora, 687; rodera, 346, 611.

S

sǣ, m., f., sea: ds. 5; as. 9.

sanct, m., saint: np. sanctas, 238, 354.

sang, m., song, singing: ns. 661; as. 233; song, 45, 142; is. sange, 144.

sār, adj., grievous: gsf. wk. sāran, 28.

Sātān, Sātānus, pr. n., Satan: ns. Sātān, 711; Sātānus, 370, 445; vs. Sātānus, 691.

sāwol, f., soul: np. sāwla, 651; sāwle, 295; gp. sāwla, 572; dp. sāwlum, 144, 265, 462; ap. sāwla, 396, sāwle, 405.

scacan, VI, hurry, speed: inf. 262.

scealu, f., throng, multitude: as. sceale, 267.

scēat, m., corner, region, surface: ap. scēatas, 3, 602.

sceaða, m., criminal, wretch, fiend: np. sceaðan, 72; gp. sceaðena, 631; sceaðana, 57.

scēawian, W2., see, behold: pret. 3p. scēawodon, 533; inf. 522.

sced, n., shade, darkness: gs. scedes, 105.

sceldburg, f., fortress, city of refuge: ds. sceldbyrig, 308.

sceppend, see scyppend.

sceððan, VI, hurt, harm: inf. 145.

scīma, m., gloom: ds. scīman, 105.

scīnan, I, shine, gleam, glitter, be bright: 3s. scīneð, 221, 351; 3p. scīnað, 212, 294, 308, 650; opt. 3s. scīne, 209.

scinna, m., demon, evil spirit: np. scinnan, 72.

scīr, adj., bright, resplendent: dsf. wk. scīran, 176; nsm. 351.

scræf, n., cavern, hollow, den: as. 128, 417, 631, 724; scref, 26, 73.

scrīðan, I, glide, go: 3p. scrīþað, 629.

scūfan, II, shove, thrust: 3p. scūfað, 631; pret. 3s. scēaf, 443.

sculan, prp., must, have to, be destined to, shall, should, ought: 1s. sceal, 48, 111, 119, 156, 170, 183, 187, 272; 3s. sceal, 193, 261, 392; 1p. sceolon, 229, 552; sceolun, 41; 3p. sceolon, 269, 504, 549, 634; sceolun, 30; pret. 3s. sceolde, 374; 1p. sceoldon, 233, 410, 417; sceoldan, 37; scealdon, 54; 3p. sceoldon, 325, 641; sceolden, 27.

scūra, m., shower: ap. scūran, 11.

scuwa, m., shadow: as. scuwan, 453.

scyldig, adj., guilty: asn. wk. scyldige, 33.

scyppend, m., Creator: ns. 242, 562, scypend, 57; sceppend, 308; gs. sceppendes, 105; as. 533.

se, sē, demon. adj., pron., def. art., that, the, he, she, it; as a rel., who, which, that: nsm. 14, 34, 125, 182, 203, 208, 241, 245, 276, 282, 287, 293, 303(2), 315, 337, 354, 370, 394, 404, 411(2), 455, 456, 464, 482, 485, 486, 492, 509, 530, 541, 574, 663(2), 703, 713, 721; nsf. sēo, 320, 403, 575; nsn. þæt, 1, 17, 20, 21, 321, 324, 354, 357, 365, 372, 373, 455, 491, 538, 545, 582, 605, 663; gsm. þæs, 173, 700; ðæs, 414, 529; þes, 714; gsf. þære, 171; gsn. þæs, 183, 229, 329, 397, 416, 432, 488, 499, 569; ðæs, 100, 245; ðes, 77, 113, 114; dsm. þæm, 237, 363; ðæm, 178, 217; þam, 255, 290, 364, 372, 502, 556, 566, 710; ðam, 74; þān, 421; dsf. þære, 176, 468, 622; ðære, 662; dsn. þæm, 519; ðæm, 201; þam, 192, 415, 517; asm. þone, 148, 177, 201, 207, 250, 331, 336, 377, 635, 641, 667, 701, 716; ðone, 30, 31, 46, 90; asf. þā, 138, 200, 457, 559, 579, 610, 693; asn. þæt, 26, 33, 73, 89, 128, 178, 192, 199, 218, 253, 289, 297, 302, 347, 352, 364, 444, 461, 471, 492, 577, 590, 626, 631, 632, 690, 724; isn. ðȳ, 119; þē, 704; np. þā, 195, 355, 446, 610, 612, 619(2), 652, 727; ðā, 480; dp. þæm, 628, 648; þām, 144, 146, 265, 382; ap. þā, 80, 147, 485, 650.

sēcan, WI., seek, go, proceed: 3p. sēcað, 265.

secg, m., man: np. secgas, 496.

secgan, W3., say, tell, relate, announce, give (thanks, praise), sing: pret. 2s. segdest, 63, 428; 3s. sǣde, 125, 469, 512; 1p. sǣdon, 155; 3p. 462; inf. 233, 521, 550, 695.

seld, n., seat, hall, home, throne: ds. selde, 172, 186, 201, 661; as. 233, 347, 587.

sele, m., hall, dwelling: ns. 135; ds. 130; as. 331.

seolf, pron., self, very, own: nsm. 308, 402, 460; sylf, 661; wk. seolfa, 4, 57, 123, 242, 258, 274, 349, 354, 394, 428, 599; seolua, 13, 711; selfa, 9; sylfa, 216, 305, 439; gsm. seolfes, 587, 684; asm. sylfne, 543; vs. seolf, 691; npm. seolfe, 23, 589; selfe, 646; seolfa, 144.

seolfor, n., silver: gs. seolfres, 577.

sēon, V, look: inf. 377.

seoððan, adv., afterwards, thereafter, henceforth: 376, 396, 418, 632.

seoððan, conj., after, since: 77, 450, 705.

serwan, WI., plan, devise, plot against: pret. 3s. serede, 15; 3p. seredon, 496.

settan, WI., set up, establish, fix, trace, travel: pret. 3s. sette, 15; inf. 188.

sibb, f., friendliness, kindness: as. sibbe, 205.

sīc, adj., sick at heart, sad: nsm. 274.

sīd, adj., broad, wide, spacious: nsm., 703; nsf. 698; dsm. wk. sīdan, 130.

sīde, f., side: ds. sīdan, 543.

*sigetorht, adj., glorious in victory: ns. 238.

sigor, m., victory: gs. sigores, 676; gp. sigora, 216.

Sīmon, pr. n.: ns. 534; ds. 521.

sinc, n., treasure: as. 577.

singan, III, sing: 3p. singað, 354.

sittan, V, sit, dwell: 3s. siteð, 579, 585; sit, 216; 3p. sittað, 645; inf. 589.

sīð, m., journey, time: is. sīðe, 75; ap. sīðas, 188.

six, num., six: 15.

snotor, adj., wise: nsm. 348; vpm. snotre, 469.

snytero, f., wisdom: ns. 490; as. 205.

some, adv., likewise: 83.

sōna, adv., soon, forthwith: 534, 628.

sorg, f., sorrow, grief, affliction: gs. sorge, 28; gp. sorga, 695; ip. sorgum, 295.

sorghcearig, adj., sad, sorrowful: nsm. 188.

sorhful, adj., sorrowful: nsm. 274.

sōð, n., truth: as. 205; ds. (tō) sōðe: truly, as a fact, really: 63, 428.

sōð, adj., true: asf. wk. sōðan, 13.

sōðcwide, m., true words, truthful speech: ip. sōðcwidum, 469.

sōðfæst, adj., righteous, just: npm. sōðfæste, 306; wk. sōðfæstan, 610.

*spearca, m., spark; ip. spearcum, 161.

*spearcian, W2., emit sparks: pret. 3s. spearcade, 78.

spēd, f., success, might, abundance: as. 621, 666.

*spellung, f., talk, conversation: as. spellunge, 636.

spreocan, V, speak, say: pret. 1s. sprǣc, 247; 3s. sprǣc, 534; inf. 78.

stǣlan, WI., lay to one's charge, accuse of, reproach, taunt with: 3p. stǣleð, 638.

stān, m., stone: ns. 515; ap. stānas, 5, 670.

starian, W2., look, gaze: inf. 139.

staðelian, W2., establish, set up, take up: pret. 1s. staðelode, 275; 3p. staðeledon, 25; staðelodon, 344.

stefn, f., voice, sound: as. stefne, 171, 236; is. stefne, 36, 600; ip. stefnum, 654.
stenc, m., fragrance, odour: ap. stences, 356.
steppan, VI, step: inf. 246.
stician, W2., pierce: pret. 3p. sticedon, 508.
stiðmōd, adj., stern: nsm. 246.
stondan, VI, stand, be: 3p. stondað, 46, 619; standað, 218; pret. 3s. stōd, 127, 718, 723.
storm, m., uproar, tumult: ns. 385.
strǣt, f., road, way: as. strǣte, 286.
strēam, m., current, stream: as. 5.
strengðo, f., strength, power: as. 2, 285.
strong, adj., strong, severe, hard, stern, fast, close: nsm. 425; strang, 246; nsn. 321; strang, 224.
stronglic, adj., firm, severe: nsm. 515; nsn. 385.
sum, pron., some, one: ns. 57; npm. sume, 262, 269, 540; dsm. sumum, 536.
sunne, f., sun: ds. sunnan, 306; as. sunnan, 4.
sunu, m., son: ns. 63, 118, 241, 351, 394, 527, 579; as. 142, 172, 526, 646.
sūsl, n., torment: ns. 691; ds. sūsle, 711; as. sūsel, 41, 64; sūsle, 722; is. sūsle, 52.
*sūslbona, m., devil of torment: np. sūslbonan, 638.
sutol, adj., clear, plain: asn. 89.
swā, adv., so, thus, likewise, such: 14, 22, 61, 65, 83, 125, 190, 254, 279, 348(2), 349, 467, 512, 527, 659, 672, 700.
swā, conj., as: 116, 278, 305, 410, 482, 523, 623, 688, 721.
swart, adj., black, dark: nsm. wk. swarta, 703; npm. swarte, 52, 638.
swāt, m., blood: as. 543.
swearte, adv., darkly, dismally, wickedly: 370, 445, 577.
swēg, m., sound, noise, hissing, music: ns. 401, 563; swǣg, 101; as. 151, 235.
swegl, n., sky, heaven, ether: gs. swegles, 23, 28, 350; swǣgles, 123; ds. swegle, 45, 142; is. swegl, 587.
swegeltorht, adj., heaven-bright: asm. 646.
swilc, pron., such, so great: nsm. 261; swelc, 79.
swið, adj., right: comp. asf. wk. swīðran, 579, 610; isf. wk. swīðran, 359, 614.
swylce, adv., also, thus, so, in such manner: 321, 426, 665.
syllan, WI., give: 3s. syleð, 291; pret. 3s. sealde, 451.
symle, adv., ever, always, continually: 285.
syn, f., sin: gs. synne, 722; as. synne, 305; ip. synnum, 130.
synfull, adj., sinful: npm. synfulle, 52.
syngian, W2., sin: pret. 1p. syngodon, 228.

T

tācen, n., sign: as. 89.
tǣcan, WI., show: 3s. tǣceð, 293.
tān, m., branch: np. tānas, 480.
teala, adv., well, rightly, righteously: 556, 593, 729.
telga, m., bough: dp. telgum, 480.
tēne, num., ten: 570.
tēona, m., injury, abuse, trouble: as. tēonan, 495.
tīd, f., time, hour: np. tīda, 708; ip. tīdum, 45.
tifer, n., victim, sacrifice: ds. tīfre, 574.

til, adj., good: apm. tile, 609.

tintrega, m., torment: gs. tintregan, 495.

tīr, m., honour, glory: ns. 92.

tō, prep., w. dat., to, into, towards, at, for, as: 63, 70, 87, 88, 91, 110, 116, 147, 148, 152, 175, 189, 195, 197, 206, 237, 247, 252, 268, 278, 287, 290, 312(with?), 314, 334, 356, 360, 361, 374, 398, 401, 413, 425, 428, 434, 435, 438, 452, 456, 459, 492, 493, 504, 525, 531, 544, 552, 561, 566, 588, 597, 617, 618, 622, 623, 631, 641, 649, 658, 670, 686, 702, 720; from: 511, 685; w. gen., to: 529.

tō, adv., to, thither: 707.

tōgegnes, prep., w. dat. obj. preceding, for, in readiness for: 692; tōgēnes, 286.

torht, adj., bright, splendid, glorious: nsm. 593; wk. torhta, 293; nsn. 556; asm. torhtne, 574.

tōð, m., tooth: gp. tōða, 338.

tōweorpan, III, overthrow, destroy, put an end to: inf. 391; tōwerpan, 85.

trēow, n., tree: ds. trēo, 415; as. 480.

trum, adj., strong, well: asm. trumne, 523.

***trumlic**, adj., firm, stable: asm. trumlicne, 293.

tūdor, n., offspring, family: as. 657.

twēgen, num., two: nf. twā, 409, 708; af. twā, 609.

twelf, num., twelve: 338, 570.

Þ

þā, adv., then: 76, 84, 159, 180, 189, 245, 246, 329, 368, 378, 383, 398, 401, 403, 405, 406, 414, 430, 435, 441, 460, 468, 472, 481, 487, 499, 524, 528, 534, 557, 563, 568, 572, 573, 667, 673, 679, 689, 710, 719; ðā, 51, 223, 254, 489, 723.

þā, conj., when: 89, 189, 191, 200, 234, 344, 374, 379, 381, 389, 404, 409, 417, 465, 467, 508, 569, 669, 723; ðā, 3, 25.

þær, adv., there, thither, in that: 174, 212, 213, 234, 308, 320, 325, 351, 353, 509, 595, 634, 645, 647, 653, 660; ðær, 24, 243, 265, 322, 338.

þær, conj., where, whilst, whereas, in that: 27, 46, 107, 142, 153, 216, 287, 296, 311, 328, 332, 360, 445, 530, 543, 552, 589, 591, 592, 617, 639; if: 232.

þæs, adv., so: 349, 515.

þæs, conj., because, that, from the time that, after: 186, 274, 484, 503, 514, 551, 576; ðæs, 172; þes, 122.

þæt, conj., that, so that, in order that, until: 2, 22, 23, 41, 54, 55, 63, 85, 100, 114, 123, 129, 140, 167, 168, 181, 194, 199, 209, 228, 245, 254, 257, 283, 316, 338, 345, 350, 369, 371, 377, 412, 422, 433, 439, 455, 462, 464, 473, 477, 480, 487, 500, 504, 517, 522, 532, 533, 541, 545, 569, 583, 594, 622, 633, 643, 668, 674, 694, 696, 704, 709, 718, 719, 722, 723; ðæt, 59.

þætte, conj., that: 428.

þanc, m., thanks: as. 550.

þancian, W2., thank: pret. 3p. þanceden, 532.

þanon, adv., thence, from there: 326, 719; þonan, 633, þonon, 473.

þe, rel. particle, indecl., who, which, that: 21, 37, 74, 88, 113, 146, 243, 260, 265, 322, 355, 382, 421, 641, 648, 667; ðe, 17, 182, 208, 282, 303, 337, 363, 364, 411, 556, 574, 619, 652, 663; with þæs (þes), þær, þonne, as conjunctions, when: 150, 514; because: ðe, 122, 186, 551, 639; that: 503.

þēah, conj., though, although: 431, 516; þǣh, 264.

þearle, adv., severely, terribly, firmly, tightly: 419; ðearle, 38.

þearlic, adj., violent, severe: asn. 634.

þegen, m., thane, servant, follower, disciple, warrior: ns. 386, 424; np. þegnas, 325, 660.

þencan, WI., think, consider, mean, intend: 3s. þenceð, 182, 363, 556; 1p. þencað, 206.

þēoden, m., prince, king: ns. 245, 386, 546, 597, 664; ds. þēodne, 532; as. 660.

þēostre, adj., dark: nsm. wk. ðēostræ, 38.

þes, pron., this: nsm. 135, 241, 385, 392; ðes, 95, 391; ðis, 102; þis, 385; ðēos, 87; ðæs, 99; nsf. þēos, 211, 261; ðēos, 83; nsn. þis, 38, 252, 385, 463, 535; dsm. þissum, 658; ðissum, 110; þyssum, 130; ðeossum, 107; dsf. þisse, 603; dsn. ðissum, 101; asm. þysne, 156; asf. þās, 607, 642; ðæs, 502; asn. þis, 179, 251, 417.

þicgan, V (w. an occasional wk. pret., as here), eat: pret. 1p. þigdon (w. gen.), 409.

þider, adv., thither: 215, 301, 529, 588, 630.

þīn, poss. pron., thy, thine: nsm. ðīn, 63; nsf. 61; gsm. þīnes, 684; asm. ðīnne, 53; dpf. ðīnum, 62.

þing, n., thing: gp. þinga, 272.

þingian, W2., plead, supplicate, sue, intercede: 3s. þingað, 445; pret. 1s. þingade, 507.

þonne, adv., then: 208, 291, 322, 355, 358, 382, 603, 608, 612, 619, 700, 704, 705, 726; ðonne, 34.

þonne, conj., when: 162, 206, 210, 275, 539, 606; ðonne, 78, 80, 716; than: 175, 211, 388, 596; than when: 150.

þorhdrīfan, I, drive or hurl forth: pret. 3s. þorhdrāf, 162.

þrāg, f., sometimes, from time to time; ip. ðrāgum: 111.

þrēat, m., troop, throng, swarm: ns. ðrēat, 94; ds. þrēate, 386; as. 335; vs. 166; np. þrēatas, 567; ap. þrēatas, 422; oppression, punishment: ns. 324.

þrēo, num., three: af. 424; an. 501.

þrītig, num., thirty: an. 501.

þrōwian, W2., suffer, endure: pret. 1s. þrōwode, 501; 3s. ðrōwade, 488; inf. 41, 393.

þrym, m., glory, magnificence: ns. 660; ðrym, 36; as. 505; vs. 163.

þū, pron., thou: ns. 53, 59, 437, 535, 656, 672, 674, 687, 690, 695, 698, 701, 704(2), 705; ðū, 55, 59, 421, 439, 688, 694, 696, 709; tū, 57, 64; ds. þē, 55, 684, 691; as. þē, 408, 420, 693; ðē, 536, 697; as. þec, 537; ðec, 60; np. gē, 249, 616, 617; gp. ēower, 112; dp. ēow, 491, 507; ap. ēow, 91, 248, 470, 627; dual n. git, 481, 484; d. inc. 486; a. inc. 482.

þurfan, prep., need, have reason to: 1p. ðurfon, 114.

þurh, prep., w. accus., through, by, by virtue of, in, because of, for: 13, 14, 390, 399, 410, 436, 470, 493, 548, 584, 588, 604, 621, 644, 666, 680, 693, 722; ðurh, 6, 53, 59.

þus, adv., thus, so: 532, 568, 655, 729.

þūsend, n., thousand: ns. 301; gp. þūsenda, 400, 419, 720.

þūsendmǣlum, adv. (ip.), in or by thousands: 234, 507, 568, 630.

þyncan, WI., seem, appear: pret. 3s. þūhte, 432, 719; ðūhte, 22, 55.

U

ufan, adv., from above, down, above: 69, 341, 494, 702.

ūhte, f., dawn: as. ūhtan, 404, 463.

unclǽne, adj., unclean, foul, impure: apm. 608.

under, prep., w. dat., under: 134, 318; w. accus., 31, 90.

underne, adj., revealed, manifest, clear: nsn. 1.

ungēara, adv., before long, soon: 393.

ungelīc, adj., unlike, different: npm. ungelīce, 149.

unrīm, n., a countless number: as. 572.

unsib, f., enmity, strife, discord: as. unsibbe, 270.

ūp, upp, adv., up, above, upward, on high: ūp, 16, 169, 243, 265, 287, 326, 401, 405, 422, 441, 456, 459, 480, 504, 510, 552, 562, 623, 633, 658, 726; upp, 528.

ūpheofon, m., upper heaven, the heavens: as. 94; vs. ūpheofen, 166.

ūplic, adj., on high, heavenly: asm. ūplicne, 361.

uppe, adv., up, above, on high: 122, 141, 198, 229, 264, 292, 329, 372, 389, 395, 590, 645.

ūre, poss. pron., our: nsm. 546; apn. 390.

ūt, adv., out, forth, outside: 5, 34, 160, 162, 518.

ūtan, adv., without, on the outside: 341; w. ymb, about, round: 153.

uton, 1p. opt. of wītan, w. infin., let us: 297, 593, 642; uta, 215, 250.

W

wā, adv., woe: 341.

wadan, VI, go, travel: inf. 120.

wǽlm, m., surging flame: ds. welme, 39; as. 30.

wǽrgðu, f., indecl., condemnation, punishment: as. 89.

wǽstm, m., fruit: np. wǽstmas, 212.

wǽter, n., water: as. 6.

waldend, m., ruler, sovereign, lord: ns. 216, 563, 584, 586, 607; wealdend, 124; gs. waldendes, 118, 194, 299, 394; wealdendes, 576; as. 187, 198, 251; np. waldend, 24.

*wālic, adj., woeful, wretched: nsm. wk. wālica, 99.

wēa, m., woe, affliction: as. wēan, 42, 184, 335, 713; wēa, 319.

wealdan, red., possess: pret. 1s. wēold, 274.

weall, m., wall: ap. weallas, 650.

weallan, red., well, surge, boil: pret. 3s. wēol, 317.

weard, m., guardian, lord: ns. 512; as. 611, 659; vs. 420.

wel, adv., well: 364.

wēnan, WI., ween, suppose, imagine, believe; hope or look for, expect: 1s. wēne, 50, 89; 3p. wēnað, 622; pret. 2s. wēndest, 674; wēndes, 59; inf. 114, 450.

weorc, n., work, deed: ns. (?p.) 490; ip. weorcum, 221, 550; wercum, 48.

weornian, W2., wither, fail: pret. 3p. weornodon, 466.

weorod, n., host, multitude: as. werud, 33; gp. weoroda, 187, 197, 563, 580; weroda, 251.

weorðan, III, become, be, befall, take place: pret. 3s. wearð, 1, 380, 710; pp. geworden, 281, 427, 451, 463.

weorðmynt, m., honour, glory: as. 151.

weotod, adj. (pp.), appointed: nsn. 691.

wer, m., man: gp. wera, 490.

*wērgu, f., indecl., misery: as. 42.

wērig, adj., weary, wretched, miserable; evil, malign: nsm. 161, 426; wk.

wērega, 125; dsm. wk. wērigan, 710; asm. wk. wērigan, 331; wēregan, 667; isf. wk. wēregan, 35; npm. wērige, 342, 447, 628; wk. wērigan, 727.
wesan, anv., be: ls, eom, 96, 129, 155, 176; eam, 167; 2s. eart, 57, 439, 535, 656; 3s. is, 17, 38, 39, 61, 95, 99, 101, 102, 135, 140, 192, 203, 212, 213, 228, 252, 256, 259, 287, 332, 354, 364, 385, 394, 425, 439, 478, 555, 582, 583, 592, 595, 647, 660, 661, 663, 691; bið, 79, 181, 263, 303, 362, 605, 624; lp. syndon, 149; 2p. sind, 616; 3p. synd, 357; seondon, 103, 708; bēoð, 355, 612, 620; pret. ls. wæs, 81; wes, 89; 3s. wæs, 76, 189, 224, 242, 245, 280, 320, 321, 322, 324, 337, 338, 341, 365, 372, 382, 403, 450, 455, 463, 485, 499, 500, 530, 541(2), 545, 557, 564, 573, 667; lp. wæron, 234, 389; 3p. wæron, 329, 383, 432; opt. 2s. sēo, 687; 3s. 211, 264, 703, 706; pret. ls. wære, 123; 2s. wære, 56; 3s. wære, 63, 516, 719; 3p. wēron, 23; imp. 2s. bēo, 729. Negative contractions of ne + wesan: 3s. nis, 40, 92, 348; pret. 3s. næs, 489, 515; opt. pret. 3s. nære, 674.
wīd, adj., wide, broad, long: nsf. 698; apm. wīde, 188.
wīde, adv., widely, far: 256, 319, 332, 384, 683; comp. wīdor, 119.
wīf, n., woman: as. 471.
wiht, f., n., creature, wight: ns. 724; gp. wihta, 124.
wilcuma, m., welcome guest: npm. wilcuman, 616.
willa, m., will, command: as. willan, 472.
willan, anv., will, intend, be willing, wish, desire; shall, will: 3s. wile, 288, 303, 390, 395, 608; 2p. willað, 249; pret. ls. wolde 172; 3s. wolde, 399, 429, 434, 462, 560; lp. woldon, 232, 254; 3p. woldon, 345; opt. 3s. wille, 108, 115, 276, 621; pret. ls. wolde, 85; 3s. 316, 369, 371. Negative: 3s. nyle, 146; pret. 2s. noldæs, 729.
windig, adj., windy: nsm. wk. windiga, 135.
winnan, III, struggle, strive, fight: 3p. winnað, 135; pret. 2s. wunne, 704; pp. gewunnon, 717.
wīnsele, m., wine or banquet hall: ns. 93; as., 319, 384.
winter, m., winter, year: gp. wintra, 418, 475, 500.
wirsa, see yfel.
witan, prp., know: ls. wāt, 180; 2s. wāst, 704; 3s. wāt, 32; imp. 2s. wite, 698.
wīte, n., punishment, torment, torture: gs. wītes, 77, 99, 102, 156, 442, 451; ds. 48; as. 492, 634; np. wītu, 225; gp. wīta, 118; dp. wītum, 80, 727; ap. wītu, 184, 335, 390, 713; ip. wītum, 161, 342, 426, 447.
wītega, m., prophet: np. wītegan, 462; wītigan, 459; gp. wītegena, 490; dp. wītegum, 586.
wītehūs, n., house of torment: as. 626.
*****wītescræf,** n., cavern or den of torment: as. 690.
wið, prep., w. gen., towards, at: 700, 714; w. dat., over, against, before: 247, 431; w. accus., against, toward: 96, 430, 704.
wiðhabban, W3., withstand: inf. 517.
wlītan, I, look, gaze: inf. 407.
wlite, m., face, countenance, beauty: ns. 221; ds. 231; as. 151; is. 209.
wlitig, adj., beautiful, fair: nsn. 212; npm. wlitige, 650; apm. wlitige, 608.
wlonc, adj., rich: gp. wloncra, 93.
wolcn, n., cloud: gp. wolcna, 563; dp. wolcnum, 607; ap. wolcn, 6.
wom, m., n., stain, spot, sin: ns. 225; ip. wommum, 156.
*****wōm,** m., wailing, lamentation, noise: ns. 332.
womcwide, m., evil word or speech, blasphemy: dp. womcwidum, 281.

won, adj., dark, lurid: nsm. wk. wonna, 713.

wōp, m., wailing, weeping: ns. 332.

word, n., word, speech: ns. 161; is. 227; np. 357; dp. wordum, 414, 628; ap. 80, 154, 484; ip. wordum, 48, 65, 125, 221, 384, 407, 512, 659, 727.

wordcwide, m., words, speech: ap. wordcwedas, 35.

worn, m., magnitude: as. 77.

woruld, f., world, universe, age: gs. worulde, 93; weorulde, 209; ds. worulde, 180, 314, 500; as. worulde, 642; woruld, 59, 222, 607; gp. worulda, 222.

wracu, f., misery, retribution, vengeance: ns. 710; ds. wrece, 492; as. wrace, 184.

wræclāst, m., exile-path or journey: ap. wræclāstas, 120; wreclāstas, 187, 257.

wrāð, adj., angry: nsm. 281, 451.

wrāðe, adv., perversely, wickedly: 315.

wrecan, V, utter: 3s. wriceð, 35.

wrōht, f., strife: as. 368.

wuldor, n., glory, heaven: gs. wuldres, 14, 24, 42, 85, 106, 118, 140, 151, 174, 231, 235, 251, 342, 390, 447, 506, 512, 555, 584, 586, 592, 616, 648, 659; ds. wuldre, 202, 368, 407; as. wuldor, 59; is. wuldre, 120, 442.

wuldorcyning, m., king of glory: ns. 114, 426; ds. wuldorcyninge, 222, 311; as. 225.

wundian, W2., wound: pp. gewundod, 156.

wundor, n., wonder: gp. wundra, 6.

wunian, W2., dwell, live, inhabit, remain: 3s. wunað, 208, 592; 3p. wuniað, 506; pret. 1p. wunodon, 235; inf. 231, 257, 296, 311, 331, 418, 475, 554.

wurðian, W2., honour: pp. gewurðad, 535.

wyn, f., delight, pleasure, joy: gs. wynne, 174, ds. wynne, 197; as. 43; dp. wynnum, 235, 506, 554, 592; ip. wynnum, 209, 648.

wynsum, adj., pleasant: nsn. 212; apf. wynsume, 357.

wyrcan, WI., make, build, accomplish, attain: inf. 364, 371, 671.

wyrhta, m., maker, creator: ns. 14, 584.

wyrm, m., serpent: np. wyrmas, 102; gp. wyrma, 335; ap. (?) wyrmas, 135.

wyrt, f., plant: ap. wyrte, 357.

Y

yfel, n., evil, misery: gs. yfeles, 373; ds. yfele, 729.

yfel, adj., evil, wicked, bad: ap. yfle, 609; comp. nsn. wyrse, 124, 174; wirse, 24; wyrsa, 140.

ymb, prep. w. accus., around, round, about: 46, 47, 135, 153, 154, 218, 233, 496, 650, 660; after: 570, before: 424.

*ymbflēogan, II, fly around: pret. 3p. ymbflugon, 567.

ymbfōn, red., surround, circle: pp. ymbfangen, 143, 516.

*ymbhaldan, red., encompass, embrace: 3s. ymbhaldeð, 7.

ymbhwyrft, m., circuit, extent: as. 701.

*ymblyt, m., expanse, circuit: as. 7.

ymbūtan, adv., about, around: 263, 351.

APPENDIX

CHRIST AND SATAN AND CLASSICAL RHETORIC

Although J. J. Campbell suggested some time ago that the critic of Old English poetry be aware of the possibility of classical rhetorical influences in the structure of Old English verse, to date his suggestion has had little follow-through.[1] This is unfortunate, since the following pages demonstrate that *XSt,* at least, yields readily to rhetorical analysis. As an end in itself, rhetorical analysis is a valid exercise which illuminates the structure of the literary work and tells something about the level of sophistication of its creator and his audience. More important, it can provide the raw material from which the critic, taking other things into account, can synthesize a literary judgment. When, for example, we discover that one of the most powerful sections of the poem, the "Ealas" which comprise Satan's lament in lines 163-171, exhibits in its structure the rhetorical figures *prolepsis, hysterology, hypozeuxis* and *anaphora,* and that this lament immediately precedes the poem's first homiletic section, we are justified in supposing that the poet consciously contrived his lines to make as strong an impact on his audience as possible, thus to support his following exhortation. Again, when we see that the last lines of the poem, from line 690 through line 719, offer examples of *anaphora, schesis onomaton, metalepsis* and *paronomasia,* we find added support for the thematic and archetectonic argument that the poem is complete: the poet manipulated his rhetoric to give his work an impressive conclusion.

I do not suggest that the poet had a rhetorical handbook to which he referred as he composed, nor that he studied rhetoric formally, though the preceding analysis of the poem's structure and theme points to a level of knowledge on the part of the poet that I think assumes something like the trivium, of which rhetoric was a part. But even if we suppose that our author had no formal rhetorical training of any sort, we are obliged to recognize that he must have come into contact with, directly by reading himself or indirectly by listening to, the normal run of homilies, gospels both canonical and apocryphal, visions, and testament exegesis, which were the stuff of monastic edification in England from the seventh through the eleventh centuries. Even assuming for the sake of argument that our poet had no Latin (but all evidence points in the other direction), he still would have become familiar, directly or indirectly, with vernacular devotional

---

[1] Jackson J. Campbell, "Knowledge of Rhetorical Figures in Anglo-Saxon England," *JEGP,* 66 (1967), 1-20; "Learned Rhetoric in Old English Poetry," *MP,* 63 (1966), 189-201. Also of interest are: A. Bartlett, *Larger Rhetorical Patterns in Anglo-Saxon Poetry* (New York, 1935); C. Schaar, *Critical Studies in the Cynewulf Group* (Lund, 1949); M. Schlauch, "An Old English *Encomium Urbis,*" *JEGP,* 40 (1941), 14-28; "*The Dream of the Rood* as Prosopopoeia," in *Essays and Studies in Honor of Carleton Brown* (New York, 1940), pp. 23-34; J. E. Cross, *Latin Themes in Old English Poetry* (Lund, 1962); B. K. Martin, "Aspects of Winter in Latin and Old English Poetry," *JEGP,* 68 (1969), 375-90.

works based on Latin originals, often hardly more than translations, and found his rhetoric there. In the event, we have the text of the poem, a text which exhibits numerous classical rhetorical features.

I have chosen Bede's *De Schematibus et Tropis* as the organ of rhetorical investigation, since it is a work which leans heavily on the rhetorical texts available in England from the eighth century on, e.g., Isidore's *Etymologiarum,* Donatus' *Ars Major,* Cassidorus' *Expositio in Psalterium,* and the grammars of Charius and Diomedes, and because surviving manuscripts indicate that it was popular.[2] For the purpose of analysis I suppose that the various laments of Part I are discrete entities, i.e., that explanations offered for the devils' sufferings in lines 36b-64 are rhetorically independent of, though thematically related to, other explanations given throughout Part I.

Bede divides his analysis of rhetoric into two large categories, *schemes* and *tropes,* the one a manipulation of words, the other a manipulation of thought. Concerning *schemes,* he writes: "It is quite usual to find that, for the sake of embellishment, word-order in written composition is frequently fashioned in a figured manner different from ordinary speech."[3] A *trope* he defines as "a figure in which a word, either from need or for the purpose of embellishment, is shifted from its proper meaning to one similar but not proper to it."[4] My analysis follows Bede's arrangement, dealing first with the schemes, then with the tropes, taking up in turn the different forms and examples of each according to his treatment. Certain schemes will not be investigated: it would be pointless to investigate *paromoeon* (alliteration). Yet others will be taken in conjunction. *Prolepsis,* a scheme, and *hysteronproteron,* a trope, are so closely akin, the one dependent upon the presence of the other, that simultaneous treatment becomes a necessity.

PROLEPSIS is defined as "anticipating or taking up in advance . . . the name of a figure in which those things which ought to follow are placed ahead."[5] Bede exemplifies this scheme by the line " 'His foundation is on the Lordly mountain / The Lord loveth the gates of Zion.' The word 'His' is used first and thereafter it is made clear that the reference is to the Lord." *HYSTEROLOGY* is "hysteron-proteron or putting the 'cart-before-the-horse'; it is an inversion of thought brought about by changing the natural word-order." He exemplifies this trope by the line " 'He shall receive a blessing from the Lord and righteousness from the God of his salvation.' God first pardons wickedness with His compassion and thus rewards righteousness with his blessings."[6]

The first line of *XSt* contains a simple *prolepsis,* since the þæt of þæt wearð *underne* is not adequately clarified until lines 2-3: "þæt meotod hæfde miht and strengðo / ðā hē gefestnade foldan scēatas." A *prolepsis* leading to a *hysterology* is found in lines 24b-33, when the poet states that the devils established a home in hell, lines 24b-25, and then proceeds to detail how they were brought to hell to so establish it. A similar structure occurs in lines 119-124, where Satan, concluding his first dramatic monologue, describes his punishment

---

[2] Ibid., p. 9; Gussie H. Tanenhaus, "Bede's *De Schematibus et Tropis*—A Translation," *QJS,* 48 (1962), 238-39. I have used this translation throughout, having checked it against the original.
[3] Tanenhaus, 240.
[4] Ibid., 244.
[5] Ibid., 240.
[6] Ibid., 248.

in four and a half lines before giving an explanation of its cause in two and a half. Exactly the same manipulation of thought is found in lines 163-175 when Satan laments his ejection from heaven and the sorrows resulting therefrom in some nine lines before revealing the cause of the ejection in four. Line 189 contains a *prolepsis,* in that its first stave remarks that Satan "turned to hell," the second stave clarifying this by stating that he was "vanquished." Even this one-line *prolepsis* seems very close to *hysteron-proteron.*

The second homiletic section of Part I indicates *hysteron-proteron* in lines 285-290 by anticipating the rewards to be gained in heaven, lines 285-288, then clarifying in exactly what manner these are to be won in lines 289-290. Another trope of the same type occurs in lines 303-305a; the first stave of 303 maintains that "he will be happy," while the remaining lines detail the conditional procedures whereby such happiness is to be gained.

In a sense, all of the second part of *XSt* up to line 511 might well be considered an extended *hysteron-proteron,* since Christ's motivation in the harrowing of hell is clarified only in his speech to the just in Paradise, lines 469b-511. Christ's attitude of charitable concern expressed in the speech finds its ultimate symbol in the personal sacrifice of the crucifixion; it is the crucifixion that effects the harrowing. Since the harrowing is treated at length before mention is made of the crucifixion, the effect is presented before the cause, the "cart-before-the-horse," and the passage becomes an extended exercise in *hysterology.* One could argue, too, that the chronological displacement of Part III is an example of structural *hysteron-proteron.* Simple *prolepsis* occurs in lines 378b-379a, since the "egsa" which the poet describes as coming to the devils is clarified in line 379a as "dyne for deman." (For *hysteron-proteron* in lines 19-20, see "Explanatory Notes," pp. 92-93.)

ZEUGMA Bede divides into two categories, defining them thus: "a joining . . . in which many ideas depend upon one word or are enclosed in one long utterance."[7] A *zeugma* of the first category, that in which "many ideas depend upon one word," can be found in lines 4-6, which state that Christ himself set the sun and moon, stones and earth, etc., the whole catalogue depending on the verb "sette." Lines 84-88 provide a somewhat more complex example of the scheme:

Þā ic in mōde	mīnum hogade
þæt ic wolde tōwerpan	wuldres lēoman,
bearn hēlendes,	āgan mē burga gewald
eall tō æhte,	and ðēos earme hēap
þe ic hebbe tō helle	hām gelēdde.

The "hogade" in line 84b governs the discourse through line 88. Though the "wolde" in line 85 is dependent upon "hogade," it too has dependencies, "tōwerpan" and "āgan." Here is a *zeugma* within a *zeugma.* Lines 303-305 have "oferhycgen" and "cwēman" of 304, and "ādwæscan" of 305a depending on "se þe æfre wille" of 303b; the "mōton" of line 311b governs "wunian" and "āgan" of lines 311b and 313a respectively.

A most complicated example of *zeugma* occurs in lines 119-121:

Forðon ic sceal hēan and earm	hweorfan ðȳ wīdor.
wadan wræclāstas,	wuldre benēmed,
duguðum bedēled,	nænigne drēam āgan

---

7 Ibid., 241.

Here the "sceal" of line 119a governs "hweorfan," "wadan," and "āgan"; the second stave of line 120 and the first stave of 121 are dependent upon and modify the "ic" of line 119a. This double *zeugma* falls into a chiastic pattern. If the staves from line 119 through 121 are lettered consecutively, a diagram of their relationship would appear as follows:

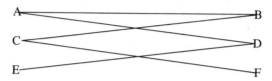

This group of lines, down through line 124, also constitutes a *hysteron-proteron*.

Bede defines *HYPOZEUXIS* as "just the opposite of the figure mentioned above, and [it] occurs where separate thoughts or words are joined each to its separate clause."[8] The finest example of this figure in the poem is contained in lines 163-171. From line 163-166, each stave is a separate thought, an isolated though related element of Satan's lament. With line 167, the *hypozeuxis* is expanded to include whole lines, and continues until line 171:

Ēalā þæt ic eam ealles lēas   ēcan drēames,
þæt ic mid handum ne mæg   heofon geræcan,
nē mid ēagum ne mōt   ūp lōcian,
nē hūru mid ēarum ne sceal   æfre gehēran
þære byrhtestan   bēman stefne . . . (ll. 167-171)

The off-verses of lines 167-170 contain that of which the devil is deprived; this is expressed with an adjective-noun construction in line 167b, essentially the same construction as object of an infinitive in line 171, with infinitives in 168, 169, 170. The balance of lines 168-170 is remarkable, and the sound patterns are quite complex. Though the alliterative pattern of the lines differs, with 168 having alliteration on the "h" and 169-170 having vowel alliteration, the nasal repetitions in the first staves of the three lines serve to bind them together, especially since the lines have similar grammatical structures. The "sceal" in line 170a appears to be a conscious variation in the sound pattern. The reader or listener would, after the balance of the previous lines, and the beginning of the same nasal pattern in this, expect a verb with a nasal sound. Instead there is the sibilant "sceal." Such a patterning could not have been the product of chance.

The lines of this particular lament continue in a well-defined rhetorical pattern. Lines 172-187a constitute what Adeline Bartlett termed an "envelope pattern," a "logically unified group of verses bound together by the repetition at the end of words, ideas, or words and ideas which are employed at the beginning."[9] In this case the explanation of the cause of the deprivations described in lines 163-171 is given in lines 172-173 and again in lines 186-187a, and thus we again have the pattern *hysteron-proteron* (see above, p. 153). The intervening material relates the sufferings that Satan believes await him. Within this envelope are two examples of *zeugma*: the "wolde" of line 172a governs the

   [8] Ibid., 241.
   [9] Bartlett, p. 9.

"ādrīfan" and "āgan" of line 173; the "ne þenceþ" of 182b governs the "heran" of the same stave and "cwēman" of 183a.

Yet another example of *hypozeuxis*, from the second homiletic section of Part I, occurs in lines 297b-300a. In Part III, lines 697b-709, the powerful catalogue of imperatives by which Christ orders Satan to hell exemplify the same figure.

SYLLEPSIS occurs "when words which do not agree in number are used together to constitute a single thought.... There may also be a *syllepsis* in the sense when a singular noun is used in place of a plural, or a plural in the place of a singular."[10] There is only one definite example of this scheme in the poem,[11] but the recognition of it clears up a textual difficulty. Line 540a contains the plural pronoun "sume," line 541a the singular "he," with its referent, Didymus, mentioned in 541b. If there be a stop at the end of line 540, and if the disparity between pronoun and noun be recognized as *syllepsis*, the sense of the lines becomes quite clear: of those who did not acknowledge what Peter and the disciples maintained, i.e., that Christ had risen, one was Didymus, etc. (see "Explanatory Notes," p. 115).

ANAPHORA, according to Bede, "occurs when the same word is used at the beginning of two or more verses."[12] *Anaphora* with the negative particle "ne" is found in lines 92-94, 137-139, 348-349, 489-490; with "hwīlum" in lines 131-135, 712-715; with "ā" signifying "forever" in line 314. The most impressive *anaphora* in the poem is that contained in lines 163-167, with the "Ēalā" repeated nine times; in lines 168-170 "ne" is repeated five times. The whole is structured as a series of *hypozeuxis*, and is quite well done.

EPIZEUXIS, "the repetition of the same word in the same line without any intervening words,"[13] yields two examples, line 222a "geond ealra *worulda woruld*," and 313a "*āgan drēama drēam.*" *PARONOMASIA*, or word-play, "the figure in which the words used closely resemble each other in sound but differ in meaning,"[14] occurs four times. Line 222 reads: "geond ealra *worulda woruld* mid *wuldor*cyning." Line 660a contains "*þegnas* ymb *þēoden,*" a possible *paronomasia*, while some lines further along there occurs "*ealra ealdor,*" 662a. Line 714a gives "*lǣhte* wiþ þæs *lāþan.*"

Bede defines *HOMOEOTELEUTON* as "a figure built on similar endings, that is, when the middle and final sections of a verse or thought end in the same syllable"; *HOMOEPTOTON* he defines as "a figure in which several words end with like sounds."[15] Added to this incipient confusion is the fact that the examples Bede provides for one figure could be included easily under the rubric of the other. But Bede is not alone in this, the same being true of Isidore's treatment of *homoeoteleuton* and *homoeoptoton*.[16] I have chosen, therefore, to use the more familiar term *homoeoteleuton* to designate the figure based upon similar endings.

[10] Tanenhaus, 241.

[11] Syllepsis might conceivably be found in lines 22-24 and 262b-265. In the former, the third person plural personal pronouns—"him," "hie"—have as a referent the singular, though collective, noun, "cyn," line 20b; in the latter, the plural pronoun "sume" is particularized in the third singular "he."

[12] Tanenhaus, 242.

[13] Ibid.

[14] Ibid.

[15] Ibid., 243.

[16] Isidori Hispalensis Episcopi, *Etymologiarum Libri XX*, PL 82, Liber I, caput 36, col. 111.

Any such figure must be handled carefully when dealing with a highly inflected language, lest grammatical requirements such as the concord of adjective and noun be mistaken for it.[17] When the poetic convention with which one is concerned is, like the Old English, traditionally formulaic, additional care must be taken lest one catalogue as the figure a half-line, say, which, though exhibiting similar endings within itself, would scarcely be recognized as rhetorical by either poet or audience. Because of these dangers, the requirement I have set for inclusion in this figure is that the sound patterns must be carried through at least two half-lines. For, while there is a possibility that such things as "sunnan and monan" (4b), "wordum in witum" (727a), and "garum on galgan" (509a) might have been recognized as rhetorical in themselves,[18] I do not think the likelihood of this is great.

Much more indicative of a conscious patterning is the series of lines comprising an *hypozeuxis*, lines 167-171:

Ēalā þæt ic eam ealles lēas	ēcan drēames
þæt ic mid hondum ne mæg	heofon geræcan
nē mid eagum ne mot	ūp lōcian
nē hūru mid ēarum ne sceal	æfre gehēran
þǣre byrhtestan	beman stefne.

The **n** sounds which terminate the off verses and the **m** sounds which terminate the first foot of the on-verses of lines 168-170, coupled with the *polysyndaton* and *anaphora* of **ne**, suggest a striving for rhetorical effect.[19]

SCHESIS ONOMATON "is a series of synonymous phrases, [in which] groups of words that differ in sound but are alike in meaning are linked together."[20] The criterion of inclusion here is the juxtaposition of half-lines. While there is no doubt that individual half-lines themselves, when constituted, say, of two substantives, e.g., "wordum and woercum" (221a), might formally indicate *schesis onomaton*, the probability that metrical and grammatical considerations are responsible for the collocation rules out counting such lines as rhetorical figures. Even so, since appositional variation was a convention with which the Old English poets worked, we find numerous examples of the figure in *XSt*:

---

[17] L. Laurand, *Etudes sur le Style des Discours de Ciceron* (Amsterdam, 1965, reprint of the edition of 1936-38), pp. 131-32, remarks of *homoeoteleuton*: "La similitude des déclinaisons et des conjugaisons latines les ramenait même quand l'auteur ne les cherchait pas; aussi est-il bien difficile de déterminer quelle sont celles qui doivent compter dans l'histoire du rythme." The same may be said for Old English.

[18] John W. Ehrstine in "Patterns of Sound in Anglo-Saxon Poetry," *Research Studies* (Washington State University), 33 (1962), 151-62, argues that since Old English was a three-stress rather than a four-stress language, every syllable was clearly audible and distinguishable. If all terminal syllable sounds, internal as well as those that end complete words, were in fact heard, then we might have to reassess the frequency of occurrence of rhetorical figures founded on the similarity of endings in Old English verse.

[19] I note the following series of lines as possibly exhibiting the figure:

Dēman wē on eorðan,	ærror lifigend,
onlūcan mid listum	locen waldendes,
ongeotan gāstlice. (ll. 298-301a)	
þæt bið daga lengust	and dinna mǣst
hlūd gehēred,	þonne hǣlend cymeð,
waldend mid wolcnum. (ll. 605-607a)	

[20] Tanenhaus, 243.

Part I: 23b-24a, 30b-31a&b, 35b-36a, 41b-42a, 44b-45a, 46b-47a, 51b-52a, 56b-57a, 70b-71a, 71b-72a&b-73a, 81b-82a, 85b-86a, 92b-93a&b-94a, 103b-104a, 115b-116a, 117b-118a, 120b-121a&b, 123b-124a, 132b-133a, 155b-156a, 159b-160a, 163a&b-164a, 165a-165b, 172b-173a, 176-177, 182b-183a, 184a-184b, 185a-185b, 186b-187a, 197b-198a&b, 199b-200a, 204b-205a, 213b-214a, 216a&b-217a, 235b-236a, 236b-237a, 238b-239a, 241b-242a, 250b-251a, 260b-261a, 277b-278a, 293b-294a, 304a&b-305a, 319b-320a, 332-333, 342b-343a, 348a&b-349a, 356b-357a&b;

Part II: 375b-376a, 378b-379a, 385b-386a&b, 391b-392a, 394b-395a, 401b-402a, 405b-406a, 412b-413a&b, 439b-440a, 451b-452a, 456b-457a, 459a-459b, 460b-461a, 482b-483a, 495a-495b, 562b-563a, 574b-575a, 585b-586a, 594a&b-595a, 597b-598a-599b, 601b-602a, 606b-607a, 628b-629a, 639b-640a, 656b-657a;

Part III: 681b-682a, 686a-686b-687a, 696b-697a.

There are some appositional variations that would qualify as *schesis onomaton* were the requirement of half-line juxtaposition waived. Here we would find:

9a-10b, 42b-43b, 104b-105b, 117a-118b, 255-256a, 259b-260b-261a, 267b-268b, 291b-292b, 308b-309b, 316a-317a, 365a-366a&b, 445a-446a, 512a-513a, 545b-546b, 557b-560a, 608b-609b, 663a-664b, 665a-666a, 680a-681a, 690a-691a, 711a-712a.

More extended examples of the figure include:

163-171, 180b-187a, 197-207, 450b-454, 455-457, 504b-507a, 589-593a, 603-604, 656-662, 663-664, 697b-709.

HIRMOS, "or connected sequence, is a figure in which the train of thought in a speech remains unbroken to the very end; neither the substance nor the subject is in any way altered."[21] Examples of this figure can be found in lines 119-124a, Bartlett's envelope pattern lines 172-188, and lines 628-632a.

POLYSYNDETON "is discourse woven together by many conjunctions."[22] The poet shows a marked preference for the **ne** in polysyndetic construction: e.g., 92b-95a, 137a-139b, 167-171, 348-349, 489-490.

Bede defines a *TROPE* as a "figure in which a word, either from need or for the purpose of embellishment, is shifted from its proper meaning to one similar but not proper to it."[23] This rather general and vague definition is concretized as Bede analyzes and exemplifies different kinds of tropes.

The first trope is *METAPHOR,* which, Bede states, "is a transference of qualities and words, and is effected in four ways: (a) from one animate creature to another animate creature; (b) from one inanimate object to another inanimate object; (c) from an animate creature to an inanimate object; (d) from an inanimate object to an animate creature."[24]

The poem contains few metaphors as such. It may appear to a modern reader that lines 78-79a—"Hē spearcade ðonne hē spreocan ongan / fȳre and

---

[21] Ibid., 244.
[22] Ibid.
[23] Ibid.
[24] Ibid.

ātre,"—contain a well-turned metaphor by which Satan is likened to his flaming environment, and himself takes on something of the fiery aspects of the regions of hell. Such an interpretation is reinforced by the intensive verb "indraf" for "speak" in the next line: "þonne hē in wītum þā word indrāf." Here it is the quality of Satan's speech that causes the sparks. But one cannot be sure. It is at least possible that both poet and audience believed this to be a literal description of Satan. One is on safer ground with lines 161b-162a, "wordum spearcum flēah / āttre gelīcost," where there is a transference from the person of Satan to the very words he utters.

Lines 39b, 70 and 317 probably contain a metaphor. Since hell in *XSt* is conceived to be a cavern, and since the cavern is thought to have a solid floor, as is suggested in Part III when Christ orders Satan to explore the depths of hell and the poet pictures him as standing on its solid bottom with the flames leaping around him, then line 39b "flōr is on welme" is a metaphor, with the "welme" actually having reference to the lake or river of fire which flows over the floor of hell. Hence line 70, "hæfdon hym tō hyhte helle flōras, / beornende bealo," becomes a metaphor, as does line 317, "Flōr āttre wēol." If, however, the poet and audience conceived the floor of hell to be in fact a sea of fire in which the devils swam, then the metaphors vanish, since a literal description would be intended in these lines. Another metaphor, one concerning which there can be little doubt, occurs in line 385, where the devils refer to Christ's coming as a "storm." This appears to be the poet's attempt to succinctly characterize the chaos wrought in hell by the harrowing.

There is a metaphoric use of images of light and dark in the poem. We move from the pedestrian statement that the devils' lost the Lord's light because of their pride (l. 68), to the assertion that whoever seeks heaven must literally "scine" (l. 209b), to the specific qualification of Christ as "Byrhtword" (l. 236b) and "sigetorht" (l. 238b). The gifts which the blessed offer to the Lord are termed "blōstman stences, wyrte wynsume" (ll. 356b-357a), a metaphor which the poet explains in line 357b: "þæt synd word godes."

Lines 540-544 contain an interesting and involved trope:

Sume hit ne mihton	mōde oncnāwan:
þæt wæs se dēora	Didimus wæs hāten,
ǣr hē mid hondum	hǣlend genōm
sylfne be sīdan	þǣr hē his swāt forlēt:
fēollon tō foldan	fulwihtes bæðe.

The Gospel of John 19:33-34, remarks that when Christ's side was pierced with a lance water and blood flowed; John 20:24-29, which deals with the "doubting Thomas" episode that the poet is following here, says nothing about anything flowing from Christ's side. It was a common Patristic interpretation that the water and blood which poured from Christ on the cross was a symbol of baptism. What we have in these lines is a conflation of the cross and Thomas episodes, with the "fulwihtes bæðe" based upon exegetical interpretations of the former. It is an example of an allegorical reading having become so prevalent that it was substituted for the literal statement upon which it was once grounded.

METALEPSIS occurs when "the true meaning of a word becomes apparent only gradually; one must reach the end of the thought before a word used earlier in the verse is completely understood."[25] Two examples of *metalepsis* occur in

---

[25] Ibid., 246.

the poem. The most impressive is the repeated use of the verb "metan" and its derivatives in Christ's curse of Satan in Part III. Bosworth-Toller[26] and Grein-Köhler[27] limit the uses and restrict the meaning of the verb to "measure." But by the repeated and emphatic use of the verb in a context which violently commands Satan to turn to the sufferings of hell, "metan" takes on the connotations of "fully experience" rather than the prescribed primary denotation of "measure." Christ orders Satan to know the pains of hell:

Wite þū ēac, āwyrgda,	hū wīd and sīd
helheoðo drēorig,	and mid hondum āmet.
Grīp wið þæs grundes;	gang þonne swā
oððæt þū þone ymbhwyrft	alne cunne,
and ǣrest āmet	ufan tō grunde,
and hū sīd sēo	se swarta ēðm.
Wāst þū þonne þē geornor	þæt þū wið god wunne,
seoððan þū þonne hafast	handum āmetene
hū hēh and dēop	hell inneweard sēo,
grim grǣfhūs.	Gong ricene tō,
ǣr twā seondon	tīda āgongene,
þæt ðū merced hūs	āmetan hæbbe. (ll. 698-709)

Hwīlum mid folmum mæt. (l. 712b)

þæt þurh synne cræft   sūsle āmǣte. (l. 722)

The sense of these lines is that Satan should come into crushingly intimate contact with hell, a hell that he has not fully plumbed in any previous sufferings.

Yet another *metalepsis* is found in Part II, lines 378b-402. In 378b the narrator explains that terror came to the devils, terror caused by "dyne for deman." In line 392a the devils themselves refer to their fear, and equate it with the "dyne." It is only in lines 401b-402a that the "dyne" is revealed as "engla sweg," the songs of the angels who accompanied Christ on his mission to hell. The poet has given two perspectives on the phenomenon of *dyne*: for the devils it is a noise productive of terror; by the just it is recognized as that which it is in fact, the song of the angels. Because the harrowing was for the devils an event which marked the destruction of their power over man, so the song was simply a noise; for the just the harrowing was a release from bondage, and hence their recognition of the angelic harmony.

Bede defines *ANTONOMASIA* as "the use of an epithet in place of a proper name."[28] This trope is well represented in *XSt*, though it must be admitted that many of the epithets the poet uses for Christ, God, the saints, Satan, and the devils are among the most common in the poetic corpus: there is nothing particularly striking in terming Christ "wuldres waldend" or the devil "awyrgda." Occasionally, as in the epithet "Byrhtword," the poet is capable of a happy formation.

[26] J. Bosworth and T. Northcote Toller, *An Anglo-Saxon Dictionary* (London, 1898), p. 681. Neither Toller's *Supplement* (London, 1921), nor A. Campbell's *Enlarged Addenda and Corrigenda to the Supplement* (Oxford, 1972), provides an additional meaning for "metan."

[27] C. W. M. Grein and J. J. Köhler, *Sprachschatz der Angelsachsischen Dichter* (Heidelburg, 1912), p. 464.

[28] Tanenhaus, 246.

Antonomasia is found:

Part I: 10b, 23b-24a, 34a, 46b-47a, 65a, 72b-73a, 76a, 85b-86a, 118b,
123b-124a, 125a, 132b-133a, 154a, 159b-160a, 163b, 182a, 187a, 190a,
197b, 198b, 202a, 216b, 222b, 225b, 235b-236a, 236b, 238b, 242a,
250b-251a, 279b, 311a, 315a, 317a, 339b;

Part II: 373a, 386b, 394b-395a, 406a, 411a, 420b, 424b, 426b, 435b, 446a,
456b-457a, 459b, 468b, 469b, 482b-483a, 512a-513a, 518b, 533b, 541a,
555, 560a, 562b-563a, 566b, 574b-575a, 576b, 585b, 586b, 615a, 626a,
638a, 639b-640a, 646b, 656a-656b-657a, 659a, 662a;

Part III: 667a, 669b, 676b-677a, 680a-681a, 682b, 690a, 694a, 696b-697a, 698a,
710a, 712a, 714a, 717b, 718a, 724a, 725, 727b.

Bede defines *SYNECDOCHE* as a "designation allowing full understanding of a thing although saying that it is quantitatively more or less than it is in
actuality. It either designates the whole by means of a part.... Or a part by
means of the whole."[29] The most obvious example of this trope is line 381, where
the blessed are said to have been joyful during the harrowing when they saw the
"hefod" of the saviour. Another is line 564b, wherein it is said that the "hand
godes" appeared in a cloud to elevate Christ to heaven.

ONOMATOPOEIA occurs when "a word is formed from its sound."[30] We
have an example of the trope in line 333, "gristbitunge and gnornunge mecga."
ASTEISMOS or *URBANITY* "is a trope of inestimable power. Every expression which is free of a rustic simplicity and has the polish of urbane elegance is
considered an instance of *asteismos*."[31] Chief among the candidates for this
accolade I would place the circumlocutory designation of time in lines 499-501:

Þā wæs þæs mæles	mearc āgangen
þæt on worulde wæs	wintra gerīmes
þrēo and þrītig gēara	ær ic þrōwede.

PERIPHRASIS, "a circumlocution ... used either to embellish and expand
a simple idea or to avoid the direct mention of an unpleasant subject,"[32] yields
two examples from Part I of the poem. The initial eighteen lines of the work are
an embellishment on the theme "He created," the purpose of which is to
adequately introduce the grandeur of the Son at the beginning of a poem that is to
deal specifically with him. The second example is the rather ironic and enigmatic
statement made by Satan in lines 256b-258a: "Cūð is wīde / þæt wreclāstas
wunian mōton / grimme grundas." In context, since the comment is made
immediately after Satan mentions that he had attempted to drive the king from
his throne, it can be understood as a periphrasis of the simple statement that "the
devils were defeated."

ALLEGORY "is a trope in which a meaning other than the literal is
indicated."[33] We have an example of this, I think, in lines 19-20 which comprise
an allegorical reference to the creation of angels and men (see notes to these
lines). As a sub-classification of allegory Bede includes *IRONY,* "a trope by

---

[29] Ibid., 247.
[30] Ibid.
[31] Ibid., 250.
[32] Ibid., 247-48.
[33] Ibid., 249.

means of which one thing is said while its exact opposite is intended."[34] As irony I classify those lines in which *hyht* with its connotations of "joyful expectation" are linked to hell and its pains, e.g., 11, 70, 334-336, and also those instances where the poet terms hell a *winsele,* lines 319a, 384a. There may also be irony in Satan's statement "Nis nū ende feor / þæt wē sceolun ætsomne sūsel þrōwian" (ll. 40b-41), when in fact he and his host are experiencing torments as he is speaking. This is a more likely interpretation than attempting to connect these lines with the harrowing or the last judgment. *SARCASM,* another sub-classification of allegory, is "hostile derision laden with hate."[35] As examples we have the devils' response to Satan's first speech, lines 53-64, and their equally genial acknowledgement of his return to hell in line 729. Most powerful is the sarcasm of Christ's words to Satan, lines 690-709.

Bede gives the name *PARADIGMA* to the trope which "use(s) . . . an example for the sake of encouragement or restraint."[36] Since the manipulation of exempla is a structural principle of the poem, it is very likely that the poet was aware of the practical, if not the theoretical, implications of this figure.

A technique Bede does not discuss is *METATHESIS,* and it is central to an analysis of *XSt. Metathesis* is neither a scheme nor a trope, and so falls without Bede's purview. It is rather a rhetorical technique or device, the manner in which an orator brings events, past or future, before the eyes of his audience and makes them live. Isidore of Seville defines it thus:

> It is *metathesis* which places the minds of judges in (contact with) things past or future, in this way: "Recall to mind the spectacle (of) the assailant of the miserable republic, and allow yourselves to see the fires, slaughter, rapine, pillaging, the harm done to the persons of free men, the servitude of mothers, the abuses of the old."[37]

Projection is the essence of *Christ and Satan,* mostly projection backward into time, and even beyond time into eternity, as when the poet treats the expulsion of the devils from heaven and their laments in hell, the harrowing and the temptation. There is only one occasion, the last judgment in Part II, where the poet brings his audience forward through time to its consummation. It is on the success or failure of the *metathesis* that the purpose of *XSt* rests. If the audience were moved by the detailed description of hell presented in the work through the eyes of an eternally wretched and suffering Satan, and could be made to feel the joy of the blessed at the harrowing, and to recognize Christ's charity and compassion for men in his speech to the just; if they could piece together some idea of heaven, grasping perhaps its ineffable brightness as opposed to the dismal gloom of hell; finally could they recognize the righteous moral indignation of the tempted Christ, the God-Man, and feel his consummate power in the curse of Satan, then the moral exhortations, for which, in a sense, the whole works exists, would be efficacious.

---

[34] Ibid., 250.
[35] Ibid.
[36] Ibid., 253.
[37] Isidori Hispalensis Episcopi, *Etymologiarum Libri XX,* Liber II, caput 21, col. 138.

SELECTED BIBLIOGRAPHY

Complete Editions (in Chronological Order)

Junius, Francis. *Cædmonis Monachi Paraphrasis Poetica Genesios ac praecipuarum Sacrae paginae Historiarum, abhinc annos M. LXX. Anglo-Saxonice conscripta, & nunc primum edita*... Amstelodami... MDCLV.

Thorpe, Benjamin. *Cædmon's Metrical Paraphrase of Parts of the Holy Scriptures, in Anglo-Saxon*. London, 1832.

Bouterwek, Karl W. *Cædmon's des Angelsachsen biblische Dichtungen*. Vol. 1, Gütersloh, 1852. Text, pp. 165-90; notes, pp. 326-27.

Grein, Christian W. M. *Bibliothek der angelsächsischen Poesie*. Vol. 1. Göttingen, 1857.

Wülker, Richard P. *Bibliothek der angelsächsischen Poesie*. Vol. 2. Leipzig, 1894.

Clubb, Merrel D. *Christ and Satan, an Old English Poem*. New Haven, 1925.

Krapp, George P. *The Junius Manuscript*, Vol. 1 of *The Anglo-Saxon Poetic Records*. New York, 1931.

Full-sized Facsimile Reproduction of the Manuscript

Gollancz, Sir Israel. *The Cædmon Manuscript of Anglo-Saxon Biblical Poetry, Junius XI in the Bodleian Library*. Oxford, 1927.

Critical and Textual Discussions, Sources, Interpretations, etc.

Abbetmeyer, C. E. *Old English Poetical Motives Derived from the Doctrine of Sin*. Minneapolis and New York, 1903.

Barnouw, Adriaan. *Textkritische Untersuchungen nach dem Gebrauch des Bestimmten Artikels und des Schwachen Adjectives in der Altenglischen Poesie*. Leiden, 1902.

Bartlett, Adeline. *The Larger Rhetorical Patterns in Anglo-Saxon Poetry*. New York, 1935.

Benson, Larry. "The Literary Character of Anglo-Saxon Formulaic Poetry." *PMLA*, 81 (1966), 334-41.

Bessai, Frank. "Commitatus and Exile in O. E. Poetry." *Culture*, 25 (1964), 130-44.

Bethurum, Dorothy, ed. *The Homilies of Wulfstan*. Oxford, 1957.

Bliss, A. J. "Single Half-Lines in Old English Poetry." *N&Q*, 216 (1971), 442-49.

Bloomfield, Morton W. *The Seven Deadly Sins*. East Lansing, 1952.

_____ ."Patristics and Old English Literature: Notes on Some Poems." *CL*, 14 (1962), 36-43.

Bosworth, J., and T. Northcote Toller. *An Anglo-Saxon Dictionary.* Oxford, 1898.

Botte, D. B. "Prima Resurrectio. Un vestige de millénarisme dans les liturgies occidentales." *RTAM,* 15 (1948), 5-17.

Bousset, W. *The Anti-Christ Legend.* Trans. by A. H. Keane. London, 1896.

Brandl, Alois. *Geschichte der Altenglischen Literatur.* Strassburg, 1908.

Bright, J. W. "Jottings on the Cædmonian *Christ and Satan.*" *MLN,* 18 (1903), 128-31.

Brooke, S. *The History of Early English Literature.* London, 1892.

Campbell, A. *Old English Grammar.* Oxford, 1959.

_____ . *An Anglo-Saxon Dictionary: Enlarged Addenda and Corrigenda . . . to the Supplement by T. Northcote Toller.* Oxford, 1972.

Campbell, J. J. "Oral Poetry in *The Seafarer.*" *Speculum,* 35 (1960), 87-96.

_____ . "Learned Rhetoric in Old English Poetry." *MP,* 63 (1966), 189-201.

_____ . "Knowledge of Rhetorical Figures in Anglo-Saxon England." *JEGP,* 66 (1967), 1-20.

Capek, Michael. "The Nationality of a Translator: Some Notes on the Syntax of *Genesis B.*" *Neophil,* 55 (1971), 89-96.

Casey, R. P. "The Apocalypse of Paul." *JTS,* 34 (1933), 1-10.

Chaney, William A. "Paganism to Christianity in Anglo-Saxon England." *Harvard Theological Review,* 53 (1960), 197-217.

Charles, R. H. *Eschatology, Hebrew, Jewish and Christian, or A Critical History of Doctrine of Future Life in Israel, in Judaism, in Christianity.* London, 1903.

_____ , ed. *The Apocrypha and Pseudepigrapha of the Old Testament in English.* 2 vols. Oxford, 1913.

Clemoes, Peter. *Liturgical Influence on Punctuation in Late Old English and Early Middle English Manuscripts.* Cambridge, 1952.

_____ , ed. *The Anglo-Saxons: Studies in Some Aspects of their History and Culture Presented to Bruce Dickins.* London, 1959.

_____ . "Cynewulf's Image of the Ascension." In *England before the Conquest: Studies in Primary Sources Presented to Dorothy Whitelock.* Ed. by P. Clemoes and K. Hughes. Cambridge, 1971, pp. 293-304.

Colgrave, B., ed. and trans. *Vita Sanctii Guthlac Auctore Felice.* Cambridge, 1956.

Conybeare, John J. *Illustrations of Anglo-Saxon Poetry.* Ed. by W. D. Conybeare. London, 1826; rep. New York: Haskell House, 1964.

Cosijn, Peter J. "Anglosaxonica III." *BGDSL,* 21 (1896), 8-26.

Crawford, S. J., ed. *The Old English Version of the Heptateuch.* EETS #160. London, 1922.

_____ . "The Cædmon Poems." *Anglia,* 49 (1925), 279-84.

_____ . "Grendel's Descent from Cain." *MLR,* 23 and 24 (1928-1929), 207-08, 63.

_____ . *Anglo-Saxon Influence on Western Christendom, 600-800.* Oxford, 1933.

_____ , ed. *Exameron Anglice or The Old English Hexameron.* Darmstadt, 1968.

Cross, J. E. *Latin Themes in Old English Poetry.* Lund, 1962.

_____ , and S. I. Tucker. "Allegorical Tradition and the Old English *Exodus.*" *Neophil,* 44 (1960), 122-27.

Crotty, G. "The Exeter *Harrowing of Hell:* A Re-interpretation." *PMLA,* 54 (1939), 349-58.

Daniélou, Jean. "The Problem of Symbolism." *Thought,* 25 (1950), 423-40.

_____ . *The Bible and the Liturgy.* Trans. by Wulstan Hibberd. Notre Dame, 1956.

_____ . *From Shadows to Reality: Studies in the Biblical Typology of the Fathers.* Trans. by Wulstan Hibberd. London, 1960.

_____ . *A History of Early Christian Doctrine.* Vol. 1, *The Theology of Jewish Christianity.* Trans. by John A. Baker. London, 1964.

Deanesly, M. *The Pre-Conquest Church in England.* London, 1961.

_____ . *Sidelights on the Anglo-Saxon Church.* London, 1962.

Deering, W. *The Anglosaxon Poets on the Judgment Day.* Halle, 1890.

Didron, A. N. *Christian Iconography: The History of Christian Art in the Middle Ages.* 2 vols. Trans. by E. J. Millington. 1851-56; rpt. New York, 1965.

Dietrich, Franz. "Zu Cädmon." *Zeitschrift für deutsches Alterthum,* 10 (1856), 310-67.

Dumville, David. "Liturgical Drama and Panegyric Responsory from the Eighth Century? A Re-examination of the Origin and Contents of the Ninth Century Section of the *Book of Cerne.*" *JTS,* 23 (1972), 374-406.

Dustoor, P. E. "Legends of Lucifer in Early English and Milton." *Anglia,* 54 (1930), 213-68.

Ehrstine, John W. "Patterns of Sound in Anglo-Saxon Poetry." *RS,* 33 (1962), 151-62.

Emerson, O. F. "Legends of Cain, Especially in Old and Middle English." *PMLA,* 14 (1906), 831-929.

Ettmüller, Ludwig. *Engla and Seaxna Scopas and Boceras.* Quedlinburg and Leipzig, 1850.

Evans, J. M. "*Genesis B* and its Background." *RES,* n.s., 14 (1963), 1-16, 113-23.

_____ . *Paradise Lost and the Genesis Tradition.* Oxford, 1968.

Farrell, R. T. "The Unity of OE *Daniel.*" *RES,* n.s., 18 (1967), 117-35.

_____ . "The Structure of OE *Daniel.*" *NM,* 69 (1968), 533-59.

Finnegan, Robert Emmett. "Christ and Satan: Structure and Theme." *Classica et Mediaevalia,* 30 (1969), 490-551.

_____ . "Two Notes on MS Junius *Christ and Satan:* Lines 19-20; Lines 319 and 384." *PQ,* 49 (1970), 558-61.

_____ . "*Christ and Satan,* 63-64." *The Explicator,* 31/2 (1972), #10.

_____ . "Three Notes on the Junius XI *Christ and Satan:* Lines 78-79; Lines 236-42; Lines 435-38." *MP,* 72 (1974), 175-81.

Förster, Max, ed. *Die Vercelli-Homilien.* Darmstadt, 1964.

──────. "Altenglische Predigtquellen, I i. Pseudo-Augustin und die 7. Blickling Homily." *Archiv,* 116 (1906), 301-307.

──────. "A New Version of the Apocalypse of Thomas in Old English." *Anglia,* 73 (1955), 6-36.

Frings, Theodor. "*Christ und Satan.*" *Zeitschrift für deutsche Philologie,* 45 (1913), 216-36.

──────, and Wolf von Unwerth. "Miscellen zur ags. Grammatik." *BGDSL,* 36 (1910), 559-62.

Fry, D. K. "Old English Formulas and Systems." *ES,* 48 (1967), 193-204.

Gatch, M. "Two Uses of Apocrypha in Old English Homilies." *Church History,* 33 (1964), 379-91.

──────. "Eschatology in the Anonymous Old English Homilies." *Traditio,* 21 (1965), 117-65.

Gillam, D. "A Method for Determining the Connotations of Old English Poetic Words." *Studia Germanica Gandensis,* 6 (1964), 85-101.

Godfrey, C. J. *The Church in Anglo-Saxon England.* Cambridge, 1962.

Grau, Gustav. *Quellen und Verwandtschaften der Älteren Germanischen Darstellungen des Jungsten Gerichtes.* Halle, 1908.

Graz, Friedrich. *Die Metrik der sogenannten Cædmonschen Dichtungen mit Berücksichtigung der Verfasserfrage.* Weimar, 1894.

──────. "Beiträge zur Textkritik der sogenannten Cædmon'schen Dichtungen." *Englische Studien,* 21 (1895), 1-27.

Greene, Richard. "A Re-arrangement of *Christ and Satan.*" *MLN,* 43 (1928), 108-10.

Greenfield, S. *A Critical History of Old English Literature.* New York, 1965.

Grein, C. W. M. "Zur Textkritik der angelsächsischen Dichter. *Germania,* 10 (1865), 416-29.

──────. *Sprachschatz der Angelsächsischen Dichter.* Ed. by F. Holthausen and J. J. Köhler. Heidelberg, 1912.

Groschopp, F. "Das angelsächsische Gedicht *Christ and Satan.*" *Anglia,* 6 (1883), 248-76.

Haddan, A., and W. Stubbs, eds. *Councils and Ecclesiastical Documents Relating to Great Britain and Ireland.* Vol. 3. Oxford, 1871.

Hefele, C. J. *Histoire des Conciles.* Vol. 3, Part 2. Trans. from the German by H. Leclercq. Paris, 1910.

Herzfeld, G., ed. *An Old English Martyrology.* EETS #116. London, 1900.

Hill, Thomas D. "Apocryphal Cosmography and the *Stream Uton Sæ*: A Note on *Christ and Satan,* Lines 4-12." *PQ,* 48 (1969), 550-54.

──────. "*Byrht word* and *Hælendes heafod*: Christological Allusion in the OE *Christ and Satan.*" *ELN,* 8 (1970-71), 6-9.

──────. "Satan's Fiery Speech: 'Christ and Satan' 78-9." *N&Q,* 217 (1972), 2-4.

──────. "Cosmic Stasis and the Birth of Christ: The Old English 'Descent into Hell,' Lines 99-106." *JEGP,* 71 (1972), 382-89.

Holthausen, Ferdinand. "Beiträge zur Erklärung und Textkritik altenglischer Dichter." *Indogermanische Forschungen*, 4 (1894), 379-88.

_____ . Review of Grein-Wülker, 2, Part 2, *Anglia Beiblatt*, 5 (1895), 227-33.

Hulbert, J. R. "On the Text of the Junius Manuscript." *JEGP*, 37 (1938), 533-36.

Hulme, W. H. "The Old English Version of the Gospel of Nicodemus." *PMLA*, 13 (O.S.) (1898), 457-541.

_____ . "The Old English Gospel of Nicodemus." *MP*, 1 (1903-1904), 579-614.

Huppé, B. F. *Doctrine and Poetry: Augustine's Influence on Old English Poetry*. New York, 1959.

Isaacs, Neil D. *Structural Principles in Old English Poetry*. Knoxville, Tennessee, 1968.

James, M. R., ed. and trans. "Visio Pauli." In *Apocrypha Anecdota I. Texts and Studies, 2 (#3)*. Ed. by J. Armitage Robinson. Cambridge, 1893.

_____ , trans. *The Apocryphal New Testament, being the Apocryphal Gospels, Acts, Epistles and Apocalypses with Other Narratives and Fragments*. Oxford, 1924.

Jones, C. W. "The Flat Earth." *Thought*, 9 (1934), 296-307.

Kahrl, Stanley J. "Allegory in Practice: A Study of Narrative Styles in Medieval Exempla." *MP*, 63 (1965-66), 105-10.

Keenan, Hugh T. "*Exodus* 312: 'the Green Street of Paradise.'" *NM*, 71 (1970), 455-60.

_____ . "Satan Speaks in Sparks: *Christ and Satan* 78-79a, 161b-162b, and the 'Life of St. Antony.'" *N&Q*, 219 (1974), 283-84.

Kelly, Henry A. "The Metamorphosis of the Eden Serpent during the Middle Ages and the Renaissance." *Viator*, 2 (1971), 301-28.

Klaeber, Fr. "Notizen zur jüngeren Genesis." *Anglia*, 37 (1913), 539-42.

Kock, Ernst A. "Interpretations and Emendations of Early English Texts." III and V, *Anglia*, 27 and 43 (1903 and 1919), 218-37 and 298-312 respectively.

_____ . *Jubilee Jaunts and Jottings*. Lund, 1918.

Kühn, Albin. *Über die angelsächsischen Gedichte von Christ und Satan*. Halle, 1883.

Larès, M. M. "Echos d'un rite Hierosolymetain dans un manuscrit du haut moyen âge Anglais." *Revue de l'Histoire des Religions*, 165 (1964), 13-47.

Lawrence, J. "On Codex Junius XI (pp 143-212)." *Anglia*, 12 (1889), 598-605.

Lee, A. *The Guest-Hall of Eden: Four Essays on the Design of Old English Poetry*. New Haven and London, 1972.

MacCulloch, John A. *Early Christian Visions of the Other World*. Edinburgh, 1912.

_____ . *The Harrowing of Hell: A Comparative Study of an Early Christian Doctrine*. Edinburgh, 1930.

Magoun, Francis P., Jr. "On Some Survivals of Pagan Belief in Anglo-Saxon England." *Harvard Theological Review*, 40 (1947), 33-46.

Martin, B. K. "Aspects of Winter in Latin and Old English Poetry." *JEGP*, 68 (1969), 375-390.

Meyer, P. "La Descent de Saint Paul en Enfer." *Romania,* 24 (1895), 357-75.

Migne, J. P., ed. *Patrologiae Graeca.* Paris, 1857-1866.

————. *Patrologiae Latina.* Paris, 1844-1864.

Morris, R., ed. *Old English Homilies of the Twelfth and Thirteenth Centuries.* EETS #29. London, 1867. EETS #34. London, 1868.

————, ed. *The Blickling Homilies.* EETS OS #58, 63, 73. London, 1967.

Mosher, Joseph A. *The Exemplum in the Early Religious and Didactic Literature of England.* New York, 1911.

Murdoch, Brian. "An Early Irish Adam and Eve: *Saltair na Rann* and the Traditions of the Fall." *MS,* 35 (1973), 146-77.

Ogilvy, J. D. *Books Known to the English, 597-1066.* Cambridge, Mass., 1967.

Patch, H. R. *The Other World According to Descriptions in Medieval Literature.* Cambridge, 1950.

Pope, John C. *The Rhythm of Beowulf.* New Haven, 1942.

————, ed. *Homilies of Aelfric. A Supplementary Collection.* Oxford, 1967.

Rieger, M. "Die Alt- und Angelsächsische Verskunst." (Zacher's) *Zeitschrift für Deutsche Philologie,* 7 (1876), 1-64.

Roberts, A., and J. Donaldson, eds. *The Ante-Nicene Fathers: Translations of the Writings of the Fathers down to A.D. 325.* American rpt. of the Edinburgh edition, revised and arranged by A. Cleveland Coxe, 10 vols., New York, 1916-1925.

Rosenthal, C. L. *The Vitae Patrum in Old and Middle English Literature.* Philadelphia, 1936.

Sala, John. *Preaching in the Anglo-Saxon Church.* Chicago, 1934.

Salmon, P. "The Site of Lucifer's Throne." *Anglia,* 81 (1963), 118-23.

Schaar, C. *Critical Studies in the Cynewulf Group.* Lund, 1949.

————. "On a New Theory of Old English Poetic Diction." *Neophil,* 40 (1956), 301-305.

Schaff, P., ed. *The Nicene and Post Nicene Fathers.* First Series, 14 vols. Buffalo and New York, 1886-1890; Second Series, 14 vols. New York, 1890-1925 (edited with H. Wace).

Schlauch, M. "An Old English *Encomium Urbis*." *JEGP,* 40 (1941), 14-28.

Shepherd, G. "The Prophetic Cædmon." *RES,* n.s., 5 (1954), 113-22.

————. "Scriptual Poetry." In *Continuations and Beginnings.* Edited by E. G. Stanley. London and Edinburgh, 1966.

Sievers, Eduard. "Collationen angelsächsischer Gedichte." *Zeitschrift für deutsches Alterthum,* 15 (1872), 456-67.

————. "Zur Rhythmik des germanischen Alliterationsverses." II and III, *BGDSL,* 10 and 12 (1885 and 1887), 451-545 and 454-82 respectively.

————. "Zu Codex Jun. XI." *BGDSL,* 10 (1885), 195-99.

————. *An Old English Grammar.* Trans. and ed. by Albert S. Cook. 3rd ed. New York, 1903.

————. "Zu Satan 42." *BGDSL,* 37 (1912), 339-40.

Silverstein, Theodore. *Visio Sancti Pauli.* London, 1935.

Sisam, K. *Studies in the History of Old English Literature.* Oxford, 1953.

Skemp, A. R. "The Transformation of Scriptural Story, Motive and Conception in Anglo-Saxon Poetry." *MP,* 4 (1906-07), 423-70.

Smetana, O. S. "Aelfric and the Early Medieval Homilary." *Traditio,* 15 (1959), 163-204.

Stoddard, F. H. "The Cædmon Poems in MS Junius XI." *Anglia,* 10 (1887), 157-67.

Tanenhaus, Gussie H. "Bede's *De Schematibus et Tropis*—A Translation." *QJS,* 48 (1962), 237-53.

ten Brink, Bernhard. *History of English Literature.* Trans. by H. Kennedy. Vol. 1. New York, 1883.

Thornley, G. C. "The Accents and Points of MS Junius XI." *Trans. Phil. Soc., 1954.* Oxford, 1955, pp. 178-205.

Thorpe, B., ed. *The Homilies of the Anglo-Saxon Church: The First Part Containing the Sermones Catholici, or Homilies of Aelfric.* 2 vols. London, 1844-46.

Timmer, B. J., ed. *The Later Genesis.* Oxford, 1948.

Toller, T. Northcote. *An Anglo-Saxon Dictionary . . . : Supplement, Revised and with Addenda by Alistair Campbell.* Oxford, 1921.

Trask, Richard. "*The Descent into Hell* of the *Exeter Book.*" *NM,* 72 (1971), 419-35.

Vacant, A., E. Mangenot and E. Amann, eds. *Dictionnaire de Théologie Catholique.* 15 vols. Paris, 1930-1950.

Van Os, A. B. *Religious Visions: The Development of the Eschatological Elements in Medieval English Religious Literature.* Amsterdam, 1932.

Warner, R. *Early English Homilies, from the Twelfth Century MS. Vespasian D. XIV.* EETS #152. London, 1917.

Welter, J.-Th. *L'Exemplum dans la Littérature Religieuse et Didactique du Moyen Age.* Paris et Toulouse, 1927.

Willard, R. "The Address of the Soul to the Body." *PMLA,* 50 (1935), 957-83.

————. "*Vercelli Homily XI* and its Sources." *Speculum,* 24 (1949), 76-87.

Wormald, F. *English Drawings of the Tenth and Eleventh Centuries.* London, 1952.

Wrenn C. L. "The Poetry of Cædmon." *Proceedings of the British Academy,* 32 (1947), 277-95.

Wülker, Richard P. *Grundriss zur Geschichte der angelsächsischen Litteratur.* Leipzig, 1885.

D5